WEBS OF TRADE
DYNAMICS OF
BUSINESS COMMUNITIES IN WESTERN INDIA

AREAS OF STUDY

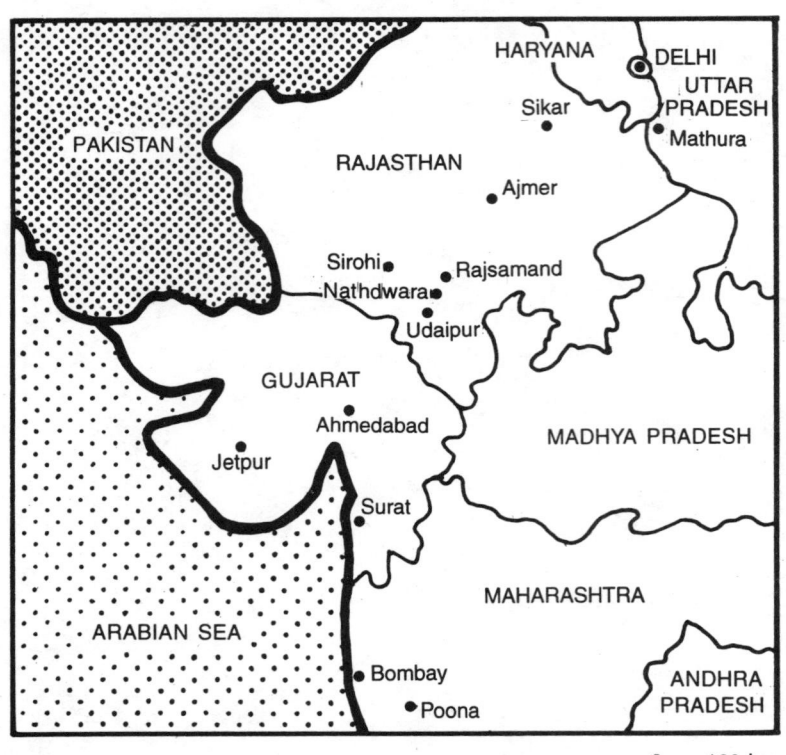

0---160 km

Webs of Trade

DYNAMICS OF BUSINESS COMMUNITIES IN WESTERN INDIA

Edited by

PHILIPPE CADÈNE
DENIS VIDAL

MANOHAR

CENTRE DE SCIENCES HUMAINES
1997

ISBN 81-7304-187-3

First published 1997

All rights reserved. No part of this publication may be
reproduced or transmitted, in any form or by any means,
without prior permission of the editors and the publisher

© Philippe Cadène and Denis Vidal, 1997

Published by
Ajay Kumar Jain for
Manohar Publishers & Distributors
2/6 Ansari Road, Daryaganj
New Delhi 110 002

Typeset by
A J Software Publishing Co. Pvt. Ltd.
305 Durga Chambers, 1333 D.B. Gupta Road
Karol Bagh, New Delhi 110 005

Printed at
Rajkamal Electric Press
B 35/9 G.T. Karnal Road Indl. Area
Delhi 110 033

Contents

Acknowledgements — 7

Kinship, Credit and Territory: Dynamics of Business Communities in Western India — 9
PHILIPPE CADÈNE AND DENIS VIDAL

The Merchant Lineage Firm and the Non-Invisible Hand: Pune, Maharashtra — 23
PIERRE LACHAIER

The Genesis and Growth of a Business Community: A Case Study of Vaghri Street Traders in Ahmedabad — 53
EMMA TARLO

Rural Credit and the Fabric of Society in Colonial India: Sirohi District, Rajasthan — 85
DENIS VIDAL

The Role of Trade and Traders in Small-Scale Industrial Development: The Example of a Textile-Printing Centre in Gujarat — 108
VÉRONIQUE DUPONT

The Part Played by Merchant Castes in the Contemporary Indian Economy: The Case of the Jains in a Small Town in Rajasthan — 136
PHILIPPE CADÈNE

Grocers and the Grocery Trade in Ratlam: Madhya Pradesh — 159
FREDERIQUE BOURGEOIS

Changing Aspects of Merchants, Markets, Moneylending and Migration: Reflections Based on Field Notes from a Village in Rajasthan
K.L. Sharma   174

Contributors   195

Acknowledgements

This book grew out of a collective Indo-French research project on business communities and entrepreneurship in western India, funded by the French Ministry for Research and Higher Education. It has been done under the auspices of ORSTOM, CNRS and the CEIAS (EHESS, Paris). The Centre de Sciences Humaines (CSH, New Delhi) has also given assistance at the final stages of publication.

Mrs A.M. Stuttle translated chapters III, V, VII as well as the introduction from French to English and also helped with the revision of other chapters. We would also like to thank Emma Tarlo and Uma Krishnan for their editorial assistance.

Kinship, Credit and Territory: Dynamics of Business Communities in Western India

PHILIPPE CADÈNE AND DENIS VIDAL

In introduction to a comprehensive collection of essays dedicated to the study of business communities of India, D. Tripathi pointed out that 'our understanding of the nature of these communities, the process of their evolution, and their distinctive contribution to the growth of Indian business system is fully inadequate' (Tripathi, 1984).[1] He also emphasised that in order to advance the terms of the existing debate about the characteristics and functions of business communities, we need further empirical studies. The essays in this volume are dedicated to fulfilling this objective. Each focusing on a specific group, activity and place, they document the ways in which traditional business communities and the networks controlled by them have confronted and participated in the major economic changes of the country. What they show is that whilst changes in the economy at large can lead to the dissolution of business communities at a local level, more often they provoke modifications, and at times they even enable the strengthening of the community in the process. The case studies are all concerned with western India, an area where business communities have left their mark on society more than anywhere else in the country.

From amongst the deeply intertwined social networks which make up the fabric of the Indian economy, the authors of this volume have paid special attention to three network systems which they consider paticularly characteristic of the functioning of business communities. The first of these is the kinship system which often plays an essential role in regulating the internal working of business circles. The second is the circulation of credit which determines the relations between members of different social milieus and different branches of activity in the production and marketing process. This is an essential aspect, the influence of which extends throughout the entire society. The third network system concerns the territorial links amongst and between mercantile groups. It relates to the ways in which business networks move in and out of different territories, sometimes spreading their influence over a well-defined geographic location, sometimes having to abandon one location in favour of another. This factor of territorial occupation throws into relief both the internal and external dynamics of business communities as they grapple to maintain their hold in local areas whilst expanding their influence further afield.

KINSHIP

Recognising the importance of kinship in structuring commercial operations in India is hardly a new discovery. The difficulty lies not so much in establishing the existence of such a connection as in determining the nature of the connection without exaggeration. From this point of view, Pierre Lachaier's article on the importance of the Kuchi Lohanas' kinship organisation in the structuring of the gunny bag market in Pune provides some interesting insights. He shows why it is impossible to understand the structure of the traders' activities if we focus merely on the existence of firms and their apparent competition in the market place. It is not only that these firms often owe their existence to tax considerations, but more importantly, that the interdependencies between them are determined by criteria that directly reflect the way in which kinship ties are organised among the Kuchi Lohanas. Such ties fundamentally shape the behaviour and operations of these traders, whose activities form an immense network covering practically the entire subcontinent.

Pierre Lachaier shows that this structure cannot be reduced either to the notion of a purely competitive market, or to the notion of an absolute monopoly. This is so, he argues, because the social organisation of the Kuchi Lohanas itself cannot be reduced either to a homogeneous whole, or to a set of isolated families. The logic which prevails in this group is more like the segmentary system. But here too we must be on our guard: it would be a mistake to jump to the conclusion that the structure of the market exactly reproduces kinship structures. Nowhere does Pierre Lachaier state that a parallel can be established, term for term, between the Lohanas' kinship structures and those of the gunny bag business. Each of these domains has its own internal logic, and an individual's position in either the economic or the familial sphere does not guarantee him the equivalent position in the parallel domain. Rather, we can say that the business and kinship spheres are mutually interconnected.

The Kuchi Lohanas provide a good example of the way in which a traditional business community can practically monopolise one sector of activity, bringing the logic of their own social organisation into play in the sector where they occupy a dominant position. But Pierre Lachaier emphasises that we should not exaggerate the significance of such a special case. It seems comparatively rare for an entire sector to be so completely dominated by one single community. We frequently encounter more variable markets, with a greater openness to businessmen and women of a more diverse social origin—although we very often find that these are still mostly drawn from the castes or communities whose mercantile vocation has always been clearly marked. Moreover there is no doubt that today many commercial enterprises are tending to 'rationalise' their activities along lines more in conformity with modern ideas about market management. But, as Emma Tarlo's contribution to this volume shows, there is always space for new entrants, some of whom are able to expand their commercial practices by manipulating the very networks of caste and kin that are generally associated with traditional business communities.

It is rarely possible to reconstruct from scratch the origin of a specific local market, especially when it has not come about through a planned intervention or been controlled by an institutional authority which might have kept a record of its emergence. So Emma Tarlo's study, dealing with the creation of the nocturnal open-air embroidery market by the Waghris of Ahmedabad provides some unusual insights. Her investigation also enables us to dispose of one of the familiar debates that has long dogged economic sociology: the nature of the relationship between individual and collective enterprise. The creation of the street market for second hand embroidery in Ahmedabad was essentially the idea of one individual whose calculation was based more on entrepreneurial insight than on long term experience. Yet this man's imaginative leap into the Gujarati embroidery trade could not have proved so successful had he not been able to mobilise his kinship network in a very short time, not only to develop a market in a specific location but also to establish a virtual monopoly for his community over the sale of second hand Gujarati embroidery on the footpath. It would be difficult to find better proof of the pointlessness of opposing 'the individual' to 'the group' in determining a society's potential for economic development. The familiar argument that it is the strength of socio-cultural ties in India that has served to inhibit economic development can surely be rejected once and for all.

But the most interesting point about the study lies elsewhere in the challenge it poses to an even more tenacious prejudice both in the sociological literature about Indian society and in the society itself. That is, our tendency to categorise as 'business communities' only those which correspond to a certain clearly defined social and cultural stereotype, thereby excluding all other groups in the process. From a sociological point of view, it is important to include not only those business communities whose collective identity is formally recognised as such, but also those to whom an identity of this kind has never really been attributed. As recent research into priesthood or rulership in Indian society shows, for a sociology of India to have a chance of making progress it is not sufficient only to identify the effectiveness of social and cultural stereotypes in the society; it is just as crucial to be able to stand back from them. Just as it is far from true that in India priestly functions are exercised exclusively by Brahmins, and that all forms of political sovereignty have always been assumed only by Kshatriyas, it is similarly true that there have always been far more business communities in India than we have been able to recognise.

So the problem is not only to enquire into the nature of the connection between business and kinship within conventionally defined business communities, but also to examine what role the establishment of such a connection plays in determining whether a group of business people are classified as a business community or not. The Waghris hardly correspond to the Indian stereotype of the Bania. Traditionally assigned a very low rank in caste society, they have indeed been engaged in varied forms of trade for a long time; but they are far from being identified—as the Lohanas could be—with the familiar image of a mercantile community: in the eyes of many Gujaratis, they would represent just the opposite. They enjoy neither the status nor the wealth nor the respectability of other business communities. Their kinship structure is also quite different. Among the Waghris, cross-cousin marriage is fairly common and the trade can be passed on both through men and women. Furthermore, unlike Bania and Marwari women, Waghri women play an essential, and at times dominant, role in the business. The only reputation which the Waghris seem to share with other business groups is that of being unbeatable bargainers—which is far from being a desirable quality in the eyes of the rest of the population.

Pierre Lachaier's research is interesting because it shows us how the interaction between business activities and kinship operates in mercantile communities. Emma Tarlo's study, on the other hand, makes us aware that our very concept of a 'business community' is an idealisation in the first place, though one which would appear to be deep rooted in Indian culture. So whenever one enquires about the future of traditional business communities in present-day India, it is important to note that they have probably always represented only one facet of India's mercantile culture, which has, in reality, been far more varied.

CREDIT

It is not enough to understand how business communities are organised internally. It is also essential to understand the kind of ties that link them to the rest of society. Two of the studies here tackle this question, each from a different angle and context. One of them explores the connections between Jain businessmen and local society in one of the former princely states of Rajasthan. The other focuses on relationships between businessmen and industrialists in a contemporary Gujarati town.

In the conventional sociology of Indian society, based fundamentally on the ideology of caste as presented in Hinduism, the position of businessmen does not create any particular problem. In spite of the wealth they often possess and the power they wield as a result, emphasis has conventionally been placed on the way in which their status remains subordinate to that of the Brahmin and Kshatriya castes which are considered ritually superior in the *varna* hierarchy. This view seems to confirm what long remained one of the fundamental postulates of the sociology of India: that the economic sphere always occupied a secondary position in traditional Indian society. This postulate was also reinforced for a long time by the hypothesis which considered monetarisation of the economy to be a relatively recent development in rural society.

Denis Vidal's study of the role of Jains in the former princely state of Sirohi (Rajasthan), however, demonstrates that a different reality underlies this surface appearance. In the first place, his investigation shows what a large degree of control the business community actually exerted over the local economy. But most of all, it stresses the importance of the role of businessmen in the fabric of Indian society. Businessmen did not occupy a merely subordinate position in caste society; they contributed significantly to the perpetuation of the system itself by enabling other social groups to fulfil the various requirements considered appropriate to their particular status. For a long time the businessman's role consisted of converting the needs connected with these requirements into an economic and monetary logic, which he regulated by means of credit. In contrast to economists, other social scientists have not always accorded enough importance to the role played by credit in social life in India. Recent researches by sanskritists and by anthropologists have now demonstrated the usefulness of the notion of debt for the analysis of Hinduism and Indian society (Malamoud, 1988; Galey, 1980). Yet there are only a few studies which have pointed out that the concept of credit is even more central not only for our understanding of business castes but also because of its influence on the society as a whole (Bayly, 1983)

Some historical investigations (Cheesman, 1982) show that when businessmen granted credit, their aim was not so much to recover the capital invested as to secure a regular income from the interest, which they usually received in kind. Credit represented for them a preferred way of obtaining inexpensive grain, which they could then resell at a profit. Rather than labelling local businessmen as 'money-lenders', it would be wiser, suggests Cheesman, to see them as 'shareholders' who invest their capital less in the hope of rapidly recuperating their funds, than with the intention of making them bear continuous fruit. The study of the Jains of Sirohi confirms this analysis. It also invites us to extend this viewpoint. The Jains of Sirohi not only held the position of shareholders in the local economy; in addition they provided it with an organisational basis which, once established, became indispensable to local society.

We can see a parallel between the organisational role played internally by the lineage structures of the Kuchi Lohanas of Pune studied by Pierre Lachaier, and the one which the business community of Sirohi fulfilled for a long time on the external plane. It would be impossible to understand the organisational principles of the gunny bag market without taking account of the role played by kinship structures within the Kuchi Lohana community, even though these would not be obvious to anyone who was not aware of their dominance in this market. In a somewhat similar way, it would be impossible to understand the functioning of the local economy in a princely state like Sirohi, if one focuses too much on the agrarian relations and the distribution of agricultural revenues, as linked with the declared distribution of land rights. Rather it is necessary to be aware of all the connections operating between the local businessmen and everyone around them who had a stake in the local economy, from the ruler to the peasant.

So, one should not assume that the businessmen's role, central though it was on the economic plane, was only confined to that. The circulation of credit did not merely allow businessmen to claim a part of the revenue; it was also decisive in defining the social standing of the people amongst whom the credit circulated. This was true first of all as far as the businessmen themselves were concerned: their reputations depended essentially on the amount of credit at their disposal, or that they could call on when required. But this was equally true for all their debtors: whether these were powerful landowners or simple peasants. Not just their living conditions, but their status and even their social identity depended largely on their capacity to call on the necessary resources when required. So we find that the businessmen, far from passively submitting to pressures exerted on them by the surrounding society, on the contrary played a decisive role in shaping it and maintaining its existence.

Thus the relationships between traders and local society are far more complex than we are apt to recognise. Not only would it be a mistake to think that the socio-cultural order existing in local society, however traditional in appearance, was ever incompatible with a monetarisation of the exchanges from which the business communities profited; on the contrary, we find the opposite. But it would equally be a mistake to think that monetarisation of the economy or the business activities necessarily tended to weaken existing traditional hierarchies. On the contrary, the businessmen's presence could contribute greatly to the stability of such hierarchies.

Must we then conclude, as some authors have done, that deep-rooted conservatism on the part of Indian businessmen is an explanation for the relatively late development of industry in India compared with other parts of the world? In the present work, Véronique Dupont's study of the textile industry in Jetpur in the State of Gujarat, demonstrates in precise detail why one has to be careful while analysing the readiness of a business community to launch into industrial investment.

In Jetpur, an initial division of functions took place within the local Khatri caste when they began to play a dominant role in the development of the textile industry during the 1950s. Some Khatri lineages became specialised in dyeing and cloth-printing, while others were engaged exclusively in cloth-selling. At this time it was mainly the artisan lineages who took charge of local factories. But it is also significant that the few traders who did take up production were particularly successful at it, because their double qualification gave them control over every branch of activity, from the manufacture of the cloth to its retailing. Since the traders were clearly quite capable of successfully entering the field of industry, Véronique Dupont's analysis raises the question of why more of them did not.

The answer is to be found, yet again, in the way in which credit coordinates a set of independent agents. As is often the case, a long chain of creditors and debtors shapes this field of activity. Credits pass back and forth from the suppliers of raw materials to retailers, via the manufacturers of printed cloth, not forgetting all kinds of middlemen who connect the links in the chain. The importance of these intermediaries increases as the local industry grows and a wider and more diverse market for these printed cloths develops. They alone are able to ensure that the range of products on offer corresponds to the varying demands of the market.

But the most revealing aspect of recent developments in the Jetpur textile industry is the emergence of professional associations for the support of all the participants at every stage of the chain of production. Their aim is not so much to keep the system as a whole functioning—there are specialised agents who take care of this—as to police the way in which credits are supplied, and attempt to exert an influence on the way that profits are distributed. In other words, these associations try to negotiate to the advantage of their members the way in which the profits, and the costs of any disfunctioning, are distributed within this localised branch of activity. Today it seems that the industrialists are gradually losing this game: they make less profits than the traders, and suffer more directly from disadvantageous terms of payment.

We may wonder whether this development provides an explanation for the lack of eagerness shown by traders to take up production themselves. Since they anyway control the credit chain all the way from the acquisition of raw materials to the sale of printed cloth, they have little incentive to become producers themselves in order to increase their control, so long as they can make others bear a large part of the costs of any slackness in the market, without allowing them a correspondingly large share of the profits.

We may also ask why the manufacturers, in spite of the associations they have formed, seem unable to obtain a better deal for themselves. The answer suggested by this study introduces a new element to the analysis: as long as the printed cloth produced was supplying a local demand, it was not difficult for manufacturers to remain independent of traders. But the very success of the textile industry in Jetpur, based on the opening up of new markets and an increasing diversification of products, has not only extended the length of the chain from the manufacture of the cloth to its distribution, and thus increased the number of middlemen involved; it has also had the consequence of increasing the interdependence of each of the links in the chain. How could small local manufacturers do without the merchant middlemen, when their expansion is becoming more and more dependent upon their capacity to suit their products to new markets of which they no longer have any first-hand knowledge?

It would be difficult to imagine examples apparently more diverse than those described by Denis Vidal and Véronique Dupont. In the first case, it was a matter of analysing a situation, now largely changed, in which a business community was the prime mover in a localised and essentially rural economy. The second is an attempt to understand the role played by a mercantile community in a rapidly expanding sector of activity which is opening up more and more to international markets. And yet both these cases demonstrate the significant influence of credit-practices, going far beyond the actual transfers of income involved, both in structuring economic activities and in shaping social identities.

Both illustrate the importance of commercial intermediaries, whose prosperity always depends on their capacity to deal with a large number of economic agents, and knowing how to coordinate their activities, however varied their respective needs and priorities may be. The extent of their creativity can be measured precisely by their capacity to invent new forms of interdependence and complementarity between these agents.

TERRITORY

The shift of activity of trading communities from villages and small towns to new centres of economic development constitutes a long-term feature of the economic history of western India. In such cases, it is important not only to understand the involvement of the communities in these new centres but also the subsequent fate of the localities and people they are leaving behind. Three of the essays investigate the contrasted situations that ensued from such movements.

Philippe Cadène's article illustrates one of these possibilities, showing how in a small town in the south of Rajasthan, half of the sons from each generation of businessmen migrate to Bombay, to set themselves up in the same type of businesses as those pursued by their families in their native place. This is not to deny that there are changes in the lives of Marwari families who settle in large cities. But unlike the businessmen of Shekavati studied by K.L. Sharma in this volume, none of the businessmen from Rajsamand, where Philippe Cadène conducted his research, have been spectacularly successful and reached the head of the large Bombay business houses. On the contrary, they more or less successfully replicate, in a few bazaars of the great Indian metropolis, the same shops that they leave behind in Rajsamand. In effect, they have transferred their activities to new territories, without introducing any radical changes in them.

While migration has enabled a significant section of the business families of north-west India to relocate their activities, it has also contributed to strengthening the position of those who have remained behind. The migrants did not leave frozen societies behind them. The causes which led them to depart also brought about profound changes in the places from which they migrated. The economic upheavals which took place in the colonial period, the economic reforms following Independence, and the rapid modernisation of the country over the last thirty years, have brought the business communities into intense competition with other social groups which were not previously engaged in business. Connection with a particular territory is a key factor in this competition, which reorganises relationships within localities. Groups who live there constitute existing social and economic networks, which get reshaped through complex marriage alliances in which caste-identity and place of origin play an important role. In the case of Rajsamand, members of the Jain community, who form the majority of the traditional mercantile families, have succeeded in maintaining their dominance in local business as a result of the fact that some members of their families are living in Bombay. From members of their own families, or others to whom they are linked by marriage, they draw the financial support they need to develop business activities in their own locality. Through kinship networks, but also through communal ties based on a shared territorial origin, they have access to sufficient capital to guarantee maximum profits in new branches of activity. The Jains of Rajsamand show no hesitation in abandoning the traditional professions of their community in order to play an active part in current economic developments. Although finance and commerce remain their main occupations, they have not failed to launch into the industrial activities which have been growing in the town over the past fifteen years. When the finance required is too much for a local family, they receive direct support from migrants of the community. The development of small marble factories in the area was initially supported by associations of this kind.

The establishment of new businesses, and access to external sources of capital contributed by migrants have enabled the traditional mercantile families of Rajsamand to resist the efforts of local Brahmin or Rajput families to seize economic supremacy of the town. Philippe Cadène's article reveals a paradoxical situation, where local developments have led a group of businessmen to depart from their traditional routine, while other members of the same families who have migrated to Bombay still stick to their traditional occupations. At Rajsamand, local roots are still an essential factor which remains unaffected by the modernisation of business activities and developing rivalries between different economic-interest groups. Moreover, each of these groups owes the strength that enables it to participate in this rivalry for local economic supremacy to its local roots.

K.L. Sharma's article also deals with the position of business communities in a locality in Rajasthan. But in this case it is a village of about 1500 inhabitants where the changes that have taken place since the beginning of the century have led to the departure of almost all members of the Jain families who used to occupy the small bazaar at the centre of the settlement. Not one of these is still in business in the village today, and their shops in the bazaar are closed. Only one member of one of these families still carries on their traditional activity of moneylender and grain dealer, without enjoying however the economic power which the Jains used to possess. Present economic conditions do not apparently provide members of this community with enough profitable opportunities in the village. The more dynamic amongst them have gone away, leaving behind only a few representatives of their families. Today most business is carried on by traders in the nearby towns, which owing to modern means of communication are now within reach of almost everyone in the locality. A few people from other communities have started small shops in the village to offer neighbourhood services, tea stalls or small groceries. But these are scattered throughout the settlement. The original bazaar is totally abandoned. K.L. Sharma focuses on this disappearance of the bazaar. The few streets where the Jains had their shops, used to form the heart of the village. With their disappearance, the webs of social relationships which gave coherence to local society have also weakened.

This point confirms the central role played by credit in shaping Indian society, of which we spoke of earlier, as well as the fundamental position of business in the dynamism of localities. But here the emphasis is on the fact that the bazaar, the place where the businessmen sit, gives the place its identity. Its disappearance weakens the coherence of the local system, which then gets integrated into a wider territorial system centred on a nearby town, whose bazaar then becomes the focal point of a new regional identity. Wealthier and better connected with large regional or national economic centres, the businessmen at the centre of this new local system are in a better position to respond to the demands of a rapidly developing economy. Drawing together a larger number of networks, the business families who dominate the bazaars of large centres are thus increasingly able to create links with other activities and to assume new entrepreneurial functions in the regional economy.

The article by Frederique Bourgeois, which deals with grocery shops in Ratlam, a medium-sized town in Madhya Pradesh, adds an additional element to this consideration of the bazaar as the focal point of a locality. After investigating the social characteristics of the shop-owners, as a geographer she describes the spatial distribution of grocery shops in this town of about 160,000 inhabitants. This type of trade forms an important part of the commercial activities which are concentrated in four areas of the town. The author shows, however, that the traditional bazaar has distinctive features. There are the oldest and largest shops, as well as most of the grocery wholesalers. But above all it emerges that the shops in this commercial centre have almost all been inherited, that the very large majority of them belong to members of traditional business communities. Whereas anyone can be a grocer in the peripheral areas, the old bazaar, where most business is still conducted, remains the privileged preserve of business communities, who strictly limit access to it. This control is obviously exercised through the communal ties linking members of the respective castes or business groups. However it is interesting to note that two-thirds of the grocers in the bazaar are members of one association, which thus provides an intercommunal forum where the shop-owners' defence strategies can be worked out. Forming a highly-structured social complex, the grocers of Ratlam bazaar are an example of businessmen who have so far been able to resist changes in the Indian economy, in a region which is still little affected by the industrialisation of the country. This article does not examine relationships between the grocers and other mercantile circles in the town. But in the light of Philippe Cadène's article on the Rajsamand bazaar, we may suppose that the shop-owners in Ratlam form a kind of base on which a reorganisation of these business families will occur, and is perhaps already going on, enabling them to adapt to changes in an evolving economy.

The validity of theoretical approaches which are not restricted to a narrow economic perspective is being widely recognised today. In India the main concern is not only to find out what form economic development will take, but also to assess what long-term consequences it will entail for society as a whole. If we want to obtain a clearer picture of the kind of choices with which modern India will be more and more directly confronted, it will be necessary to undertake more investigations which make the old distinction between 'economy' and 'society' completely obsolete. Such, at least, is the view which has prompted these essays.

NOTE

1. The terms, 'business community', 'trading community' and 'merchant community' are used to refer to those social groups traditionally associated with trade in Indian society. While one term may be more accurate than another in a specific context, we have decided to retain the use of 'business community' in the introduction because it is the expression most commonly used in the literature on the subject.

REFERENCES

Bayly, C.A., *Rulers, Townsmen and Bazaars, North Indian Society in the Age of British Expansion 1770-1780*, Cambridge University Press, Cambridge, 1983.

Cheesman, D., 'The omnipresent Bania: rural money lending in nineteenth century Sind' in *Modern Asian Studies*, vol. 16, 1982.

Galey, J.C., 'Le créancier, le roi, la mort: essai sur les relations d'interdépendance au Tehri-Garwhal' in *Purushartha 4*, EHESS, Paris, 1980.

Malamoud,C., 'Dette et devoir dans le vocabulaire sanscrit et dans la pensée brahmanique' in Malamoud, C. (ed.), *Lien de vie, noeud mortel. Les représentations de la dette en Chine, en Inde et dans le monde indien*, EHESS, Paris, 1988.

Tripathi, D., *Business Communities of India*, Manohar, Delhi, 1984.

The Merchant Lineage Firm and the Non-Invisible Hand: Pune, Maharashtra

PIERRE LACHAIER

I happened to meet Gulab in Pune, the second largest agglomeration in the most industrialised Indian state, Maharashtra. Gulab had just bargained for quantities of used gunny bags for dispatching vegetables and cereal crops. I wondered how the second-hand bag market functions, and investigated the matter. I discovered something that was both self-regulating and regulated—let's say something not unregulated. Neither Adam Smith's Invisible Hand, nor A. Chandler's Visible Hand could be of help. I have been trying to find some model that could illustrate how it works, and I think I can simply sum it up like this: when a sense of I-ness opposes a stronger sense of We-ness in the hearts of competing kindred people, the resulting pattern of relationships is likely to be a kind of segmented structure, latent or actual. I am suggesting that, from an anthropological point of view, the organisation of this Indian bag-business, seen as a whole, exhibits many features which are reminiscent of the way the Japanese industrial economy and organisation are working today: there is neither any 'Bags-Business Incorporated', nor any simple Invisible Hand.

INTRODUCTION

On the whole, Indian merchant castes and communities have remained relatively unstudied as such, although we have evidence of their existence at least since the classical period. Many of the largest modern Indian merchant and industrial groups have sprung from these castes and communities.[1] Here we will describe briefly some socio-economic features of the merchant 'communities' in

Maharashtra that specialise in handling gunny bags, the most important of them being the 'Kutchi Lohana'.

As is well known, Adam Smith in his day envisaged the overall socio-economic structure of a national entity as resulting from the actions of a multitude of individual entrepreneurs, each of them competing with each other in an open market which was supposed to be globally self-regulating, a virtue that called forth the metaphor of an *invisible hand* as a symbolic administrator. This Invisible Hand has remained to this day a paradigm to be used and misused in many discussions about how not to organise national economies, while it has been rejected by collectivist doctrines.

Alfred D. Chandler is one of the well-known specialists on modern firms and organisations who has contested the relevance of such a paradigm in the modern economy. He deliberately named his classic work on the history of the emergence of the modern American big business: 'The *visible hand*: the managerial revolution in American Business'.[2] He found that until about 1840, most of the economic agents acting on the American scene were family businesses, rather small in size and narrowly specialised, and that they were dealing in a market that was indeed regulated by an 'Invisible Hand'. Gradually, modern organisation substituted itself for these market mechanisms, coordinating economic activities and allocating resources. In many sectors of the American economy, the Visible Hand of managers, a newly appeared class of salaried specialists, started to replace the Invisible Hand of the market, and the integrated multi-divisioned companies that appeared by 1920 became the model for the modern large-scale big organisation we know today, which has established itself all over the world. According to A. Chandler, conspicuous warnings of an almighty and ubiquitous Invisible Hand have today become more or less rhetorical, although in the West, and in the United States in particular, the general importance of the open, self-regulating end-users' market cannot be denied.

These paradigmatic games of hands—visible and invisible—have more often than not inspired, explicitly or otherwise, economic and sociological field-surveys about the Indian world of traditional small-scale firms and companies,[3] not, however, without raising some embarrassing questions about the troublesome social phenomena that has been called either 'Business Community' or 'Community Business', depending on whether the observer was predominantly a sociologist or an economist. Some other observers, preferring a more neutral approach, have contrasted the 'firm' with its closest social environment, categorised as a 'reserve group'.[4]

After all these various specialised attempts to define the structure and organisation of the Indian firm, the anthropologist finds himself left with no way to distinguish himself except one that is certainly more in accord with Indian culture: a 'non-dualistic' socio-economic approach to the merchant firm, which is one-in-many and many-in-one, segmentable, and therefore not characterised by fixed clear-cut external or internal contours. I found that the 'organisation' of such 'firms', as well as the way they 'organise' transactions, can ultimately be traced to social institutions which are playing the role of some *non-invisible hand*.

I was first able to observe Indian firms and enterprises in 1979-82. Specific field surveys were carried out in Maharashtra in 1985-6, especially in Bombay, Mulund and Pune.[5] Most of my information about the Kutchi Lohana merchants and their commercial activities has been obtained from interviews, through direct observation of their professional life and setting, and from their own literature.[6] Representatives of their local association, Mahajan, in Pune and Mulund kindly supplied me with their recently compiled directories. Among much other valuable and informative documentation, these directories contain a detailed census of the associations' members, and some full-page advertisements without which it would have been extremely difficult to understand how their bag-business is 'organised'. All these different sources of information have been cross-checked with each other.

Kutchi Lohana behaviour and representations being rather archaic in comparison with those of other present-day Indian merchants and industrialists I happened to know, I compared my data about them with the few other available sociological and historical descriptions of merchant 'firms' based on material dating from the last century.[7] The Kutchi Lohana type of 'firm', which I have called the 'Merchant Lineage Firm', is certainly disappearing today. Nevertheless, apart from its importance for historical and theoretical studies, it may also help us to understand how the modern industrial and commercial firms and enterprises which have emerged from it have been organised in India.

This comparison between the modern type of big organisation and the Kutchi Lohanas' rather archaic form of business enterprise might at first sound a bit far-fetched. However, I think that the big organisational model described by A. Chandler has been showing some signs of obsolescence over the last ten years throughout the world: many of today's big organisations are desperately engaged in a process of modernisation, which consists mainly of adapting to the more efficient Japanese model of organisation.[8] As is well known, the Japanese modern organisation exhibits many traditional Japanese features. This is relevant for the anthropologist, who can now comparatively investigate modern and traditional 'firms' in a new and wider perspective.

The western theory of the firm can hardly be separated from the theory of the market as a self-regulating institution. I thought it convenient to imagine a character, Gulab, who has apparently endorsed such a point of view. Gulab is not purely a product of my imagination: he also represents many real people whom I have met during my survey. Gulab's role is to introduce us by proxy to the bag-business as if we were one of the end-users.

THE INVISIBLE HAND SEEN FROM THE END-USERS' BAG MARKET

Gulab, the son of a well-to-do Maharashtrian farmer living in the vicinity of Pune, is about to harvest various vegetables. He will need second-hand gunny bags to pack and carry them to the market yard: 120 small broad-woven cheap ones, 40 strong normal ones, and 3 of a closer weave for a special variety of peas. Gulab decides to go and purchase them in Pune, in the Bhavani Peth area, where many bag-merchants and dealers have concentrated their shops. Bhavani Peth is the old wholesale market quarter. It is very crowded and busy: trucks, bicycles and bullock-carts are constantly trying to make their way through a dense throng. All kinds of artisans are practising their crafts in small shops and often on the pavement.

Certain streets harbour many similar-looking gunny bag shops, which may stock up to 40 different types of bags, available in rolls of 10, or by the piece. A few larger shops would not consider any deal below some hundreds of bags. Prices vary according to quality and quantity. After shortly bargaining here and there, Gulab had found all he wanted at a price which suited his purse.

A week after Gulab had sold his vegetables, a young Kutchi he did not remember having met before bicycled by his farm and proposed to buy any empty gunny bags he had left, for less than half the price he had bought them for—because the bags had been damaged and needed to be mended, said the youngster. Gulab did not find this proposition very sound and refused it. He had taken a good decision, for two days later an 'untouchable' Mang from another hamlet came to him and offered him 20 paise more per bag.

On another occasion, Gulab had been requested by the farmers' cooperative, of which he and his father are important members, to purchase bags for dispatching the cereal crop. Three quarters of it could be sent in about 10,000 second-hand gunny bags to a local mill. Part of the rest had to be packed in 3,000 new bags to be delivered to a Bombay wholesaler. Last but not least, 250 bags of a special size and quality were needed for exporting the very best of the crop to the Gulf.

Gulab sought the advice of a Marwari grain merchant he knew a bit, and received these precise tips:

— for procuring the 10,000 bags, the best way would be to select two or three rather large bag-merchants from amongst those who advertise in a well-known business directory of Pune, and let each of them bid for a share of this number.
— for procuring the 3,000 new bags, it was worth going to Bombay, Masjid Bhandar area, and looking there for the best offers (Gulab was given some phone numbers and addresses).
— for procuring the 250 special gunny bags, it was better to contact a bag-broker in Pune who would arrange everything, instead of going to Nasik where such bags are manufactured (Gulab got the addresses of a bag-broker in Pune, and of the so-called 'King of the Bags' in Nasik).

No need to say how relieved Gulab felt after he had finalised all these transactions. All the bags were delivered in due time by a Kutchi transporter. In addition, his new friend the Marwari merchant had been kind enough to allow Gulab to use his company telex to speed up the business. Gulab remembered one of his B.Com. teachers speaking about Adam Smith's famous Invisible Hand—no doubt, it too had been working in his favour!

As a matter of fact, the merchants I met in various places, both big and small, from various caste-groups, and dealing in various goods, all stated that they do usually compete with each other. Competition is even admitted among closely-related people, even sometimes those belonging to the same joint-family: for instance, a father will consider it his duty to advance money to his son, even though he knows that the son may use it for a transaction that is detrimental to his own business.

However, there is normally no 'cut-throat competition' among related members of the same caste-group. In order to avoid fierce competition, members of the same Kutchi Lohana 'family' may enter into a partnership with each other for a defined transaction. They may also conclude partnerships with members of other 'families'. Since these 'families' are most of the time dealing in the same sort of goods, they will also compete. In the bag business, related people usually try to minimise the competition, by specialising in certain types of bags (I would rather consider this 'specialisation' as a mere differentiation within the bag-business speciality), or by working in different geographical areas (where they will however have to compete against less closely related caste-members).

Whatever these precautions, it is not unusual to find that in a given caste-group or sub-group, some merchants are successful while others may go bankrupt. I have actually come across such a case of a merchant having gone bankrupt twice. Each time he could recover and start again, in a smaller town, with a lower level of capital, and with the financial help of other merchants of his caste-group. Finally, having become a minor partner in someone else's 'company', he decided to give his sons such an education that they could make their own way out of the traditional family business. His partnership was transmittable to them. Competition or cooperation? Both. Ultimately it all depends on what the informants had in mind when they said 'family', 'related members', 'caste-group' ..., etc.

Gulab has not really been cheated. There is no organised bag-lobby as such. His Marwari friend has been sincere and loyal. However, after a peep in backstage, we may wonder whether Gulab has not been dealing with an octopus of a kind neither Adam Smith nor A. Chandler could have thought of!

VISIBLE HANDS

REGIONAL SPECIALISATIONS

Most of the Kutchi Lohana, now living in Maharashtra came from Kutch and Pakistan around 1947, at the time of Partition. Today they are settled in Bombay, Mulund, Nasik, Pune and in the Satara area.

In Bombay their shops and 'firms' are concentrated in the overcrowded Masjid Bhandar market area.

Mulund is a new township on the outskirts of Bombay. It counts about 600,000 inhabitants, of whom around 100,000 have migrated from Gujarat. According to the Mulund section of the Kutchi Lohana Association, Mulund is considered their World Capital, because the world's highest concentration of Kutchi Lohanas live there, that is around 10,000 individuals. The Pune Kutchi Lohana section counts about 1,500 people, and the Satara section some 130. A few wealthier Kutchi Lohanas from Karachi have settled in Nasik.

The degree and type of Kutchi Lohana specialisation in the bag business tends to depend on the area. Most of Pune's Kutchi Lohanas are purchasing second-hand gunny bags and reselling them locally (some wealthier merchants also procure them in large quantities in Orissa). A few of them have tried to make their living from other occupations or businesses: one or two are accountants, one is a physician, one is running a hotel, one or two are transporters ... Kutchi Lohana firms or merchants of average size often employ workers from the 'untouchable' Mang caste-group in addition to their own caste brothers. Mangs are usually employed for mending damaged bags. This group is to be found in all Maharashtrian villages, and could become a threat to the Kutchi Lohana's quasi-monopoly in the near future. But the Kutchi Lohanas do not seem to fear them. They rather tend to support them to a certain extent. A similar situation, observed in Bombay and Mulund, gave me an understanding of the kind of relationship that exists between the Mangs and the Kutchi Lohanas.

In Bombay-Mulund, many Kutchi Lohanas who used to have the same type of bag business as their Pune brothers, have now diversified their occupations. They may be dealing in various goods, such as surgical instruments for instance. A few of them have even founded small-scale industrial enterprises. These better-off Kutchis may retain some interest in bag businesses. Bombay-Mulund's Kutchi Lohanas are nowadays also dealing in new gunny bags, which involves a bigger capital. Seen from Pune, new bag-businesses are the Bombay Kutchi Lohana's typical speciality. Many, if not most, of Bombay-Mulund's present second-hand bag dealers actually belong to the Bhansali caste-group, and one might wonder whether the Kutchi Lohanas and the Bhansalis are not fiercely competing here. However, many of these Bhansalis have taken over Kutchis' businesses, with their financial help: it is part of the Kutchi Lohana's collective strategy of social promotion to progressively abandon the bag business, which they find 'dirty', in order to enter more dignified commercial fields. Kutchi Lohanas who have succeeded in getting out of the second-hand bag business often continue to lend money to these Bhansali firms, and therefore have an interest in their clients' success. Kutchi Lohana and Bhansali firms or merchants employ Bhansali workers, whom they recruit from Kutch. Bombay-Mulund's Kutchi Lohana companies are generally larger than the Bhansali ones and those of their Pune brothers. The few Kutchi Lohanas settled in Nasik specialise in making new gunny bags. They employ a number of local people, at their homes.

Kutchi Lohanas have responded differently to the local commercial opportunities they found. However this most often leads them to diversify their speciality within the bag business. Clearly enough, these local sub-specialities are complementary: merchants who sell new bags often know where used bags can be found, and vice versa, so they can cooperate if need be, although business information is reserved, if not 'privatised'. Accounts can be balanced in different places on a basis of mutual trust. At the same time Kutchi Lohanas do speculate and compete against each other. Cooperation and competition are possible at the same time only if they take place at different levels of kinship, as we shall see. There is no discernible central or leading business organisation as such.

PROFESSIONAL ASSOCIATIONS

Gunny bag dealers' non-caste based professional associations exist in Bombay and in Pune. Most of their members are Kutchi Lohanas, other members being Bhansalis in Bombay and Mangs in Pune. Most members of both these caste-groups are clients of the Kutchi Lohanas. The few other members are often from Marwari castes. In Pune (but also in various other Kutchi professional associations in Bombay), the elected president of the 'Gunny Bags Association' is also the elected President of the local caste-group association, the Mahajan. Although few Marwaris may be involved in the bag business, they tend to be respected because they are well-connected with the Indian jute business. They will know well in advance about market trends in new jute material, according to which the pricing of old gunny bags fluctuates. Kutchi Lohanas are thus eager to maintain good contacts with their Marwari brokers, in order to get timely business information from them for speculation. Some Marwaris may possibly be financing some of the larger Kutchi 'firms', especially the broker ones, in the same way as rich Kutchis are financing Bhansali 'firms'. But this cascade of caste-to-caste financing does not really endanger the business of a given segment of it; on the contrary, Marwaris certainly like the Kutchis to be successful, as much as the Kutchis like their Bhansali and Mang clients to be successful—up to a certain point.

These independent local professional associations may arrange certain things in the common interests of their members. They are certainly able to unite all or most of them in cases where the bag-business as a whole would be endangered (state regulation of the jute quota to be exported or not, for instance). Most frequently, they are able to arbitrate professional disagreements among members. However these professional associations cannot be seen as central organs regulating the bag-business as a whole: their members are also competitors, and there is no single leadership.

PUNE'S COMMERCIAL NETWORK

Pune's Kutchi Lohanas are specialised in the second-hand bag business. They have concentrated their '100' shops and 'companies' in the area around their caste association building, their Mahajan, which is located almost in the centre of Bhavani Peth, the wholesale-market quarter where Gulab met them. From the commercial and economical point of view, the Pune Kutchi Lohana's bag business considered as a whole cannot be said to be 'organised'—because there is no central authority, no single 'management', and no department that could possibly 'rationalise' the transactions between their shops and 'companies', big and small. Yet, seen as a whole, all these competing agents acting in their own commercial interests do build up a coordinated commercial network that has its own rationale, because they do organise their supplies and sales with each other to a certain extent.

Used bags are normally to be found in a number of scattered places, most of the time in small quantities. Their availability varies during the year depending on the agricultural work going on, and on the place and time of consumption of bagged goods. It is therefore necessary to have a ramified network of collecting agents, each with a minimum working capital at his disposal, to go and pick up the bags. On the other hand, big merchants or 'companies' which can deliver huge quantities of bags of given qualities, according to particular delivery schedules, would normally have to maintain large stocks of bags; this implies that the dispersed bags have already been collected, sorted out and mended if necessary. All these necessary operations involve and immobilise correspondingly larger fixed and working capitals. Retail, collecting and wholesale operations have opposing requirements in terms of kinds of capital, human resources, qualifications, and management abilities. So we would rather expect these two complementary types of business to be clearly separated. This is not exactly what happens among Kutchi Lohana bag merchants or 'companies'.

The structure that emerges from observation of the way Pune's Kutchi are working is in fact a graduated multi-level one. I have found it more convenient to distinguish large wholesale 'firms' or merchants, average-sized ones, and 'shop-firms', although it would certainly be possible to find as many intermediate categories as wanted. The bigger 'firms' or merchants will give loans roughly equivalent to their working capital to many average-sized 'firms' or merchants to collect bags for them. These average-sized 'firms' or merchants do the same with even smaller 'firms' or merchants, and so on down to the end of the chain where single operators are taking daily advances from a 'shop-firm' which they will supply with the bags they have collected during the day. These basic operators, closely linked with their patron-shop, are used to collecting bags, sometimes piece by piece, in and around Pune. They may ride a bicycle of their own or one bought with a loan (Kutchi Lohana operators may be granted loans for this purpose by their Mahajan), and they may also use, in addition to the advances from their patron, their own small working capital.

In this way, money roughly covering the working capital of smaller 'firms' or merchants flows from the bigger ones in successively smaller streams. Conversely, a multitude of tiny rivulets of bags are converging upwards and mingling together into streams that get larger and larger in a pattern that is reminiscent of an inverted tree, until they may finally be assembled in a few godowns of the largest 'firms' or merchants when these happen to need them for a wholesale delivery.

However, it should be underlined that every branch of this

inverted tree likes to come into leaf individually, while at the same time receiving loans from bigger ones and possibly granting loans to smaller ones. Each operator, merchant or 'firm' is at the same time the buyer for his client-suppliers, the supplier for his patron-buyers, and, whenever possible, his own master, using his own capital to finance transactions with final end-users so as to maximise his profits. A small operator will save money, invest it little by little in transactions of his own, until his capital and regular income have grown big enough, so that he can afford to buy a share of a shop, or share the rent of one with a partner. This small operator may, for instance, be a younger son whose father is already well established in business. In this case the son will probably get most of his credit from his father and supply him with bags he has either collected himself, or had collected by his own client-collectors, who may be Kutchi Lohanas who are poorer or less experienced than himself (maybe a cousin, or even a younger brother, or friend, or an in-law, or a secondary partner), or Mang clients. This means that it is rather difficult to classify these operators, 'firms' or merchants, in a general way as retailers or wholesalers or 'general merchants', as clients or as patrons. It all depends on what we consider as the business unit. If we consider the son and his father as 'associates' or even 'partners' of one single business unit, then we have to admit that this unit is also differentiated when operating as retailer and as wholesaler.

Whatever their position in this commercial hierarchised network, all these agents normally consider themselves self-employed (rather than 'independent') businessmen. To be self-employed is dignified. An employee may be a trustworthy relative; he would then consider his work 'service' (*seva*). Only casually-employed porters are non-Kutchi or non-Mang; they are remunerated for the given task and do not participate in the network (they are the only truly 'independent' workers in it, if I may say so: patrons do not feel tied to them, and vice versa).

Larger 'firms' or merchants do not mend the collected bags themselves; they get this done by smaller Kutchi agents or by untouchable workers from the Mang caste-group. Overall, the Pune Kutchi Lohanas employ hundreds of Mangs, sometimes in large familial units. Some of these Mangs who have been collecting bags for them may even be able to develop their own bag businesses with the financial help of their Kutchi Lohana patrons.

Some of the larger Kutchi Lohana 'firms' tend to specialise in brokerage; they balance offers and demands according to the season, and find themselves in the best position to speculate. Brokerage requires a higher capital, a wider network of contacts, and a good access to information channels that may lie outside the business world (it is an advantage to have a relation who is employed in a bank, for instance). Every 'self-employed' merchant will also try to speculate provided he has the financial means for it. This speculation occurs within the bag-business sector; and it may hurt some badly-informed Kutchi Lohanas much more than the end-users.

If we exclude the few Marwaris operating in Pune (less than 5 per cent in number), Kutchi Lohanas as such, together with their Mang clients, do enjoy a kind of 'monopoly' over the second-hand bag business in the Pune area. They have spacious godowns, specialised shops, trucks for large heavy deliveries. But the word 'monopoly' is not really accurate, for the Kutchi Lohanas do not constitute any 'organised body' or 'corporation' as such. Neither do Marwaris, Kutchis, Bhansalis or Mangs. Visible Hands of these many 'self-employed' agents are certainly co-ordinating flows of bags and money, supply and demand, and they do appear to constitute a closely integrated commercial network. Yet nobody's hand in particular can claim even to regulate it, let alone to administer or manage it.

THE NON-INVISIBLE HAND

THE KINSHIP ORGANISATION OF THE KUTCHI LOHANA

According to their mythical history, the so-called Lavrana migrated in very ancient times from Afghanistan to northern India where they founded the town of Lohagadh. The Lavranas who administered Lohagadh were then called Loharanas. Driven on by Muslim invaders, the Lavrana-Loharanas resumed their migration southwards and became known as Lohanas. During this migration they diverged into two main branches: one headed by Shri Kanaksen settled in Saurashtra and founded some small kingdoms there,[9] the other went into Sindh, where they repeatedly had to fight against the Muslims, who persecuted them and forced them to conversion. These Lohanas from Sindh finally settled in Kutch. There they erected a temple that has remained important to them to this day. It is dedicated to Shri

Daryalal, also called Jhulelal, after one of their heroes who distinguished himself in opposing the Muslim authorities that were oppressing the Lohanas. Today Lohanas from these two main branches have hardly any contact with each other. They do not intermarry. By convention, I call the main flow of Lohanas which issued from Afghanistan, still remembered in this myth and in certain rituals, a 'Caste', and 'Subcastes' its endogamous branch subdivisions. We will be concerned only with the branch established in Sindh and mainly in Kutch.

This Lohana subcaste is again subdivided into many endogamous sections usually called *jati*, such as the Kutchi Lohanas one we have been talking about. Other endogamous Lohana *jatis* are also established in Bombay and some of these are said to run rather bigger businesses than our Kutchi Lohanas. The *jatis* are again subdivided into local sections—therefore not according to kinship—located in Bombay, Mulund, Pune, Satara, and Nasik. At least three of these sections have founded their own local associations called Mahajan, on which I will expand more later. Kutchi Lohanas allow intermarriage between different local sections. Membership of a given local section normally does not restrict matrimonial alliances (there are no local alliance circles such as *gol* in Gujarat).

According to the census lists and information published in the directories of the Mulund and Pune local sections, the Kutchi Lohana *jati* is again subdivided into some 85-6 common exogamous clans called *gotras*. These *gotras* have been listed in an order that 'tends' to be alphabetical, seemingly to neutralise as far as possible differences of status (certainly in an effort at modernising the *jati*). However Kutchi Lohanas certainly still think of these as hierarchised. *Gotras* are generally assumed to be descended from revered ancestors, sometimes a hero or one of the mythical Lohana kings, which means that they are considered to be of Kshatriya origin in terms of status. But some of them in the same list are marked out as being of mixed origin, Kshatriya and Brahmin, and would therefore tend to be considered of a different ritual status. A footnote in the Pune directory explains that in ancient times Kshatriyas and Brahmins did exchange girls and food. A quotation from the *Vishnu Purana* is offered in support of this legitimising claim.

These *gotras* are again subdivided into lineages called *nukhs*. Their number varies depending on the *gotra* (*gotras* may have up to 16 *nukhs* in the Pune list. The Mulund list is less detailed in this respect). In the census lists of the Pune directory, for every person enumerated the *nukh* is followed by a denomination of origin called *gam* or *mul vatan* (i.e., hamlet, village, or root-land). These *gams* normally correspond to real villages in Kutch, and occasionally even to its capital, Bhuj. In Pune many different *nukhs* originate from the same *mul vatan*, and conversely, many Kutchi Lohanas originating from different *mul vatans* share the same *nukh*. *Nukhs* are strictly exogamous subdivisions. However, since most of the *gotras* do not subdivide into the same *nukhs*, it is the *gotra* which can generally be considered the widest possible exogamous subdivision. *Mul vatans* or *gams* are not factors which could compulsorily define some bar to intermarriage. But they certainly influence particular matrimonial strategies.

In addition to his *gotra*, *nukh* and *mul vatan*, a married Kutchi Lohana is also called by a *nam*. *Nams* are the most currently used denominations. The *nam* is made up of two terms, 'A' and 'B'. The 'B' term of a man's *nam* is the 'B' term of his mother's *nam*, and his 'A' term is the 'B' term of his wife's *nam*.

From the practical point of view, it is to be noticed that since a Kutchi 'firm' or 'company' is often advertised and denominated under the *nam* of its headman, kinship relations between apparent Kutchi 'firms' or 'companies' can hardly be detected by a Maharashtrian like our Gulab, whose own denomination is usually completely patrilineal.

Census lists are actually called *vasti patraka* in Mulund (something like 'list of inhabited places') and do actually register residential units in Mulund and in Pune. They have not been established according to any alphabetical order, but according to the geographical proximity of the registered residential unit to the Mahajan building, which contains a shrine dedicated to a Kutchi Lohana god. Mulund's shrine is dedicated to Shri Daryalal, with a perpetually burning flame that is said to have been brought from Pakistan. Pune's list counts 278 residential units, the largest of them housing 24 people. Residential units frequently, but not systematically, correspond to a family, nuclear or joint. Some joint families, however, may be living in nuclear subdivisions residing separately as distinct residential units. Most of the adult males have occupations related to the bag business. Only a few of them have attended school beyond the primary level.

THE ORGANISATION OF KUTCHI LOHANA LOCAL ASSOCIATIONS (MAHAJANS)

The 'Shri Kutchi Lohana Mahajanwadi, Mulund' was founded in 1945, and Pune's 'Shri Kutchi Lohana Mahajanshri' a few years later. They are both officially registered as 'charitable trusts'. As such they are entitled to receive donations from their members, and can take legal action. Mahajans are important collective 'real organisations' of the Kutchi Lohana *jati*. By calling them 'real organisations' I want to emphasise that while these associations are managed by democratically elected councils and individuals, they are primarily associations of the members of the Kutchi Lohana *jati*. Mahajan associations as legal 'real organisations' are deeply embedded, as K. Polanyi would have said, in the *jati* itself.[10] The President and executive council members of Pune's Mahajan are elected according to detailed rules published in the directory and certainly widely known. A candidate may not be among the richest merchants of the association, but he certainly has to be among the 'most honourable' ones.

In Pune,[11] the 'Shri Kutchi Mahajan Shri' is registered on the census list as the very first member of the association (that is: He is a member of Himself) with the following attributes: His *nukh* is 'Kutchi Lohana', His *mul vatan* is 'Kutch', he is residing in the building of the Mahajan (the shrine), His occupation is to serve the community (*seva*), He has no real age since, He is immortal (*amar*). In other words the Mahajan is conceived of as a divine legal entity. As such He encompasses all local subgroups or individual members: His place of origin is the area containing all possible places of origin of the members (*gam* and *mul vatan*), and His lineage is deeper than any member's lineage because He is also assimilated to the *jati* divinity: Shri Daryalal or Sri Jhulelal. Immanent and transcendent, He nevertheless also has His ultimate principle in a more ancient divine figure: Varuna.

The organisation of Pune's Mahajan is described in detail in a 30-point list of regulations. This indicates an agenda for the main festivals and rites, gives a list of Brahmins from Kutch (registered according to their proximity to the Mahajan), stipulates two categories of sacerdotal and ritual rates, fixes the taxes to be paid to it on the occasion of certain rituals and so on. The ritual of marriage is dealt with in articles 11 to 27 and can be considered as the most important subject of concern. The Mahajan recommends its members to respect the legal minimum age for marriage, but it also takes the initiative of prohibiting remarriage for members over 48 years old.

In Pune Mahajan building houses the *karyalaya* (executive office), a large kitchen, a patio that can be covered for marriages and other ceremonies, flats rented to members, and a library that is open to all members for a yearly fee of Rs. 3, and to non-members for Rs. 15. Its shelves may contain a few thousand books, 'public' newspapers from Kutch, as well as other papers and reviews written by Kutchi Lohanas for their own use.[12] The Mahajan regularly organises lectures for the education of younger members and women. Subjects include the history of the community, the *Bhagavad Gita*, etc. Children attending local public schools (normally Marathi speaking, although Gujarati-medium schools are preferred) can be financially supported. The Mahajan organises medical-checks (eyes, lungs, etc.) and helps the destitute (particularly widows, among other socially deprived people). It can grant loans at reduced interest rates for buying bicycles or sewing machines, which are both very useful for the daily work. Young Kutchi starting their own business can be granted a so-called 'seeding capital'. The Mahajan maintains records of births, deaths and marriages. Unlike the association in Mulund, the Pune Mahajan can still sentence offending members to outcasting (which is certainly very detrimental to their business activities).

The Mulund Mahajan claims to act as 'primus inter pares'. Its President, a physician who wants to develop and modernise his community, has been trying to loosen the endogamous circle by encouraging inter-*jati* marriages among the Lohanas. For this purpose, he has organised formal meetings of Mahajans representing different Lohana *jatis*. This inter-*jati* assembly, called the 'Lohana Mahasabha Parishad' takes non-binding decisions and does not sit regularly. As a whole, the Lohana subcaste, subdivided into endogamous *jatis*, each with its own rather independent local association, has no formal overall political institution, nor any specialised organ of coordination. Its relationships with other higher or lower caste-groups used to be regulated by what may be called a 'caste-system' originating in Kutch. Only bits and pieces of this may possibly still persist in Mulund where the Gujarati population is rather numerous.

The local Mahajans are the only bodies of the *jati* which are real organisations. But they are built on a principle of locality which is subordinate to the kinship principle. Mahajans do not organise the bag-business, and every self-employed Kutchi Lohana may manage his business as he wants. The internal '*jati* organisation' is essentially kinship based, the kinship structure being mainly hierarchised according to generation, age, sex and ritual status. It is the very backbone of the whole Kutchi Lohana bag business. Such a Non-Invisible Hand is not normally envisaged in the theory of the firm, or it is considered informal and dysfunctional.[13]

THE MERCHANT LINEAGE FIRM, WHERE HANDS VISIBLE, INVISIBLE AND NON-INVISIBLE MEET

THE MERCHANT LINEAGE FIRM

We started by approaching the bag business from outside with the help of Gulab. Then, after examining it from a regional point of view, we focused our attention on the way it is 'organised' in Pune's local section. Then we described the kinship system of the Kutchi Lohanas, which we characterised as the backbone supporting their commercial and business networks. Here we will again adjust our focus, onto a smaller kinship and/or business segment which I have called 'the Merchant Lineage Firm' or MLF for short. Information about this has been obtained mainly in Pune.

Up to now, I have been using terms such as 'merchants', 'firms', 'company', or 'agents' in a rather loose way, because it is not easy to specify what corresponds to these familiar concepts or notions of our modern world of business and management in the Kutchi Lohana context.

Let us first remind ourselves that there is no genuine equivalent of the terms 'firm' or 'company' in Indian languages. Entities designated by these terms in colonial India correspond more to something like a 'concern', that may stand for all the affairs affecting the interests of a joint family. Account books of merchant families of the last century include items such as expenses for the gods, for the ghats, for pilgrimage, etc., in such a way that it seems difficult to separate the 'real business' accounts from other 'private' ones.[14]

Secondly, no clear-cut distinction can be drawn between single and collective Kutchi Lohana economic agents. An individual 'firm' or 'company' cannot be taken a priori as a unit bounded by limits that would allow us to know precisely where it starts and where it stops, what pertains to it and what does not. The Kutchi Lohanas' so-called 'companies' are usually not registered. The MLF is both a kinship and a business segment of a larger lineage, and is itself subdivided into smaller 'firms' (which cannot be equated with 'divisions' or 'departments'). Basically it has no solid 'external' interfaces with other larger encompassing segments, nor any 'internal' ones with its encompassed 'sub-units', the next shorter possible segment being an individual agent. The 'borders' of a MLF and of its sub-segments vary, depending on the point of view chosen by the observer and on the level at which the observation is made. The external/internal opposition is segmented here.[15] From the practical and methodological point of view, this means that it is impossible to figure out the precise number of business units, or 'firms' in existence. Longer lineages are constantly fissioning into elder/younger shorter lines, and so are business 'concerns', because they are not absolutely separable from the kinship structure. Alliances would conversely tend to coalesce business 'concerns' from different exogamous lineages. The MLF is a lineage segment seen from the point of view of the commercial occupation of its members. It may correspond to a joint-family.

As a whole, the bag business of the Kutchi Lohanas is Janus-like. On the one hand, we have an integrated and gradually stratified system of retailers-wholesalers, founded on contractual linkages and clientelism. On the other, we have a hierarchised kinship system that has been both inherited and built up over the centuries (genealogies have been arranged). These kinds of systems are usually seen as antagonistic, and our main preoccupation here is to understand how they may articulate with each other. The hierarchised kinship network and the stratified business one actually do not, and cannot, coincide because they are founded on different principles. For instance, we may find a high-status Kutchi Lohana who has a poor business record, and vice versa. Moreover, a young Kutchi Lohana merchant may start his professional career almost from scratch, even though he is the son of an already established merchant: he will first have to learn how to collect bags, how to mend them or have them mended. True, he will be helped by his kinsmen, to an extent that depends on their business position. But younger brothers do not normally inherit the larger part of their father's business: they will either work for elder brothers, or try to start on their own with whatever lesser means they have. Nothing will guarantee that their business performance will constantly be up to their lineage status.

Then, a boy will certainly tend to be married according to the business position of his closest relatives. But the rules for matrimonial alliances are primarily based on kinship, and not on business position; nothing precludes a high-status poor retailer's boy being married to a low-status wealthy wholesaler's daughter.

And finally, the heads of the Mahajans, whether in Bombay, Mulund or Pune, are not elected on the basis of their success in business, but because they are considered amongst the 'most honourable' members of the local association.

In general in the Kutchi Lohana community, a person's business position is seen as an important but subordinate dimension of his status. In other words, as Pocock has aptly said in his study about the *Patidar*, 'standing' is here not to be equated with 'status'.[16] These can rather be seen as two faces of a single coin, one bearing a quantitative sign and owing its economic value to the other, which bears a socially symbolic one.

The offices, godowns and advertisements of the Kutchi Lohanas exhibit some common features in their spatial conception, which we can analyse briefly in order to illustrate this articulation.

In Bombay the offices are located in apartments in large old multi-storied buildings. Rooms are subdivided into narrow cells furnished with one or two desks and boards. Given the scarcity of habitable space in Bombay, this fragmentation is not surprising. However, these cells are occupied by people belonging to different 'firms', or at least to business segments each with their own boss and 'official' designation.

In a similar way, godowns are many-in-one. The Bombay godown I saw is a long building with a single entrance. This gives access to a long walled corridor with many doors on both sides. Each of these locked doors gives access to a 'privatised' box to store bags and various other goods. These boxes belong to different 'firms'. The godown I saw in a suburb of Pune was a similar long building, but each of its boxes had its own locked door directly accessible from outside, without the central corridor and common main entrance. In all these cases, a group of Kutchi Lohana merchants have collectively invested in facilities which they have later subdivided according to their 'individualised' and competing professional requirements.

Collective full-page advertisements published in the Mulund and Pune Mahajan directories are similarly subdivided into five clearly defined areas, each one dedicated to a particular 'firm' designed by a 'company name', a single merchant's 'name', or a composite of both. Some of these 'companies' may be shown as partnerships. All these 'individualised firms' are usually dealing in gunny bags, ropes and other kinds of packaging material, and are therefore in competition with each other. What could not immediately be perceived in the cases of offices and godowns here is striking: the surface area of these advertisements is wholly and clearly hierarchised. Apparently the most important merchant has his logo printed in thicker type and occupies a larger part of the page, while the other merchants occupy correspondingly smaller and smaller surface areas. All these 'firms' or 'merchants' tend to be kin, members of one lineage (or of branches of a patrilineal lineage). From the top to bottom of the page, they tend to be separated by three generations. The spatial hierarchy of the advertisements corresponds to the kinship hierarchy. These full-page representations can be seen as two-dimensional projections of what I have called the MLF. The MLF does not necessarily coincide with a joint-family. Advertisers may be members of two or more domestic units. But they are from the same kinship segment.

In a given MLF, one is therefore likely to find younger and older 'self-employed' individuals, beginners and well-established merchants, the latter controlling a larger capital than the former. Some members of the MLF will operate as small-scale collectors, mending and retailing for the other members, from whom they take loans. At the same time, these MLF members are also trying to maximise their own profits and share of the market; they may be in competition with each other (we should not forget that the MLF is bound to segment when its elder people disappear). Individually they can enter into partnership, deal with members of other lineages, and act to promote the business interests they consider their own. They may also take money advances from merchants belonging to other MLFs (in-laws, for instance) and deliver to them the bags they have collected with it, or build up their own network of client-suppliers (with friends happy to get this opportunity, for example). Transactions between 'merchants' belonging to the same MLF are normally negotiated at the market price, that is to say that theoretically and technically they are not distinguished from other normal transactions with other Kutchi Lohanas. However, these 'self-employed' merchants are also subordinate to their elder relatives and owe respect to them, starting from the elder of the line, who will also be the principal merchant of the MLF unless he has retired. The merchants' functional sense of I-ness is then necessarily limited by their social sense of We-ness, and competitive contractual business structures are only possible to the extent that they are kept within the frame of the more resistant and more valued structure of kinship relations. In other words, the individualistic business behaviour of the MLF members has to remain embedded in the primary group structure, in the same way as office cells, storage boxes, individual advertisements, and last but not least, Mahajan associations do. Otherwise it would be difficult to account for the durability of the *jati* as such.

Related merchants may compete and cooperate at the same time, but do so in business situations which have to be related to different levels of the kinship structure. For instance, 'Ravi' will compete against his father's brother's son of the same MLF when both are collecting bags in order to resell them on their own. They may also compete when they are collecting bags to supply to their own fathers in the MLF. But at the same time, they will cooperate when both of them have to supply their common grandfather so that he can make a wholesale delivery that will be profitable for the whole MLF. Obviously, depending on how particular MLFs are built, this intra-MLF competition/cooperation is also bound to occur between two MLFs, for instance between the elder and the younger branches of a larger lineage. This behaviour of competition/cooperation is typical of segmented kinship structures, which have been observed in various parts of the world. Here it is clearly apparent that such a mechanism works when the members of a kinship structure have to harmonise the interests of their closest group with the interests of a higher level group that they also belong to. This can only happen when the kinship hierarchy makes sense for its members, when their sense of I-ness is embedded in a sense of We-ness, or when individual members rather spontaneously subordinate their own interests to those of their kin-group. The larger kinship hierarchy may be latent, or more or less accentuated, according to circumstances.

Kinship and business structures can be analytically distinguished in the Kutchi Lohana bag business, but they cannot be understood independently. Business linkages have been built up into a network of retailers and wholesalers which can be represented as a systemic construction with its own rationale. However, this systemic construction is not autonomous. It keeps on emerging out of a hierarchic system of kinship relations in which it is rooted and which ultimately constitutes its real backbone.

WHERE BOTH HANDS MEET

At this point, we are still missing the key-stone of the whole edifice. We will now enquire about what kind of principle silently makes the two faces of this coin hold together, if not exactly coincide.

Let us first notice about these collective advertisements that: (a) they are not primarily intended to emphasise the quality of the goods dealt in (all the advertisers are dealing in more or less same ones); (b) they are published in directories which are normally reserved for the Mahajan members, who are kindred people who know each other more or less well, and not intended for the end-users; (c) the surface area of the advertisement that is dedicated to the leader of an MLF very often contains a picture of a god or a goddess such as Lakshmi, or a symbolic sign that has a religious meaning, under whose auspices the whole MLF is being placed.[17] So, what are these advertisements for?

As we have said, these advertisements actually represent a segment of a lineage through the occupational activities of some of its members. It is then the lineage-segment as such which is being advertised, for the purpose of heightening the social recognition of its status and credit among other kin members. From the business point of view, the higher the prestige of the lineage, the higher its status, the more confidence its members will certainly inspire in potential Kutchi Lohana loan-givers or investors. Prestige, status and credit-worthiness are linked. It has been usual in the past for a 'merchant family', an MLF I would say, to take collective responsibility for any bad debts incurred by its members.[18] These debts have been transmissible from generation to generation, along with positive assets and credits. This inter-generational collective responsibility for real debts has often been amalgamated with the ritualised debts Hindus are customarily born with.[19] These debts tend to position the people in their society as well as in the cosmic order. Such debts are due to one's ancestors up to the third ascending generation, according to the ancient Yajnavalkya school.[20] This is certainly why these advertisements generally spread over three generations of male kindred. In some cases advertisers did not hesitate to show a male infant as a merchant with his own company. Since the people who are supposed to read these advertisements will certainly get to know about it, this child-promotion can only be for the sake of having a formal 3-tier lineage advertisement. It is then a 'public way to guarantee potential loan-givers that the MLF already has the means to transmit its real debts to a male who is at the same time bound to repay his ritual debt to the present leader of the MLF. The *karta*, the oldest male member of the lineage, is also its head man and the leading merchant of the MLF. It is in this double capacity that the *karta* will offer *pinda* to his ancestors during the ritual called *shradha*. *Shradha* means confidence, credit, and designates the ritual offering of *pinda* to the three generations of *sapinda* ancestors. These ancestors will finally coalesce with the common mass of Kutchi Lohana ancestors represented by Daryalal, Jhulelal and Varuna: there lineage debts and business debts finally amalgamate, and Invisible, Visible and Non-Invisible Hands meet.

CONCLUSION

The Kutchi Lohana segmented type of organisation appears to have hardly anything to do with the Western family firm, nor with the modern type of the big organisation, nor with any Western model of organisation I know of. So a real comparative analysis of it is hardly possible here. I will only shortly contrast some features of the big organisation with their non-equivalent counterparts in the segmented organisation, from a perspective which I think is relevant for the anthropologist.

A segmented system is not centralised but poly-centred. Seen as a whole, it is not a federation of independent familial units that could be better coordinated: segmentary subdivisions are self-coordinating while competing with each other. Since a segment has no real internal or external fixed perennial limits, the question of internalising transaction-costs does not really make sense. Neither is there any need for a class of salaried managers. Every male Kutchi family-head is supposed to be or to become 'self-employed', and I may say that in that respect, the Kutchi system gives individuals more chances to become entrepreneurs than a system of competing big organisations: Indian merchant communities are a well-known reservoir of entrepreneurs. In short, most of the arguments adequately developed by A. Chandler to explain how the familial type of enterprise gave way to the big organisation do not, and cannot, apply here.

Chandler's history convincingly recounts the story of the big organisation that first appeared in the United States of America and was then exported to Europe and later to the rest of the world, including India and Japan. According to him, the managers appeared with the organisation itself to coordinate flows of material and immaterial inputs and outputs, functions, processes and also other men. Internal hierarchies of functions and competencies were designed mainly on the basis of functional linkages and contractual relationships. Other kinds of social relationship not prevalent in the structure of modern Western societies are not supposed to intervene: they have been thought of as informal and dysfunctional in the architecture of the big organisation. The segmented organisation of the Kutchi Lohanas is primarily based on the kind of social relationships that prevail in Indian society. The Kutchi Lohanas do not have to design and build up a huge artificial functional organisation, because their whole business is structured by the existing social kinship hierarchy itself: in this respect, and from the point of view of 'social engineering' technology, their business networks are much more sparingly constructed.

From the point of view of the big organisation, workers, employees and managers are considered as 'human resources', that is to say as a production factor, or a consumable input to make the organisation work. The organisation is in fact a huge machine made up of things material and immaterial, with people acting mainly as functional parts of it. 'Human resources' then appear to be inserted in this machinery and one cannot account for any system of possible relationships between people within the organisation without having first understood the organisational machinery itself. As we have seen, the reverse is true in the case of the Kutchi Lohanas: we cannot fully account for the way their business networks function without having understood their kinship system. Whereas their business networks are embedded in their social system, the reverse is true in the case of the big organisation: social relationships are inserted in the machinery. In other words, we are dealing here with relations between people and things, and this attitude ultimately depends upon the way people see themselves in their society and on what their primary aims are. Kutchis have been aiming at improving their status while increasing their 'standing'. Westerners tend first to administer things.

Case-based archaic business organisations such as the Kutchi Lohanas' are certainly residual in India today. That does not, however, mean that the Indian social texture has become such as to allow for the easy transplantation of modern big organisations. As a matter of a fact, Indian specialists do recognise that modern big organisations generally do not function properly in India, and new management and organisational models that would be more suitable are being investigated.[21]

All Western specialists are doing the same, since, as I said rather abruptly in the introduction, the Western model of organisation and management has become obsolete because it has proved to be not as efficient as the Japanese one. Managers have been prompt to react, and are nowadays taking lessons in Tokyo.[22] Some specialists are of the opinion that the Japanese are simply better at applying a model of organisation and management that is basically universal (so Westerners can learn from them how to improve their own methods). Other experts think that the Japanese organisation and management model is rooted in Japanese society and ideology (so Westerners can hardly be successful in imitating it).[23] None of them are really supporting their opinions by decisive arguments. Whatever their disagreements, however, most of these various specialists do generally admit that the way Japanese people behave in a group is one of the most important factors in their superior organisational efficiency ('groupism'). The Japanese do seem to spontaneously exhibit a stronger sense of We-ness, that appears rather strange to Westerners.[24]

One other remarkable feature of the Japanese organisation is that relations between people appear to be more valued than relations between people and things, material and immaterial. For instance, the big Western organisations used to have a reduced Personnel Department which has grown more important only recently, whereas Personnel Departments have always been most important in Japanese organisations. People are not hired primarily because of their technical specialisation, but because of their potential ability to integrate themselves into a particular organisation.[25] Contrary to what happens in the typical Western big organisation, people's qualifications are not primarily defined by and derived from the specific requirements needed to fulfil more or less standardised functions in the machinery.[26] Japanese organisations have historically been engineered with a relatively high content of prevailing hierarchised social material:[27] interpersonal relationships are normally hierarchised in Japan, and this social characteristic has been (deliberately or otherwise) retained in the organisations, where it has had to combine with the organisational hierarchy of functions. Japanese enterprises are themselves usually operating in hierarchised networks of interrelated and rather exclusive linkages between principals and subcontractors.[28]

These features are strikingly reminiscent of the traditional Indian type of organisation as illustrated by our Kutchi Lohana bag businesses. According to the well-known Japanese sociologist Chie Nakane, Japanese industrial organisation and society is actually functioning as a segmented system.[29]

I am, of course, not saying that traditional Indian networks should be reanimated. I am just pointing out that studying them in a certain perspective may help us to understand better why the Japanese system is working so efficiently, why some Indian organisations are not, and in which direction investigations may be more fruitful. From the anthropological point of view, modern Japanese and traditional Indian systems, however different they may be, may actually prove to be much closer to each other than either are to the Western one. This is a point of view that may be shared by a few management specialists in India. So far, it has not been supported or documented in a fully convincing way.[30] Organisations may or may not be embedded (in the sense I have used this word) in the social system: this will be better recognised through comparative anthropological and social analysis. If they are, then they can only be thought out after the social system itself has been understood, the reverse process being much more difficult. The matter is of importance because the Japanese have demonstrated that big organisation of the West can really be efficiently acculturated into a non-Western society. However, it does not look as if the product resulting from this acculturation process still has much to do with its original model: it can hardly be transferred back as such into Western countries without being 'transculturated'.

It is quite a long time since the West acculturated some decisive technology. In the near future anthropologists may find themselves confronted with a challenging task that is quite new to them!

NOTES

1. R.K. Hazari, *The Structure of the Corporate Private Sector: a Study of Concentration, Ownership and Control*, Asia Publishing House, Bombay, 1967, p. 400.
2. Alfred D. Chandler, *The Visible Hand: the Managerial Revolution in American Business*, Harvard University Press, Cambridge, Mass. USA and London, UK, 1977.
3. James J. Berna, *Industrial Entrepreneurship in Madras State*, Asia Publishing House, Bombay, 1960, p. 236. In this classic work the author did see linkages between the entrepreneurs of his sample, but did not consider them when representing Indian entrepreneurs in general.
4. P.G. Gadgil, *Origins of the Modern Indian Business Class*, Institute of Pacific Relations, New York, March 1951. As far as I know, Gadgil is the first to have raised the question of the Indian 'Business Community', or 'Class' as an economist. See also Thomas Timberg, *The Marwaris: from Traders to Industrialists*, Vikas, Bombay, 1978. Timberg is the first author to have reported on a business community as such, although he did not really try to analyse social relationships typical of Indian society and preferred to speak of 'resource groups'. The following articles by him have been extremely useful to me: 'A Study of a Great Marwari Firm: 1860-1914', in *Indian Economic and Social History Review*, vol. III, no. 3, 1971, pp. 264-83; and 'Three Types of the Marwari Firm', in *Indian Economic and Social History Review*, vol. X, no. 1, 1973, pp. 1-36.
5. Pierre Lachaier, *Réseaux marchands et industriels au Maharashtra (Inde): castes, sous-traitance et clientelisme*, Ph.D. for the EHESS, Paris, 1989. An anthropological description of the Kutchi Lohana networks is to be found in Pierre Lachaier, 'Le capitalisme lignager assigné aujourd'hui: les marchands Kutchi Lohana du Maharashtra (Inde)', in *Annales*, nos. 4-5, July-October 1992, Armand Colin, France.
6. Sri Kutchi Lohana Mahajan, p. 78, Mulund, 1970; Pune, p. 170, 1984, printed in Gujarati.
7. C.A. Bayly, *Rulers, Townsmen and Bazaars, North Indian Society in the Age of British Expansion, 1770-1870*, Cambridge University Press, Cambridge, 1983. The book contains two important chapters devoted to the description of Indian merchant firms.
8. William Ouchi, is amongst the best known authors who started deriving new methods of management from Japanese organisations: *Theory Z, How American Business Can Meet the Japanese Challenge*, Avon Books, New York, 1982 (this is an effort to understand, and then to adapt or imitate the Japanese way of management and organisation started at the beginning of the eighties. These efforts have become less obvious in the nineties.
9. Shri Kanaksen is certainly the merchant Kharagsen whose life has been described by Banarasidas, himself a Jain merchant living in the seventeenth century, in his 'Ardha Kathanak'. See Ramesh Chandra Sharma: 'The Ardha Kathanak: a neglected source of Mughal history', in *Indica*, vol. 6, 1969, pp. 49-73 and vol. 7, 1970, pp. 105-20.
10. Karl Polanyi, *The Great Transformation*, 1944. I have borrowed from Polanyi the word 'embedded'.

11. The Pune directory contains three lists: one for Pune, a much shorter one for its surrounding area, and a list of Kutchi Brahmins serving Kutchi Lohanas.
12. G.S. Ghurye, has mentioned the Kutchi Lohana caste association and newspaper 'The Lohana Hitechu', in *Caste and Race in India*, Popular Prakashan, Bombay, 5th edn, rptd 1986, p. 443.
13. Clifford Geertz, *Peddlers and Princes: Social Development and Economic Change in Two Indonesian Towns*, The University of Chicago Press, 1963, p. 162. In this earlier work, which has become a classic in the field of entrepreneurship, Geertz attempts to compare the bazaar as an open network type of business with local Westernised, rationalised, closed private firms. The paradigm of the firm as an 'Organisation' plays a dominant role in this analysis. Was the author perhaps confronted with some sort of segmented type of network?
14. See C.A. Bayly, ibid.
15. The first description of a segmented system was made by E.E. Evans-Prichard about people living in south Sudan: The Nuer, The Clarendon Press, 1937. French trans. *Les Nuer: description des modes de vie et des institutions politiques d'un peuple nilote*, Gallimard, Paris, 1968. Preface by Louis Dumont. A more recent description of a segmented system can be found in E. Gellner, *Muslim Society*, Cambridge University Press, Cambridge, 1981.
16. The opposition of status versus standing is from David Pocock, F. Kanbi and A. Patidar, *Study of the Patidar Community of Gujarat*, Oxford University Press, 1972.
17. Cf. Florence Caillet, *La Maison Yamazaki: la vie exemplaire d'une paysanne japonaise devenue chef d'une entreprise de haute coiffure*, Plon, 1991. The author has written a biographical account of a Japanese woman who after the war founded an important chain of hairdressers shops in Tokyo. The author reproduces a calligraphic picture representing the harmony of the company: directors are shown around the founder as well as gods to whom everyone has to be loyal. All of them are in a bubble, to the bottom part of which the sign for 'Harmony', 'wa', is attached. This rather conservative private company is managed according to the 'familialist' doctrine.
18. Here I am referring to C.A. Bayly's 'merchant families', ibid.
19. See the review *Purushartha 4: La dette*, EHESS, Paris, 1980, particularly the contributions of Ch. Malamoud, L. Dumont and J.C. Galey.
20. See L. Dumont in *Purushartha 4*, ibid.
21. For instance S.K. Chakraborty, *Managerial Effectiveness and Quality of Worklife, Indian Insights*, Tata McGraw-Hill, New Delhi, 1987. The author contrasts an Indian way of working based on a sense of duty—the Hindu debts—with the way Westerners work egocentrically, with a sense of their own rights. The Indian doctrine of management he is suggesting would be closer to the Japanese one.
22. See for instance the very popular French book G. Archier and H. Serieyx, *L'Entreprise du 3ème Type*, Le Seuil, Paris, 1984.
23. See Serge Airaudi, 'Peut-on faire une théorie du "management japonaise"?' in Jean-François Sabouret, *L'Etat du Japon*, ed. La Découverte, Paris, 1988, p. 403.
24. See W. Ouchi, ibid.
25. See W. Ouchi, ibid. and Masaru Yoshimori, *Les entreprises japonaises*, PUF,

2nd edn, 1987. This author has produced many works in Japanese about the ideology and behaviour of European, German, and French enterprises.
26. Laurent Schwab and Thiercelin Patrice, *L'Economie du Japon: performances et internationalisation*, Nathan, Paris, 1990. 'Contrairement à l'organisation taylorienne, le poste de travail n'est pas le support de la qualification de la personne. La qualification est attachée à l'individu', p. 125.
27. P. Beillevaire, 'Le Japon, une société de la maison', vol. 1, pp. 479-517; and 'La famille: instrument et modèle de la nation japonaise', vol. 2, pp. 237-65, in A. Burguière *et al.*, *Histoire de la Famille*, Arman Colin, Paris, 1986. A description of the key concepts and notions relating to the pre-war social hierarchy is to be found in Ruth Benedict, *The Chrysanthemum and the Sword*, Houghton Mifflin, 1946 and R.G. Freeman, 1974.
28. Schwab and Thiercelin, ibid., give a good description of the linkages between enterprises, pp. 53-73. Yveline Leclerc has studied subcontracting linkages, 'Un système productif fondé sur la sous-traitance', in J.F. Sabouret, ibid., pp. 260-3. Such subcontracting systems have also been developed in India, see P. Lachaier, ibid. and 'Employeurs-employés et employés-employeurs dans les Firmes Lignagères industrielles du secteur de la mécanique de Pune', in *Purushartha 14*, EHESS, Paris, 1992. This study is based on the industrial engineering network in Pune.
29. Chie Nakane, *Japanese Society*, 1970.
30. A.V. Srinivasan, *Japanese Management: The Indian Context*, Tata McGraw-Hill, New Delhi, 1990, p. 205. See also S.K. Chakraborty's *Indian Doctrine of Management*, ibid. Indian specialists used to working according to US management methods seem to experience the same kinds of difficulties as their Western colleagues when trying to transfer Japanese methods.

REFERENCES

Airaudi, Serge, 'Peut-on faire une théorie du "management japonaise"?' in Sabouret Jean-François, *L'Etat du Japon*, Ed. La Découverte, Paris, 1988.
Archier, G. and Serieyx, H., *L'Entreprise du 3ème type*, Le Seuil, Paris, 1984.
Bayly, C.A., *Rulers, Townsmen and Bazaars, North Indian Society in the Age of British Expansion, 1770-1870*, Cambridge University Press, Cambridge, 1983.
Beillevaire, P. 'Le Japon, une société de la maison', in Burguière A. *et al.*, *Histoire de la Famille*, Arman Colin, vol. I, Paris, 1986.
——— 'La famille: instrument et modèle de la nation japonaise', in Burguière A. *et al.*, *Histoire de la Famille*, Arman Colin, vol. 2, Paris, 1986.
Benedict, Ruth, *The Chrysanthemum and the Sword*, Houghton Mifflin, 1946.
Berna, J. J., *Industrial Entrepreneurship in Madras State*, Asia Publishing House, Bombay, 1960.
Caillet, Florence, *La Maison Yamazaki: la vie exemplaire d'une paysanne japonaise devenue chef d'une entreprise de haute coiffure*, Plon, Paris, 1991.
Purushartha 4: La dette, EHESS, Paris, 1980.
Chakraborty, S.K., *Managerial Effectiveness and Quality of Worklife, Indian Insights*, Tata McGraw-Hill, New Delhi, 1987.
Chandler, Alfred D., *The Visible Hand: the Managerial Revolution in American*

Business, Harvard University Press, Cambridge, Mass. USA and London, UK, 1977.

Evans-Prichard E.E., *Les Nuer: description des modes de vie et des institutions politiques d'un peuple nilote*, Gallimard, Paris, 1968.

Gadgil, P.G., *Origins of the Modern Indian Business Class*, Institute of Pacific Relations, New York, March 1951.

Geertz, Clifford, *Peddlers and Princes: Social Development and Economic Change in Two Indonesian Towns*, The University of Chicago Press, Chicago, 1963.

Gellner, E., *Muslim Society*, Cambridge University Press, Cambridge, 1981.

Ghurye, G.S., *Caste and Race in India*, Popular Prakashan, Bombay, 5th edn, rptd 1986.

Hazari, R.K., *The Structure of the Corporate Private Sector: a Study of Concentration, Ownership and Control*, Asia Publishing House, Bombay.

Lachaier, P., *Réseaux marchands et industriels au Maharashtra (Inde): castes, sous-traitance et clientelisme*, Ph.D. for the EHESS, Paris, 1989.

————, 'Employeurs-employés et employés-employeurs dans les Firmes Lignagères industrielles du secteur de la mécanique de Pune', in *Purushartha 14*, EHESS, Paris, 1992.

————, 'Le capitalisme lignager assigné aujourd'hui: les marchands Kutchi Lohana du Maharashtra (Inde)', in *Annales*, nos. 4-5, July-October 1992, Armand Colin, France.

Leclerc, Y., 'Un système productif fondé sur la sous-traitance', in Sabouret Jean-François, *L'Etat du Japon*, Ed. La Decouverte, Paris, 1988.

Nakane, Chie, *La Société japonaise*, Armand Colin, Paris, 1974 (orig. *Japanese Society*, London, Weidenfeld and Nicolson, 1970).

Ouchi, W., *Theory Z, How American Business Can Meet the Japanese Challenge*, Avon Books, New York, 1982.

Pocock, David, Kanbi, F. and Patidar, A., *Study of the Patidar Community of Gujarat*, Oxford University Press, Delhi, 1972.

Sabouret Jean-François, *L'Etat du Japon*, ed. La Decouverte, Paris, 1988.

Sharma, R.C., 'The Ardha Kathanak: a neglected source of Mughal history', in *Indica*, vol. 6, 1969 and vol. 7, 1970.

Schwab, L., Thiercelin P., *L'Economie du Japon: performances et internationalisation*, Nathan, Paris, 1990.

Srinivasan, A.V., *Japanese Management: The Indian Context*, Tata McGraw-Hill, New Delhi, 1990.

Timberg, T., *The Marwaris: from Traders to Industrialists*, Vikas, Bombay, 1978.

————, 'A Study of a Great Marwari Firm: 1860-1914', in *Indian Economic and Social History Review*, vol. III, no. 3, 1971.

————, 'Three Types of the Marwari Firm', in *Indian Economic and Social History Review*, vol. X, no.1, 1973.

Yoshimori, Masaru, *Les entreprises japonaises*, PUF, 2nd edn, Paris, 1987.

The Genesis and Growth of a Business Community: A Case Study of Vaghri Street Traders in Ahmedabad

EMMA TARLO

The problem of how to comprehend the relationship between individual and collective economic enterprise has long plagued sociologists, anthropologists and economists working in non-Western societies. At its most crude, this debate used to be summarised in terms of a simplistic opposition between formalist and substantivist theories: the formalists suggesting that the classical Western economic theory of the market is universally applicable; the substantivists claiming that it is inappropriate to those societies where economic relations are embedded in the social structure. The former theory gave birth to the familiar and controversial figure of Homo Economicus, the rational, self-seeking, profit-oriented individual, who existed in a world of scarcity, governed by the laws of demand and supply, and making choices to satisfy his personal needs. The latter gave birth to the equally one-dimensional model of Non-economic Man, an altruistic being who, living in a world where scarcity was barely perceived, acted according to social and moral obligations rather than personal choice.

It has long been recognised that this simplistic opposition does not correspond to the reality of socio-economic behaviour either in capitalist or non-capitalist societies. Furthermore the assumption that strong social and moral obligations necessarily stand in the way of rational economic advancement has also been shown to be largely erroneous. The success of various traditional trading communities in India is sufficient proof of the fact that socio-religious bonds such as caste can operate as an asset in economic development. Yet at the same time the fact that there are well established business communities with a history of trade and, in some cases, a virtual monopoly over certain types of goods, also reminds us that the market in India is far from being an open playing field. Clearly it is a complex arena born out of the interaction between individual and collective enterprise, and if we are to understand how such interaction works, we need to analyse more closely the process by which individuals and groups manipulate social and economic relations to their advantage.

The particular example I wish to discuss is that of the footpath embroidery traders at Law Gardens in Ahmedabad city.[1] Every night of the week, these traders can be seen lining the pavements with elaborate local embroidery from the towns and villages of Gujarat. Situated opposite the College of Law in the salubrious western quarter of the city, Law Gardens is a well established evening leisure spot. One attraction is its large selection of food stalls and snack bars which specialise in local favourites such as *pau bhaji* and Jain vegetarian pizza. The other is the embroidery market which stretches along one of the pavements, creating a dazzling display of silk, cotton and mirror work. Arriving in the early evening, the footpath traders spread out their wares, converting the Garden railings into an embroidered backdrop for their stalls. Seating themselves on a mud platform and surrounding themselves with further piles of embroidery, they launch into persuasive sales banter which goes on well into the night. As *kharid-walas* begin to give way to *khanne-walas*,[2] the traders start to pack up their goods and prepare for home. By eleven o'clock most of them have climbed into rickshaws and sped off into the darkness.

Ahmedabad's embroidery market may be unusual for being held at night, but otherwise it bears much resemblance to street markets for Gujarati embroidery all over India. The most famous of these is the street market just off Janpath in Delhi where Gujarati women sell embroidered clothes and hangings to a mixture of tourists, fashion designers and trendy urban youth. In Goa, male and female traders gather under the trees near the beaches in 'flea markets', catering to a mixture of ageing hippies and Indian and foreign tourists, whilst in Bombay, Calcutta and Pune they apparently sit on the pavements like their counterparts in Delhi and Ahmedabad.[3] There are, of course, street traders all over India dealing in various textiles including embroidery, but those dealing specifically in Gujarati village-style embroidery[4] are invariably members of the Vaghri community from Gujarat.

At a superficial level, the Vaghri traders would appear to display many of the features typical of a traditional Indian business community. They have a highly specialised profession centred around a distinctive product; their markets occupy fixed spaces in various cities throughout the country; their business operates through extensive kinship networks, and such networks are intensified through intermarriage which helps to perpetuate the link between caste and profession. Yet this apparent uniformity of identity is deceptive when one realises these traders have only entered the profession in dribs and drabs since the 1950s and that, as a group, they do not have any historical links with the embroidery trade. Furthermore, they have entered the trade from a number of different occupations, some of which had nothing to do with commerce at all. How these men and women have homogenised their activities to create a new form of caste specialisation is the initial focus of this article. Concentrating on the street market in Ahmedabad, I shall demonstrate how it came about through the efforts of a single entrepreneur, who, by introducing his relatives to the trade, was able to transform his individual actions into a collective enterprise, involving 120 participants (children included). I shall then go on to examine the extent to which the footpath embroidery trade has provided the basis of a new collective identity for the traders, and shall question whether becoming a 'business community' has in any way inhibited their scope for entrepreneurship. But in order first to give some idea of the diverse backgrounds from which the traders have emerged as a collectivity, I shall begin by introducing the Vaghris as a social group, indicating the types of occupation they were pursuing earlier this century.

THE VAGHRIS OF GUJARAT:
A MUCH MALIGNED IDENTITY

There is a certain amount of confusion in the sociological literature concerning the identity of Vaghris, a group which seems to escape simplistic distinctions between 'caste' and 'tribe', 'settled' and 'nomadic' populations. *The Gazetteer of the Bombay Presidency* of 1884 contains just a single paragraph on the subject, stating without further substantiation that: 'Vaghris are one of the early tribes' (*GBP*

1884:158). It goes on to outline their various activities: as poaching, hunting,[5] begging, thieving, growing water melons, selling babul sticks, making stone handmills and tattooing women. *The Gazetteer* of 1901 contains a considerably more detailed entry and tries to place this miscellaneous[6] community within the context of Gujarati society. 'The Vaghris of Gujarat', it suggests, 'probably belong to the Bagri tribe inhabiting the Bagar country, a tract between the south-western border of Hariana and the Shara in the North-West provinces. . . . Originally they were Rajputs but they have degenerated to a very low social position. . . . Vaghris are superior to Dhedas but inferior to Kolis'[7] (*GBP* 1901: 510-11). *The Gazetteer* remains confused as to whether to interpret the Vaghris as a 'tribe' which has absorbed Hindu elements or a 'caste' which has sunk to a degraded position, but what it is clear about is the fact that Vaghris occupy a very low position in society, living in small mud huts and pursuing a variety of petty enterprises. To the occupations already listed in 1884, the new gazetteer adds sheep and cattle rearing, trading in livestock, painting, working as carriers and field labourers, fishing, farming, trading in green parrots and renting trees in order to sell their produce. Other less reputable activities include begging in the guise of *jogis* or astrologers and catching wild birds in order to make wealthy Hindus pay for their release. What is evident from such descriptions is that Vaghris do not have any single fixed occupation and that even those who apparently belong to specific occupational subgroups, such as the Datanias, (babul stick sellers), vary their activities during the year.

If British administrators and ethnographers were unable to define the Vaghris either by their origin or their occupation, they nonetheless found a means of classifying them according to their reputation and reported behaviour. In 1879 the Vaghris, along with various other miscellaneous groups were officially classified as a 'criminal tribe'. Writing some thirty years after the Criminal Tribes Act was introduced, M. Kennedy, Deputy Inspector General of Police in the Bombay Presidency, included a description of the Vaghris in his much discussed directory of the 'criminal classes'.[8] Here again, there is confusion about who the Vaghris are and what they do. On the one hand we are told that they 'are not a nomadic tribe'. On the other hand we are informed that some of them 'wander in small gangs', leading the 'lives of Gypsies' whilst others 'travel about the country' putting up in *dharamsalas* or temples when permitted.

Kennedy estimates that there are somewhere around 60,000 members of this marginal group in the Presidency as a whole. He refers to them as 'practically outcasts', a phrase which seems to sum up the ambiguity of their position.

There is, of course, much blatant stereotyping in Kennedy's description of the language, customs and amoral behaviour of the so called 'Criminal classes'. But rather than directing yet another arrow at this obvious and well-worn target, I want to try to elucidate some possible areas of interest. One point that is worth considering is that if the Vaghris ended up being classified as criminal, this was no doubt partly because educated Indians had defamed them to such an extent that the appellation seemed, to the ignorant British, appropriate. It is, of course, impossible to disentangle retrospectively the relationship between Gujarati and British stereotypes in the nineteenth century,[9] but what is clear is that Kennedy's description of Vaghris as 'dirty and slovenly', 'poorly clad', 'naturally lazy', and 'addicted' to crime differs remarkably little from the types of description given by both rural and urban Gujaratis of most classes today. To what extent the British use of the label 'criminal tribe' has influenced these local perceptions it is difficult to judge. The fact that most contemporary Gujaratis seem entirely unaware of the creation and destruction of the category, 'criminal tribe' would suggest to me that the negative reputation of the Vaghris may have as much to do with old Gujarati attitudes as it has with British ones. Whatever the origin of the stereotype, the image of the Vaghris remains very negative even today, a fact that is highlighted in the frequent use of the word 'Vaghri' or 'Vaghran' as an insult in Gujarat.

A second point of interest from Kennedy's account is that despite his attempts to classify Vaghris into occupational subgroups, they nonetheless continue to display an extraordinary heterogeneity of activity. Of those classified as lime burners and cultivators (Chunarias), we learn that they also keep pack bullocks and deal in old bricks which they obtain from ruins. Of those who sell toothsticks, we learn that they are also drummers during the wedding season, as well as being cultivators and hawkers in the rainy season. A third type of Vaghri alternates, we are told, between cultivating, selling reed tatties, trading in bamboo or tobacco pipes, and keeping male buffaloes for stud purposes. It seems pointless to go into all of the activities listed for each subdivision. But what comes across from Kennedy's description is that the Vaghris, motivated no doubt by poverty and necessity, seem highly versatile and capable of pursuing a variety of different types of work simultaneously.[10] To the activities listed in the gazetteers, Kennedy adds castrating bullocks, hewing wood, working as watchmen, dealing in mangoes and mhowra flowers, exhibiting peep shows and assuming guises in the pursuit of organised crime, an activity he describes at length. He does, however, point out that many Vaghri men and women have settled in Ahmedabad where 'some earn an honest livelihood by working in mills or support themselves by rearing small live-stock, fishing and snaring' although 'others again wander about begging' (ibid.: 160).

A clearer picture of these Ahmedabad Vaghris can be gained from the work of P.G. Shah, writing some half a century later.[11] He suggests that Vaghris initially came to the city in search of employment and that some of them had previously owned small plots of land which they lost during the British period out of fear of having to pay taxes if they declared it (Shah 1967: 2). He claims that in the 1960s many Ahmedabad Vaghris farmed rented land or worked in the textile mills. Others were successful in a number of conventional 'semi-commercial' activities such as selling ghee, vegetables, fruits and tooth sticks. To these Shah adds yet another 'traditional and popular occupation of the Vaghris', that of obtaining second-hand clothes in exchange for steel vessels, and repairing the former for sale to other poor communities. This activity had clearly become something of a Vaghri speciality by the 1950s and it may well be a very ancient profession. Certainly Vaghri men and women were bartering with brass and copper vessels long before the introduction of stainless steel. Writing in the 1990s, Kalima Rose paints a grim picture of the life of those involved in the profession today. Like the vegetable vendors of Ahmedabad, most of whom are also Vaghris, the used clothes vendors suffer not only from poverty and indebtedness but also regular police harassment. Rose adds: 'Because of the widespread belief that they are thieves, Vagharis can be arrested, beaten, sentenced and fined summarily, without evidence to implicate their guilt' (Rose 1992: 43).[12] This observation reveals the extent to which, even today, being a Vaghri in Gujarat means living with a damning reputation.

The above account is sufficient for revealing that clearly Vaghris do not have the classical background of the successful Indian business community. Far from concentrating their attention on a single trade, they have a history of diversifying their activities in numerous directions, taking up whatever occupation appears most lucrative at the time. Some of these occupations are adopted on a full time basis and become caste professions, but many of them are temporary or seasonal. The result is that a single individual may earn money by several different means during the year whilst members of a single family often do not share the same profession. It is from this background of occupational diversity, combined with low social and economic status and a widespread negative reputation, that members of the Vaghri community have succeeded in forging a new identity built around the footpath embroidery trade. In order to demonstrate how they have entered the trade and made it a new caste specialisation, I shall first begin by tracing the history of Dharamsingbhai, the individual entrepreneur behind the creation of Law Gardens embroidery market in Ahmedabad.

THE EMERGENCE OF A VAGHRI ENTREPRENEUR

Dharamsingbhai[13] was born around 1943 in Dholera Bhander, a village in the southern tip of the dry zone of the Ahmedabad district. After only two years of schooling he abandoned education and, at the age of 13 or so, he married Champaben. Together the young couple worked as farm labourers until the severe drought of 1957-8, which prompted them to leave the village and to set out for Ahmedabad in search of water and employment. One can get an idea of their lack of material resources from Champaben's recollection of the period which, though somewhat stereotyped, is none the less revealing:

When we left home, we had only 10 rupees. Out of this we paid 9 rupees and 25 paisa for the train fare. So we had only 75 paisa when we arrived in Ahmedabad. With this we bought some kindle for 25 paisa and some rice and lentils for 50 paisa. With this I cooked some *kitcharee* by the roadside, and we slept. The next day we had to find work.

Like many a migrant couple before them, they found their first employment in the construction industry, an industry renowned for taking on casual unskilled migrant labour. But after spending some time shifting loads, they made contact with other Ahmedabad Vaghris whom they eventually joined in the vegetable business. Champaben recalls:

After some time [shifting loads] we saved a little money. With this money we would buy fresh vegetables in the early morning and sell them during the day. There were other people of our caste doing this thing so we sat with them on the pavement and learnt the trade.'

Learning the trade meant not only buying and selling vegetables but also cultivating them in the dried up river basin of the Sabarmati, another activity in which Ahmedabad Vaghris were well experienced. Champaben, comparing those early vegetable-vending days to her current situation as an embroidery trader, remarked to me in 1988: 'Now we still sit on the pavement, but we sell embroidery. Things have changed. We came with 75 paisa and now we have a two-storey house, a car, a rickshaw and a house in the village.'

This leap from being poor vegetable vendors to comparatively prosperous embroidery traders was accomplished largely through the entrepreneurial exploits of Dharamsingbhai. Not content to remain a vegetable vendor all his life, he abandoned the trade and found individual employment as the handyman of a Brahman merchant, his principal task being that of a driver. There was nothing unusual about this occupational shift. As we have seen, there were plenty of rural and urban Vaghris who drifted from one activity to another, depending on the benefits of the moment. But in Dharamsingbhai's case, he was to use this shift as the stepping stone for launching a new personal career. His employer was initially exporting mill-made textiles, but shortly after employing Dharamsingbhai, he decided to branch into the embroidery business, a trade which was proving a great success with another Ahmedabad merchant called Manubhai. How Manubhai had entered the trade and how the Brahman merchant succeeded in imitating him are subjects I have discussed elsewhere within the context of wider national and international embroidery merchant networks [cf. Tarlo: forthcoming]. My aim here is to concentrate specifically on how Dharamsingbhai was able to secure a unique role for himself within the business.

The distinctive feature of the Gujarati embroidery trade as it was developing in the 1950s and 60s was that the embroidered cast-offs of Gujarati villagers were collected for a pittance from rural areas and resold in a new urban or foreign context where they attained the status of 'ethnic arts'. These embroidered items consisted primarily of clothing, animal regalia and decorative wall hangings which Gujarati village women made for use by themselves and their families. They not only wore colourfully embroidered skirts and bodices on a daily basis, but they also accumulated large stocks of embroidered items for their trousseaux. The result was that most reasonably prosperous rural families had considerable reserves of embroidery stored away in cupboards, sacks or chests.[14] Access to this embroidery was gained through the intervention of *pheriyos*, (wandering traders) who would offer women small items like stainless steel vessels or plastic buckets in exchange for their old embroidery. They would move from house to house usually in rural areas, and once they had accumulated sufficient stocks, would hand these over to their employers for export. Since many Vaghris were involved in the second-hand garments trade, a business which also used kitchen utensils as a medium through which to obtain old clothes, it was members of the Vaghri caste who were mostly enlisted as *pheriyos*. Being poor and of low social status, Vaghri women were almost as free as their husbands to move about out of doors and were often considered particularly skilled barterers.

When Dharamsingbhai's employer first entered the embroidery trade, there were several such *pheriyos* working for Manubhai on a commission basis. The Brahman merchant simply observed their techniques and followed suit, using Dharamsingbhai in the dual role of driver-cum-*pheriyo*. Soon the latter was driving his employer around the rural areas of Saurashtra and Kutch on embroidery-gathering tours. Although Dharamsingbhai had no personal experience of the trade, he had access to the considerable knowledge accumulated by other Vaghri *pheriyos* and bartering traders. Furthermore, he had substantial kinship networks on whom he could rely in towns and villages throughout Gujarat. Caste etiquette ensured that other Vaghris were always willing to provide him with food and shelter when he came to their villages in search of embroidery. Whatever their *gotra* or lineage, as 'caste brothers' they were, according to Dharamsingbhai, expected to offer hospitality. Soon Dharamsingbhai's employer, recognising his driver's superior bargaining talents, sent him to the villages of Kutch and Saurashtra alone, whilst he himself concentrated on the export side of the industry. Unlike other *pheriyos*, who usually travelled by train and foot, Dharamsingbhai had the use of his employer's car and was therefore well placed for rapidly acquiring knowledge of the embroidery-producing terrain. Through observing his employer's transactions, he also accumulated knowledge of the market for embroidery, knowledge which he could not have obtained so easily from members of his own caste. In particular, he learnt that it was mainly foreigners or wealthy urban Indians who wanted to buy these village products and that amongst this category of people, the fact that embroidery was old often increased its 'artistic' and monetary value. This made the embroidery trade far more prosperous than the second-hand sari business. The Indian repugnance at the idea of wearing second-hand clothes meant that only poor people ever purchased rejected and repaired garments, with the result that the trade operated right at the bottom end of the economy. Embroidery, by contrast, was an upmarket product, sold to foreigners or to exclusive, educated Indians who were willing to pay well for what they considered 'folk art'.[15]

Eighteen months of working as a *pheriyo* was sufficient for Dharamsingbhai to recognise that he had all the knowledge necessary for being a dealer in his own right. He therefore approached his employer saying that he wanted to become a business partner or at least to gain a greater share of his master's profits. When the merchant refused this arrogant suggestion, Dharamsingbhai decided to leave the security of his employment and to launch out alone with the aid of his wife. He recalls the moment of the decision as follows: 'At that time, we had 800 rupees. My wife was still selling vegetables. But I told her to sell embroidery. I gave her 400 rupees and some embroidery to sell. I myself took the other 400 rupees and went to Baroda.'

Here Dharamsingbhai stayed with relatives and encouraged some of them to trade with him. Together they sat on the pavement and found their buyers in the students and staff of the Baroda Art School who were beginning to take an interest in the rural crafts of Gujarat. Dharamsingbhai acted as chief supplier, but when a relative died without paying for his order, he lost money and returned to Ahmedabad where his wife was hawking embroidery from door to door in prosperous residential areas. It was at this period, somewhere around 1966, that they first decided to settle on the pavement of Law Gardens and to try to attract the customers to come to them. Despite their lack of financial assets, they had the advantage of dealing directly both with village suppliers and with urban consumers. This enabled them to undercut the prices charged by the more affluent export merchants.

In many ways, Dharamsingbhai's actions conform to the typical

The Genesis and Growth of a Business Community 63

behaviour of a self-styled entrepreneur, as classically defined. He was not afraid of taking numerous risks: leaving his native village, quitting the vegetable business and deserting his employer in favour of establishing a business of his own. Neither was he afraid of the making maximum usage of caste connections and expertise. It was fellow Vaghris who taught him the workings of the vegetable business, gave him information about how to barter in exchange for embroidery and provided him with hospitality in towns and villages throughout Gujarat. In fact Dharamsingbhai was quite prepared to exploit whomever he met, whether they were caste-fellows or anyone else. Hence, he used his role as the driver-cum-*pheriyo* of an export merchant as a means of acquiring knowledge with which he could later set himself up in competition. And when his employer failed to grant him a substantial pay rise, he seized the opportunity to break away and establish an alternative trade of his own on the footpath.

Dharamsingbhai's skill was in making the maximum use of caste resources whilst at the same time carving out a unique niche for himself and his wife. By becoming footpath embroidery traders they were carefully steering the narrow path between two well-established Vaghri professions, that of the *pheriyo* and that of the second-hand clothes dealer. Whereas *pheriyos* played merely an intermediary role in the embroidery business, Dharamsingbhai and his wife expanded this role to include the retail and eventually wholesale aspects. Like the second-hand clothes dealers, they collected their supplies by bartering with steel and sold the end-products for cash, but, unlike the latter they dealt in a product which attracted wealthy foreign and Indian consumers rather than the urban poor. And while there was nothing new about trading in second-hand embroidery as such, there was none the less something new about selling it in the streets by night at prices that even students and hippies could afford.

However, unlike the typical self-styled entrepreneur of formalist persuasion, Dharamsingbhai and his wife were to transform their individual achievement into a collective enterprise for themselves and their immediate relatives. Soon, two of his cousins and one of hers had joined them on the footpaths, and by 1988, at the time I was conducting fieldwork at Law Gardens, the market consisted of 23 stalls, involving at least 120 participants, all of whom could trace some relationship to Dharamsingbhai. As I have described elsewhere, the trade had spread horizontally within generations and vertically from one generation to another (cf. Tarlo forthcoming). As many as 80 per cent of the stalls contained direct descendants of Dharamsingbhai's paternal grandparents, the rest containing relatives of in-married members.

FROM DIVERSITY TO UNITY: THE CREATION OF A BUSINESS COMMUNITY

That the Law Gardens' footpath embroidery trade has developed along the lines of caste and kin may come as no surprise to sociologists familiar with the workings of traditional business communities in India. But what I have tried to show is that Vaghris, as a group, differed considerably from such communities by their tendency either to cluster in unlucrative petty trades (such as selling tooth sticks, vegetables and second-hand clothes) or to shift from one activity to another, scrambling a livelihood as best as they could. Furthermore, Dharamsingbhai, as we have seen, was not following an already established profession but was inventing a new role for himself and his family. The fact that his relatives abandoned all sorts of different activities in order to join him reveals the extent to which they previously lacked a common occupational foundation. Two of Dharamsingbhai's paternal uncles had been bullock traders based in Dholera Bhander. Their two eldest sons had abandoned this profession in favour of vegetable vending in Ahmedabad. They were Dharamsingbhai's first cousins and were the first to join him in the embroidery business, followed shortly by Champaben's cousin who was an itinerant ghee seller and part time *pheriyo*. Dharamsingbhai's brothers, meanwhile, had settled in Bombay, Calcutta and Pune. Of the two in Calcutta, one was employed as a chauffeur and the other as a factory hand. The former's wife was a ghee seller and the latter's wife a dealer in second-hand saris. All of these activities were abandoned when they made the decision to join Dharamsingbhai at Law Gardens. Other relatives left jobs in the spice trade whilst yet others came directly from their villages where they were either working sporadically as labourers or cultivating their own small plots of land.

The fact that the market now contains so many of Dharamsingbhai's relatives should not mislead one into thinking that they all left their various occupations simultaneously or for the same reasons. The two couples who initially joined did so at their cousin's request when the street market was still little more than an experimental idea. They may be considered as founding members of the market, men and women who shared some of the entrepreneurial zeal of Dharamsingbhai. Champaben's cousin, however, seems to have joined the line without being invited, transforming his initial role as one of Dharamsingbhai's suppliers into the role of trader in his own right. Others, like Dharamsingbhai's brothers from Calcutta and his sister from a village in the Ahmedabad district, joined Law Gardens at a time when the market had already proved to be successful. In the two brothers' cases, they had weighed up the benefits and concluded that the embroidery trade was more lucrative than their current professions. In his sister's case, the trade had seemed a useful supplement to her husband's agricultural activities, so she and her son established a stall, leaving the rest of the family back in the village. More recently still, others had been motivated to join the market by the crippling drought conditions of 1985–3 when alternative labour was unavailable and the embroidery trade afforded a means of survival. But whatever the reasons for the convergence of these various relatives within the footpath embroidery market, the result of their convergence has been the forging of a new sense of collective identity and action.

This identity is built around the product (embroidery), the space (Law Gardens) and the unique timing of the market. To begin with the product, all of the traders have acquired a well-developed connaissance of Gujarati embroidery. This connaissance is largely new to most of the traders who came from families who could ill afford the luxury of making or wearing embroidered cloth.[16] Vaghris were neither significant producers nor consumers of embroidery in rural Gujarat. Now, like any other specialist business community, they have an exhaustive knowledge of the different aspects of the product. They know where to get cheap supplies of old embroidery which they obtain either from villagers, *pheriyos* or wholesale merchants in towns and cities throughout Gujarat. They are skilful at recognising the embroidery styles of different regions and good at transforming redundant items such as bullock blankets and horn covers into cushion covers, yokes and purses for sale. They are also experienced at commissioning new hand and machine-embroidery which is rapidly taking its place alongside old handiwork in the market. Their trading networks stretch not only through Kutch and

Saurashtra where they obtain much of their supplies, but also to major cities throughout India where they act as suppliers, often to other Vaghris who trade on the footpaths, and some of whom are related to Dharamsingbhai and his cousins. In short the Law Gardens traders are more than simply embroidery vendors. They are active in every aspect of the trade which has become, for most, a full time occupation. They now refer to themselves as *'bharatkam-walas* (embroidery people), and this is also how they are perceived by most of their customers in the market.

The collective identity of the Vaghri embroidery traders is reinforced by the fact that they are the only group to have made the embroidery business into a form of caste specialisation. In Ahmedabad the strength of their position is recognised, and to a large extent resented, by other embroidery merchants, none of whom have been able or willing to expand their businesses through mobilising such extensive networks of caste and kin. These merchants complain, perhaps exaggeratedly, that it is now almost impossible to sell embroidery retail in Ahmedabad since all the potential local consumers go to Law Gardens where the prices are lower owing to the lack of over-heads.[17] The merchants have two different ways of dealing with this virtual Vaghri monopoly. Either they decide to become wholesale suppliers to Law Gardens, or they concentrate largely on the export end of the market, an area which is still largely outside the reach of the footpath traders. There are various merchants in Ahmedabad who perform one or other of these functions, and there is at least one merchant who performs both.

While embroidery merchants, along with police officials, love to stress all of the conventional stereotypes about Vaghris, arguing that they are essentially quarrelsome cheats selling shoddy goods, this is not the image that the general public holds of the Law Gardens traders. Many consumers, most of whom are from a middle class urban milieu, actually mistake the traders for village peasants or 'gypsies' who have come from the rural areas to sell their own handiwork. This gives the traders a romantic aura and results in them being associated with 'authenticity', even though in some cases they are selling new machine-made products from Ahmedabad. Buying from them is not only considered cheaper than buying from a shop, but it is also considered more 'genuine', although it is recognised that ferocious bargaining is a prerequisite to obtaining the 'real thing'.[18] This myth of authenticity is of considerable benefit to the traders, who often do not bother to disillusion their clients about their real identity. In this sense, the Law Gardens traders' intimate association with embroidery has not only provided a new collective activity but has also led to the emergence of a new semi-mythical identity with relatively positive connotations when compared to the conventional stereotypes about Vaghris. To what extent these connotations spring from the image of the product itself, it is difficult to judge. But perhaps it can be argued that just as a craftsman who works with gold has a better status than one who works with leather, so a dealer who trades in embroidery has a better status than one who trades in vegetables, tooth sticks or second-hand saris. After all, such products are hierarchically ranked in India as elsewhere, and Gujarati embroidery, which is perceived by the urban middle-classes as a luxury and artistic product, rates well in this ranking system.

If embroidery is the product around which the footpath traders have built their new collective identity, then Law Gardens is the location through which this identity has taken on a concrete and recognisable form in Ahmedabad. If the traders had been dispersed throughout the city, it is unlikely that they would have been able to coordinate their activities and unlikely that they would have earned the reputation of being embroidery specialists. But the fact that the embroidery vendors have hijacked the pavement next to Law Gardens, making it their own exclusive and distinctive space, reveals their sense of collective solidarity. This unity is further evident from the fact that traders return to the same spots every night,[19] taking up fixed positions in the ordered assembly of embroidery stalls. Furthermore the embroidery is arranged in such a way that those stalls which contain very similar contents are reasonably dispersed at different intervals in the line. This line appears, however, as a continuous spread,[20] with vendors collectively making the maximum use of all the space available to them on the pavement and the fence behind. They have also built themselves a mud platform which stretches right along the street and, despite not having licences to trade, they are planning to introduce electric lighting to the market. In this way they are structuring a dramatic collective stage for themselves and their embroidery, a stage which gives their product higher visibility than any shop or emporium could offer. They may have to palm off the local police every few days, but this does not in any way affect their attachment to the space. They have, in short, monopolised the area, a fact which is evident from the rapidity with which they band together to kick out impostors who occasionally attempt to trade from the same spot. Finally the fact that the market is held at night further distinguishes it from other embroidery outlets in Ahmedabad, making it a unique feature of the city. It is this collective agreement as to the timing, location and contents of the market that has enabled the participants to define themselves as *bharatkamwalas* and to distinguish themselves both from other embroidery sellers and from other street vendors, many of whom are Vaghris.

EMBROIDERY TRADERS AS DISTINCT FROM OTHER VAGHRIS

Distinction is, of course, a subtle process, difficult to document in any decisive way. But there is a clear sense of collective pride amongst those who have joined Law Gardens, a pride which leads them to look disparagingly at some of the more traditional Vaghri occupations, including the ones they themselves used to follow. Vegetable vending is now considered by them to be a poor person's trade, one which involves the strenuous labour of obtaining supplies, sitting all day in the hot and congested old city for a few rupees. By comparison, men who sit at Law Gardens claim to be leading 'the raja's life', taking it easy all day long, trading only in the cool of the evening, and accumulating money 'just by sitting'. When I tried to suggest that they and their families did in fact work during the day, repairing old embroidery and buying and commissioning new stocks, they retorted that such activities were not very demanding and could mostly be done at home. Besides, the time was theirs to do with as they pleased. In reality, most older women and some young men were kept fairly busy with embroidery-related work during the day. But the fact that their activity took place within the home or just outside it led them to perceive it more as leisure than work.[21]

It is therefore possible to detect at least two strands in the process through which the Law Gardens traders are dissociating themselves, if not from other Vaghris as such, then at least from the old stereotypes about Vaghris.[22] On the one hand, they are beginning to emphasise their distance from the poverty of their own past, redefining themselves as successful business people. On the other, they are increasingly distancing themselves from the present poverty of the numerous other Vaghris who trade in the city. Such other

The Genesis and Growth of a Business Community 69

Vaghris which include vegetable, ghee and tooth stick vendors trade essentially during the day, either in the highly congested walled city or wandering from house to house with their wares on their heads. In both cases it is not only their circumstances that compare unfavourably to those of the embroidery traders, but also their reputation. For whereas the vegetable, *datun* (tooth sticks) and used clothes vendors are generally known to be Vaghris, with all the connotations that the name implies, the embroidery traders have, as we have seen, a more ambiguous identity. That their distinctiveness is not only conceptual, but also material, can be gauged from comparing the businesses and life-styles of embroidery traders to those of second-hand clothes vendors.

The immediate factor that strikes one in making such a comparison is that the two groups did at one time perform almost identical activities: both obtained used textiles by wandering from house to house, using vessels as a means of exchange. And both resold their second-hand goods on the streets of Ahmedabad after having carried out necessary repairs. The embroidery trade in its embryonic state was in fact little more than a specialist branch of the used garments industry. But whereas most of the embroidery traders have shed the more arduous and demeaning aspects of their trade by sending *pheriyos* to get supplies for them or buying directly from merchants in cash, or even commissioning new embroidery work from producers, the used clothes vendors continue to wander the streets in search of supplies, walking some 10 to 12 km a day in the burning sun with a basket of vessels on the head and a bundle of old clothes over the shoulder. The fact that the vessels with which they barter are usually obtained on a credit basis which is paid at an interest rate of 10 per cent per month, means that many get sucked into severe indebtedness (Rose 1992: 42). Their financial difficulties are compounded by the fact that the products they sell are of little market value and they regularly lose money to the police in fines or petty bribes.[23] The Law Gardens traders also suffer from police harassment, but to them a pay-off of Rs 10 is less significant since the products they sell are considerably more valuable and the profit margin more substantial. In 1988 second-hand embroidered bullock horn covers, for example, could be obtained from an Ahmedabad merchant at the cost of Rs 15 each. After slight alterations to make them into decorative yokes for the *salwar kameez* (tunic and trousers) they could be sold for Rs 45 at Law Gardens. Selling newly-made machine embroidery was not as profitable, but the turnover was more regular. A single bed sheet could be obtained for Rs 60 and sold for Rs 80 to 100 to a local consumer. If an unsuspecting foreigner came along, however, the trader might be able to extract Rs 200 for the same product, depending on the foreigner's experience. But unlike the Janpath traders operating in the heart of the central tourist zone of Delhi, the Law Gardens traders could not rely on regular custom from foreigners. Nonetheless, occasional tourists provided a welcome financial bonus when they did appear. Second-hand clothes dealers also sold the occasional sari to foreigners, but even when they charged double the usual price they still only received a few rupees extra profit since their prices were so low in the first place.[24] Added to this, the used clothes vendors did not constitute a tourist attraction and it is likely that most tourists who visit Ahmedabad are not even aware of their existence.

With the profits they have obtained over the years, the Law Gardens traders have considerably improved their houses and their general standard of living. Most have built themselves *pucca* homes of at least two rooms in new Ahmedabad suburbs. Although these homes cannot be considered lavish, they certainly compare favourably to the homes of the used garment dealers, most of whom live and work in the so called 'inner city slum' of Raikhad (Rose 1992: 42). They also compare favourably to the Vaghri houses described by P.G. Shah in the 1960s. His survey reveals that most Ahmedabad Vaghris were living in desultory conditions, often in only one-room *kutcha* construction of mud, tin and cow dung (Shah 1967: 35-9). Their standard of living was so low that few could afford to go to the cinema, and their possessions consisted of little more than a few cooking pots and the odd *charpai*. By comparison most Law Gardens young men today are regular, and in some cases, daily cinema goers. And those families who have been in the trade right from the start now live in fairly comfortable circumstances. Some have been able to purchase televisions and sewing machines. And all, except one, stress that they are living in much better circumstances than in the past. Unlike the second-hand clothes dealers who seem both to live in poor conditions and perceive themselves as poor, the embroidery traders live in improved conditions and seem to perceive themselves as a community with a rising income and status.

Whether the Law Gardens traders' apparent distance from other Vaghri vendors is incidental (stemming merely from the way their occupations and life-styles have diverged) or constructed (being deliberately reinforced through restrictions on interaction) it is difficult to tell. But I was informed many times that it would be inappropriate for an embroidery trader to marry off his daughter to a second-hand clothes dealer, *pheriyo* or tooth stick vendor. In reality, there was some blurring of categories since the immediate relatives of two Law Gardens vendors were still in the spice and ghee trades. Nonetheless, as far as I could gather, all of the marriages that had taken place in the past ten years were either to fellow embroidery traders (in Ahmedabad or elsewhere) or to village Vaghris who came from families with some land. Of the marriages and engagement ceremonies I attended, one was between a boy and a girl who already worked at Law Gardens, whilst the other two were between Law Gardens boys and village girls. Two out of these three alliances were cases of cross-cousin marriage in which the groom was marrying his mother's brother's daughter. Such intermarriages have the obvious effect of reinforcing the collective identity of the traders as a distinctive group.

A BUSINESS COMMUNITY WITH A DIFFERENCE

I have so far argued that by converging their activities in the market and by distancing themselves from other groups, the footpath traders at Law Gardens have succeeded in building a new identity for themselves as a *bharatkamwalas*. Their well-defined product, their monopoly of a fixed space, their temporal coordination and their endogamous tendency all suggest that they have become a business community in their own right. But this does not mean that they necessarily function and reproduce in the same way as those communities we usually associate with the term. At first sight, the fact that almost every stall (at least 80 per cent) contains someone who shares the same paternal grandparents as Dharamsingbhai, would seem to suggest that what is emerging is the conventional lineage structure which is often perceived as forming the backbone of traditional trading communities in India (cf. Lachaier, this volume). If this were the case then we would expect the Law Gardens market to contain all the male descendants of the ancestral couple (Raganbhai and Laliben), along with their wives and children. The trade would pass effectively from seniors to juniors and from fathers to sons. There are plenty of cases in the market where precisely this has happened. Of the three first men to sit at Law Gardens, all have passed the profession on to their sons who now sit in the market. But to describe this pattern of transmission as typical would be to create an unrealistic picture of the way the market has expanded.

The first point to note is that although the market did indeed originate with the male grandchildren of the ancestral couple, these men had wives who participated in the trade, not as assistants but as partners in the true sense. When, in the early days, the traders would themselves collect embroidery from rural areas, it was often only one member of the couple who would go in search of embroidery whilst the other would remain in Ahmedabad concentrating on sales. Once a woman had large numbers of children, then it was more common for her husband to travel whilst she remained in Ahmedabad, but this gave her total control over the market aspect. Still today, it is women who keep the family earnings gained in the market whilst men deal only with the supply and export side of the business. Whilst men are the nominal heads of the business, women may be considered the principal force behind the trade. It is generally they who organise their children into an efficient workforce during the day and it is usually they who dominate transactions in the market at night. Not surprisingly, their powerful role has consequences for the transmission of the trade which can be passed on not only through the male line but also the female one.

A brief survey of the organisation and transmission of the trade in Dharamsingbhai's immediate family clarifies the matter. Although for many years both husband and wife would attend the market whenever they were both in Ahmedabad, now it is only Champaben who comes to Law Gardens while Dharamsingbhai sits at home smoking his hookah and taking life easy. He goes 'out of station' in search of embroidery or a business order once or twice a month, but he no longer bothers to go to villages. Rather he collects his stock from merchants in various towns in Gujarat. His main preoccupation seems to be 'taking it easy', a fact that he summarised by the phrase: 'I put my stomach first and then the business.' To this Champaben retorted with irony: 'I put the business first and then my stomach.' Champaben's powerful role in the business has been accentuated (willingly or unwillingly) since Dharamsingbhai took himself a second wife a few years back. This has freed Champaben entirely from domestic activities and left her in full control of their stall at Law Gardens.

Dharamsingbhai and Champaben have ten children, all of whom participate in the embroidery trade. But whilst, in a conventional patriarchal structure, only the sons would have inherited a place in the market, here both sons and daughters have established their own stalls after marriage. Hence when Dharamsingbhai's eldest daughter married a man from the village of Bhyla, she did not go to join him in his native village as would be the case if the custom of virilocal residence were respected. Rather, her husband came to live with her and her parents in Ahmedabad until eventually the young couple were able to build a home of their own. Her husband's younger brother has since married her younger sister. And following these marriages, the brothers' parents and their cousin and even their cousin's son have established stalls at Law Gardens. What is clear from such an example is that the trade is being retained and transmitted through both men and women which gives it the potential to expand at double the rate of the conventional lineage structure.

But it would be wrong to assume that all the men and women who have access to the embroidery trade necessarily follow the profession. Dharamsingbhai was in fact more effective at mobilising his paternal cousins than his own siblings when he first entered the trade. Today, out of his four brothers and three sisters, two of the former and one of the latter trade at Law Gardens with their partners. His other siblings are mostly scattered in Bombay and Pune where some of their children trade in embroidery. Of the siblings who have settled in Ahmedabad in recent years, all would appear to be passing the trade on to their children. Dharamsingbhai's sister's son has in fact recently married Dharamsingbhai's brother's daughter, thereby reinforcing the continuity of the business. But such continuity is not inevitable. Amongst Dharamsingbhai's paternal cousins, there is one couple who have dropped out of the embroidery trade altogether. This couple has returned to selling ghee and second-hand clothes, apparently because they could not master the complexity of the embroidery trade now that it no longer consists of simply selling old village embroidery. Another of Dharamsingbhai's paternal cousins, though a successful trader himself, arranged for two of his daughters to marry men who lived outside Ahmedabad. One married a Bombay embroidery trader and the other a village boy involved in the diamond cutting industry. However, the former's marriage only lasted a couple of years, after which the girl returned to Ahmedabad where she now shares an embroidery stall with her brother.

What is clear from these examples is that the structure of the embroidery trade is both flexible and unpredictable. It can, in fact, expand in any direction, whether through sons, daughters or affines (people related through marriage).[25] This makes it very different from the tightly structured lineage-based units that would appear to organise more conventional business communities. The general pattern in Law Gardens, if indeed there is one, is that those children who marry (whatever their sex) and remain in Ahmedabad, tend to follow the embroidery trade. Whilst it is more common for boys to remain in Ahmedabad after marriage, there are plenty of girls who, as we have seen, do the same. When both the bride and groom are already working at Law Gardens prior to marriage, then the trade can be said to be passing down through both male and female lines of descent simultaneously. Once a new couple establishes itself, then it usually, either immediately or shortly after marriage, sets up its own stall. The result is that although the market contains the elements of a vast extended family, it is none the less divided into smaller units for business purposes. As with all families, closeness in kinship terms does not necessarily signify closeness in business terms. In the final section of this paper I shall trace the extent to which different branches of the extended family have been able to expand and diversify their businesses at different levels.

UNITY TO DIVERSITY: ENTREPRENEURSHIP WITHIN THE BUSINESS COMMUNITY

I have suggested that the term 'business community' is appropriate for describing the Law Gardens traders if we are prepared to adjust our notion of how a 'business community' is structured. Similarly, the term 'family business' is appropriate once it is recognised that different branches of a single family may pursue their own interests in relatively small semi-independent units. The Law Gardens traders perceive themselves as one big family when it is convenient for them to do so, but they also perceive themselves as rivals in a competitive market at other times. As a result they do not automatically share their knowledge of embroidery sources. Neither do they like to share their major clients, if they can help it. This was evident from the fact that all of the stall holders wanted me to enter into an export deal exclusively with them. Needless to say, all were disappointed.

The fact that Law Gardens market does not function as a collectivity when it comes to economics, highlights the weakness of the assumption that in 'tradition-bound' societies potential entrepreneurs are 'held back' by social and moral ties. According to this view the embroidery market would appear to represent the ultimate in altruistic businesses, since it is little more than one vast and expanding family. But examination of the way in which different family units within the market have been able to expand their businesses in divergent ways reveals the potential for entrepreneurship within the family business. Since I have already spoken much of Dharamsingbhai's personal exploits, I shall concentrate here on other branches of the family, showing how their success is as variable as their business acumen.

The first example I want to discuss is that of one of Dharamsingbhai's cousins. He and his wife have been trading at Law Gardens for approximately 25 years, during which time they have produced eleven children. Between them and their children, they run five different embroidery stalls in the market. Of these, one is run by the original couple, one by their eldest son with his wife, one by their second son with his wife, one by their eldest daughter with her husband, and one by their second daughter without her husband. This last daughter, whose marriage has broken up, returns her earnings to the parental purse at the end of each week, but the three young couples run separate businesses from their parents. This nuclearisation process is also reflected in their living space which consists of four adjoining houses, each containing two rooms.

Over the years, the parental couple, along with their children, have diversified their business in several directions. Like Dharamsingbhai, they have long since ceased to collect old embroidery from the villages themselves. To do this job they employ 15 *pheriyos* who work for them on a commission basis. But the *pheriyos* are not their only source of old village embroidery. The family also gets supplies in bulk from merchants in Ahmedabad. They have, therefore, organised their business in such a way that the embroidery comes to them rather than vice versa. In the old days, they would repair damaged embroidery and sell the rest as it was, but nowadays they are also active in the recycling process.

Recognising that old village embroidery does not necessarily correspond to customer demands, they have for some years been cutting up old embroidery and refashioning it into new items.

These adaptations of old products began on a small scale basis, but they have now become an important part of the family's business. To perform such tasks, the parental couple have purchased two sewing machines which the boys of the family use for stitching during the day. Supervised by their mother, they make bags, letter racks, pockets, yokes, table cloths and cushion covers out of old embroidered door hangings, wall hangings, horse blankets and bullock horn covers. The result is that although the parents' stall contains mainly the old style of embroidery, it none the less offers the sort of items that fashionable urban customers are likely to buy.

Those members of the younger generation who have their own stalls specialise less in reworkings of old products than in new products that have been made either by hand or machine. Some of the latter are produced in rural areas and have to be ordered through the managers of the businesses concerned. But others are made in Ahmedabad, in which case it is possible for the traders to communicate directly with the producers. The two eldest sons of this particular family do in fact make regular trips to a production centre in the city where they have access to 15 machine-embroiderers and take orders from them on a regular basis. These machinists make mainly cushion covers, TV covers and letter racks. These are considerably cheaper to obtain than the old village embroidery which represents hours of painstaking labour. Since villagers are now aware of the potential economic value of their work, they no longer part with it at throw away prices. A discriminating buyer at Law Gardens will often prefer the intricate workmanship found in the old village embroidery. But most consumers are not discriminating and just want something reasonably cheap. Many cannot even distinguish the handiwork from its machine made counterpart, so it pays to offer both on one's stall. Between their five stalls, this family sells most of the possible variations in embroidery quality, style and form. If one couple has a captive customer, then often their brothers and sisters will pass pieces of embroidery from their own stalls down the line, so that the couple can offer the full range to their potential consumer. There is, therefore, much interaction between the owners of the five stalls.

Taken as a whole this branch of the family has, therefore, entered into the production process in two ways: firstly as repairers and converters of old products and secondly as designers and commissioners of new products. Although they run five separate stalls and keep the profits of four independently, there is much give and take as well as a noticeable sharing of assets. The sewing machines can be used by any male member of the family who is old enough to use them, as can the auto rickshaw-van which members of the family have purchased collectively. The van is used to transport the embroidery of all five stalls to and from the market every evening. Since all of the family members live in adjoining houses, they do not have any difficulties in sharing these assets. In general, it can be said that this branch of the Law Gardens traders has been highly successful at expanding its business both on individual and collective lines. The monopoly of five spaces in the market, the investment in sewing machines, the well established links with producers and suppliers of old and new embroidery all suggest that the families have been well able to adapt to the changing requirements of business as the demand for embroidery has expanded. Added to this the younger generation has been able to anticipate new demands by designing and commissioning new products, some of which they sell in Law Gardens, and others in bulk to merchants, boutique owners and exporters in Delhi and Bombay.

A similar success has been achieved by Dharamsingbhai and by his cousins. In fact between them, these three cousins with their wives and children make up 13 different stalls in the market. In each case they have successfully mobilised their immediate families into smallscale units of production, with young girls repairing old embroidery, young boys operating sewing machines and the older generation of married children organising their own stalls. Although there is an element of business rivalry between these three branches of the family with each accusing the other of stealing their ideas, there is also an element of mutual respect for each other's entrepreneurship and success. The three men who head these families always invite each other to their childrens' weddings, and there is evidence of the women discussing and sharing ideas amongst themselves. True, as cousins, they are all closely related, but so too is Dharamsingbhai's brother. Yet the latter and his wife were noticeably not invited to weddings and engagement ceremonies and seemed to keep their business very much to themselves. In particular, the brother's wife was accused of selfishly concealing her major source of supply. Her stall contained a large number of old embroidered *chaniyas* from the Bhavnagar district. No other trader had such a good selection of this particular type of embroidery and it seemed that she was going to make sure that things remained that way. But she and her husband were relatively new members of the market, having left Calcutta only three years before. What about the other two couples who came to Law Gardens shortly after Dharamsingbhai?

The first of these is a man named Prabubhai and his wife. This couple had originally been supplying embroidery to Dharamsingbhai as *pheriyos*, but decided to become footpath traders instead. According to some traders, Prabubhai's first wife was killed whilst she was touring the villages in search of embroidery. Today he lives with his fourth wife, nine daughters and three sons. Prabubhai, a somewhat wizened man, sits in the market every evening without his wife but also with two of his daughters. The organisation of the trade in his branch of the family is very different from that of the three cousins described above. Firstly, unlike the others, they still obtain their old embroidery by travelling in the rural areas of Kutch and Saurashtra. And, perhaps because Prabubhai is old and frail, it is his wife who travels with her baby in search of supplies. This means that the old village embroidery they sell is obtained more cheaply than that sold by other traders who all buy from merchants and *pheriyo*s. Prabubhai still reasons according to the old logic that the best deal is achieved when old village embroidery is sold for a handsome profit. He, therefore, bides his time, waiting for foreigners to come to the market, and he is fairly successful at attracting their attention when they do. His relatively empty stall contains only old wall hangings, door hangings, skirts and animal decorations. It is invariably these old and faded looking pieces that appeal to the foreigner's sense of the authentic. Prabubhai has learned this and sticks tenaciously to the old *desi* image. But not enough foreigners come to Ahmedabad and Prabubhai has been unable to expand his business as successfully as those traders who cater to all types of consumer.[26] As a result he is the only trader who has not succeeded in upgrading his standard of living. Despite being in the market for over 25 years, he and his offspring have only one stall and no sewing machine. They have very little to do with the other traders at Law

Gardens and it is quite probable that when Prabubhai dies, his branch of the family will cease to trade in embroidery. As it is, none of his married children have taken on the trade and most of his close male relatives still earn their living selling spices.

The final example I wish to discuss is that of Sunderben. On the scale of success, she rates somewhere between Prabubhai and the three male cousins described above. She is in fact a female cousin of Dharamsingbhai who has been trading in embroidery for over 20 years. At first, she used to trade with her parents, but they never took to the work and eventually returned to selling ghee. So it was Sunderben who persisted in the embroidery business with some participation from her husband. Sunderben has thirteen children, of whom ten are girls and three boys. One of the girls is married and lives with her husband outside Ahmedabad, but the rest are living with their parents. Sunderben can usually be seen in the market surrounded by four or five infants and two teenage daughters. The rest of the children remain at home under the supervision of their father. He has very little to do with the trade but his younger brother has a stall next door to Sunderben. Sunderben's success has been to develop a specialist niche for herself. Like Prabubhai she does not sell any modern machine embroidery, but unlike Prabubhai, she is adept at giving old pieces a new form. Her stall has the largest selection of yoke pieces in the market and, therefore, attracts a steady stream of college girls for whom such yokes are a fashionable component of the *salwar kameez*. Even when she was nine months pregnant with her thirteenth baby, Sunderben preferred to tend the stall herself, leaving her husband at home. Since most of her clients were female, she felt that they preferred to buy directly from another woman and this was no doubt part of her success. By making her stall a specialist place for obtaining accessories for women's dress, she had been able to hold her own in the market arena.

Sunderben's business does not have any of the complexity of those of Dharamsingbhai's and his two male cousins. She buys all of her supplies from two city merchants, both of whom are based in Ahmedabad. At home, she cuts the embroidery into suitable shapes for yokes, pockets and borders, and gets her son to stitch them into finished products on the machine. He, a boy of less than twelve years, sits at the machine most of the day whilst some of the daughters help their mother with repairing damaged embroidery work. Although Sunderben and her offspring have only one stall in the market, it is a fairly thriving one, as is evident from the fact that she and her husband have been able to build a *pucca* house and invest in a sewing machine of their own.

Examination of the diversity of ways in which different traders organise their businesses demonstrates that although all share the same collective occupation and identity, they do not necessarily act in unison. The market has space for them all but this does not necessarily mean that they all help each other in the market. It is not unlikely that most family businesses operate in a similar fashion, with segments of a family cooperating on certain points and fragmenting on others. When a SEWA[27] activist tried to encourage the traders to organise their activities to combat police harassment, this lack of unity was evident. Only one trader in the market was a SEWA member at the time. She was one of Dharamsingbhai's cousin's wife and a proud outspoken woman. One day, she asked me to accompany her to SEWA to discuss the problem of how to obtain a trader's licence. An experienced activist informed her that unless the Law Gardens traders formed themselves into a cooperative and approached SEWA as a group, SEWA was not prepared to help them. The trader claimed to show an interest in this idea, but I found out later that she had only informed Dharamsingbhai's two cousins' wives about the visit, even though all traders were anxious about the license issue. I do not know the precise reasons for her reluctance to speak with the others, but it betrayed a certain lack of solidarity. As a SEWA member, this woman had been able to acquire bank loans in the past, and perhaps she did not want this opportunity to be open to all the other traders. Or perhaps it was simply that the embroidery traders were not as poor and desperate as the used garment dealers and vegetable vendors who have successfully united and, with the help of SEWA, obtained the right to trade in the Ahmedabad streets.

I began this article by suggesting that the relationship between individual and collective economic enterprise needs to be examined in more detail. Through documenting the growth and development of Law Gardens embroidery market in Ahmedabad, I hope to have provided clarification of the complexity of the various strands that make up such a relationship. But above all, I hope to have highlighted the fact that there are many more business communities in India than we are apt to recognise. The fact that the Law Gardens traders conduct their business on the streets and that they come from a notoriously low socio-economic milieu has been sufficient to draw our attention away from their role as a business community. Yet if one speaks to more '*pucca*-looking' embroidery merchants, shopkeepers, exporters and foreign dealers, they will all emphasise the significance of the Vaghris as a community which has had its finger on the pulse of the trade since its very inception. How long, one might ask, do traders have to specialise in a single product and monopolise a single geographic space before they are recognised as a business community? My suspicion is that as long as they continue to trade in the streets, we are prone to perceive them as temporary, even when they have monopolised the same spot and dealt in the same product for generations and generations. But if we open our eyes to these 'other' business communities, then we may find that our entire picture of the Indian economy blurs. We can no longer argue definitively that traditional trading communities are losing their hold on the economy when new communities are clearly coming up along traditional or familial lines. I would suggest that it is only through including these various forms of specialist traders in our analysis that we can get a clear idea of the functioning of business communities in India today.

NOTES

1. The following research was conducted in 1988-9 and this paper does not discuss how the embroidery trade has developed in Ahmedabad since this date. I am grateful to the Economic and Social Research Council for supporting the initial fieldwork on which this research is based, and to the School of Oriental and African Studies and the British Academy for supporting the writing of this article.
2. These were favourite terms used by traders to distinguish between those who came to buy embroidery (the *kharid-walas*, literally 'buyers') and those who came just to hang out and eat snacks (the *khanne-walas*, literally 'eaters').
3. My own research has been restricted to the street market for Gujarati embroidery in Ahmedabad although I have spoken at some length with traders in Delhi, and briefly with traders in Goa and Mahabalipuram. I have, however, been unable to visit the street markets in Pune, Bombay or Calcutta so my knowledge of the latter is based only on what Ahmedabad traders have told me. Some Ahmedabad traders have relatives who deal in embroidery in these two cities.
4. This embroidery is characterised by its bright colours, use of mirrors and Gujarati folk motifs. For a classification of different local embroidery styles, see Nanavati *et al.* (1966), Dongerkery (1960) and Irwin and Hall (1973). For a discussion of the adaptation of embroidery to the market, cf. Tarlo, forthcoming.
5. Hunting is generally considered by Vaghris to have been their 'original

occupation'. Most Vaghris today interpret their caste name as meaning 'tiger-like'. Scholars, however, are apt to argue that the term 'Vaghri' stems from the Sanskrit 'vaghur' meaning 'nets'. This makes the Vaghris a 'tribe of netters'(cf. Shah 1967: 7-8). Yet others suggest that the name has nothing to do with hunting or bravery, but stems from 'Vagad', an area of sandhills in Rajasthan (cf. Enthoven 1922: 399). But the fact that Vaghris in the south became known by the Tamil name Kuruvikkaran (bird-catchers) and by the Telegu name Nakkala-vandlu (jackal people) suggests that hunting was indeed an important part of Vaghri identity and may well explain the origin of the name (cf. Thurston 1909: 181-2).

6. The information in *The Gazetteer* of 1901 is divided into 14 sections with 3 appendixes: appendix A: 'The foreigner'; appendix B: 'The Gujar' and appendix C: 'Miscellaneous'. The Vaghris are classified in the last section under the subheading, 'Castes'.

7. Dhedas was the Gujarati term for an 'untouchable' weaving caste in Gujarat. Many Dhedas later adopted the name Wanker and are now referred to as Harijans or Dalits. The Kolis have a highly ambiguous status in Gujarat. Those living along the coast are mostly fishermen and women whilst those on the mainland are either small scale peasant farmers or poor labourers. Whatever their occupation, their general status is generally considered to be low.

8. Cf. M. Kennedy, *The Criminal Classes in India*, Mittal Publications, Delhi, 1908 (rpt) 1985, pp. 155-65.

9. One would need to know more about how Kennedy's information was compiled to asses this relationship convincingly. One thing that is clear is that much of his information stems from *The Gazetteer* of 1901.

10. Edgar Thurston even encountered Vaghris in Madras where, apart from the common occupations of keeping pack-bullocks, collecting firewood, hunting and working as watchmen, they were also hawking needles, glass beads and 'spurious jackal horns'. The community was locally known by the Tamil name, Kuruvikkaran (bird-catchers), but Thurston states: 'Among themselves they are known as Vagiri or Vagirivala' (Thurston 1909: 181-2). Clearly their reputation in south India was not much better than in Gujarat, for Thurston states: 'Wearing the bodice like a Kuruvikkaran woman' is considered a taunt' (ibid.: 185).

11. Cf. P. G. Shah, *Vimukta Jatis: Denotified Communities in Western India*, Gujarat Research Society, Bombay, 1967.

12. Rose's account is based on a report compiled by SEWA (The Self-Employed Women's Association) in 1988-9. She goes on to record how women in the second-hand clothes business have been able to improve their livelihood to some extent, with the help of the organisation, SEWA, which has fought for their rights to trade in the streets. For an account of the struggle and protests of the Vaghri vegetable vendors, see Rose 1992: 68-74.

13. I have previously discussed Dharamsingbhai's role in an article which situates the footpath embroidery trade within wider national and international trends, cf. Tarlo, forthcoming. Here the focus is on the organisation of the local market and in particular, on the emergence of Vaghris as a business community.

14. There is no space here for discussion of the importance of embroidery in rural Gujarat nor of women's willingness to sell their handiwork to *pheriyos* in the

The Genesis and Growth of a Business Community 83

      1960s. For an understanding of the former issue, cf. Tarlo, 1996, and for an understanding of the latter, cf. Tarlo, forthcoming.

15. For a discussion of changing consumer tastes and an analysis of the process by which Gujarati embroidery became popularised in India and abroad from the 1960s onwards, see Tarlo forthcoming.
16. The extent to which Vaghri women wore embroidered clothes varied according to the wealth of their families. Those traders whose families were very poor had scarcely ever worn embroidery, whilst those who were slightly wealthier claimed to have owned a few embroidered *chaniyas* at the time of their weddings.
17. A similar complaint is heard from the shopkeepers at Janpath (Delhi) who resent the presence of Vaghri footpath embroidery traders almost at the doorstep of their boutiques.
18. Gurjari, the Gujarat State Government Craft Emporium was also thought to sell the 'authentic' article, but it was considered much more expensive than Law Gardens. Furthermore many local people still perceived it as being 'essentially for foreigners' even though it had considerably revamped its image in recent years and captured some of the internal market.
19. In 1988, I was visiting the market almost every night for five months, and never witnessed any change of layout in the order of the stalls. None the less one would anticipate that it must have changed in the five years following this research period.
20. Displaying the embroidery in such a way that one stall ran into another was partly a way of trying to minimise police harassment. If a mother and son presented their stalls separately, then each had to pay fines and bribes to the police. But by visually merging their products, they could claim that they had only one stall and, therefore, had to pay only one fine. This means that the number of stalls in the market was deliberately ambiguous.
21. This is, of course precisely the attitude which womens' organisations are trying to combat in India and elsewhere, arguing that unless people learn to perceive work in the home 'as work', then women will continue to act as an underpaid invisible labour force as well as being a target for exploitation.
22. This dissociation process was even stronger amongst the Gujarati embroidery traders of Goa, many of whom claimed to be Kolis (a group with higher social status in Gujarat), but who later turned out to be of Vaghri origin. The ignorance of the local Goanese and other foreigners (Indian or otherwise) seemed to have provided them with greater scope for redefining their identity in relation to the others, and for distancing themselves from the Vaghri-stereotype.
23. An idea of the negative reputation of Vaghri hawkers can be gained from Strip and Strip's caricatural description of Bombay Vaghris in the 1940s. They claim that Vaghri women 'pose as' sellers of tooth sticks, ropes, beads and trinkets 'but while posing as hawkers . . . they direct their activities towards the commission of petty thefts. . . . They also practise the elusive craft of fortune-telling' (Strip and Strip, 1944: 40). Here the Vaghris are described as 'the Gipsies of India' who are in their habits 'almost an exact prototype of their Western cousins, the Romany' (ibid: 39).
24. On the three occasions that I purchased second-hand pure silk saris from such traders, they never charged more than Rs 15 despite my foreign appearance.

25. The footpath embroidery traders who sit in the lane just off Janpath in Delhi have also passed on the trade along male, female and affinal lines. In this case it is almost exclusively women who trade in the market which is held during the day whilst the men are busy obtaining supplies and re-dying or stitching embroidery. These women consist of an original five daughters and five brothers' wives along with their daughters and daughters-in-law. The market contains three generations and around eighty traders. Unlike the Ahmedabad traders, these women rarely bring young children to the market.
26. That different types of embroidery appealed to different types of consumers was recognised by all the traders. Essentially it was foreigners, museum collectors and the owners of exclusive boutiques who were the primary buyers of old village embroidery, while new hand and machine embroidery tended to appeal more to the local middle class Ahmedabad consumer, who generally favoured cleanness and cheapness.
27. SEWA: The Self-Employed Women's Association which has a flourishing base in Ahmedabad as well as in other major Indian cities.

REFERENCES

Ahmedabad District Gazetteer, Government of Gujarat, Ahmedabad, 1984.

Gazetteer of the Bombay Presidency, vol. VIII, Kathiawar, 1884.

Gazetteer of the Bombay Presidency, vol. IX, part I, Gujarat Population: Hindus, 1901.

Dongerkery, K., *The Romance of Indian Embroidery*, Thacker & Company, Bombay, 1960.

Enthoven, R.E., *The Tribes and Castes of Bombay*, vol. III, Goverment of Bombay, Bombay, 1922.

Irwin, J. And Hall, M., *Indian Embroideries*, Calico Museum of Textiles, Ahmedabad, 1973.

Kennedy, M., *The Criminal Classes in India*, Mittal Publications, Delhi, 1908 (rpt), 1985.

Nanavati, J., Vora, M. and Dhaky, M., *The Embroidery and Beadwork of Kutch and Saurashtra*, Museum Monograph Series, Baroda, 1966.

Rose, Kalima, *Where Women are Leaders: The SEWA Movement in India*, Vistaar Publications, New Delhi, 1992.

Shah, P.G., *Vimukta Jatis: Denotified Communities in Western India*, Gujarat Reseach Society, Bombay, 1967.

Strip, P. and Strip, O., *The Peoples of Bombay*, Thacker & Co., Bombay, 1944.

Tarlo, E., *Clothing Matters: Dress and Identity in India*, Hurst & Co., London and Penguin, India, Delhi, 1996.

———, 'Traders as Trendsetters: The marketing of "village embroidery" in Gujarat', in Haynes D. and Byfield J. (eds), *Cloth, The World Economy and the Artisan*, (forthcoming volume resulting from a Conference of the same title, held in Dartmouth, Hanover, April 1993). In press.

Thurston, E., *Castes and Tribes of Southern India*, vol. IV, Government Press, Madras, 1909.

Rural Credit and the Fabric of Society in Colonial India: Sirohi District, Rajasthan[1]

DENIS VIDAL

How did indebtedness grow to such proportions in India that from the nineteenth century onwards it has been generally considered one of the major scourges afflicting the Indian countryside? This question is still being debated; and it is made more difficult to answer by the fact that rural indebtedness varies enormously in kind, depending on the period, the area and the communities involved. For this reason, I intend to approach this problem from one specific angle, referring to the case of one district in Rajasthan (Sirohi). Nevertheless I hope to show that some of the conclusions I have reached make it possible to cast a certain light upon this question which is so crucial to Indian society.

In the abundant literature devoted to rural credit in India, some strong stereotypes continued to prevail right up to the 1980s. There was a consistent emphasis upon the negative aspects of rural credit, from the exploitation of rural society by moneylenders to the unproductive nature of the spending facilitated by this kind of credit. As a result, the declared aim, first of the colonial administration from the middle of the nineteenth century onwards and later of the government of independent India—which changed little from this point of view—was always to develop a system of banks and cooperatives which would make it possible in the long run to completely eliminate the hold exercised by moneylenders and financial middlemen of all kinds over rural Indian society. But despite the increasingly thorough methods deployed to realise this aim (especially the nationalisation of the banking system in 1969), this policy has not achieved all the hoped-for results.

Thus, in a district of Rajasthan (Pali) immediately adjoining the one to be examined here, moneylenders were still providing 61 per cent of all rural credit in 1989 (Rajasekhar and Vyasulu, 1991). This is not an exceptional case, and we should not be too ready to attribute it to the backwardness of economic conditions in this semi-arid part of Rajasthan. In fact, according to available statistics, in 1982 more than two-thirds of all rural credit was still being supplied outside any institutional form of lending (Bouman, 1989, p. 17). Even more significant is the fact that the same situation is to be found in the Punjab, where agriculture has undergone an unprecedented economic development; there, all classes of cultivators without exception, from the richest to the poorest, stated a preference for using informal credit rather than any institutional form of lending, whether by banks or cooperatives (Chandra, 1993). But even this is not really a new discovery; the increasing indebtedness of all classes of farmers in the Punjab was already puzzling the British administration at the beginning of the century. Reversing the classical thesis, M.L. Darling even concluded, rather hastily, that this increase was not a consequence of the farmers' poverty, as usually believed, but on the contrary, of the relative prosperity which the Punjab was beginning to experience in the early years of this century (Darling, 1925). And it should be noted that in this respect India is no exception amongst developing countries. According to Padmanabhan, 'in most developing countries, informal sources still meet 50-80 per cent of the credit needs of rural people' (Padmanabhan, 1988).

These facts help to explain why the 1980s have witnessed a gradual questioning of the most established dogmas about non-institutional forms of rural credit. For example, in the case of India, more attention began to be paid to studies which challenged the idea that moneylenders necessarily demand extortionate rates of interest, or even rates very different from those current in the banking system (Harris, 1980). Instead, a greater emphasis was placed upon the various factors which would explain the grounds for this (transaction costs, opportunity costs, risk costs, etc.). Rather than condemning such practices out of hand, economists have gradually begun to try to place them within a wider network of causality. It was noted, for example, that the amount of interest charged by moneylenders should be seen in the light of the fact that sums which could never have been borrowed on other terms enabled the borrowers to achieve rates of profit that very soon exceeded the rates of interest charged (Ghate, 1992, p.114). Similarly, the idea that this type of borrowing never gave rise to productive investments has been increasingly challenged (Bouman, 1989).

Today, development experts are viewing the relationship between institutional and informal credit-sources in rural society more and more in terms of complementarity between different sources of possible finance, rather than purely in terms of one replacing the other. From the methodological point of view, however, it must be stated that this change in the economists' evaluation of non-institutional credit practices has not been accompanied by a corresponding change in the conceptual framework on which their analyses are based. Economic thinkers have justified first their condemnation and then their reassessment of non-institutional credit-practices by practically the same concepts of rationality or productivity. It is also surprising to see how, going from one extreme to another, the very idea that peasants might in fact be exploited by moneylenders seems now to have been so lightly set aside, although it was the focus of all discussion for so long. Yet it is not really possible to address such a question without also understanding the actual functions fulfilled by merchants and financial middlemen in rural society in exchange for the share of its produce that they appropriated for themselves.

One might suppose that anthropologists, traditionally less susceptible to the attractions of economic reasoning, would long ago have suggested an alternative idea about the role of non-institutional credit practices in rural India. Yet this is not the case, for reasons exactly the opposite of those affecting economists. In fact it has taken a very long time for anthropologists to finally become convinced that the socio-economic logic at work in rural society—even at the most localised level—could never be explained exclusively or even primarily by the *jajmani* system (Fuller, 1989; Mayer, 1993; Vidal, 1993). So, apart from a few exceptions where more emphasis is laid on the concept of debt (Galey, 1980), there are still very few anthropological or sociological studies which accord full importance to the concept of credit in analysing the socio-economic and cultural fabric of rural society in India.

It is in the work of historians (Cheesman, 1982; Bayly, 1983; Hardiman, 1987; Bose *et al.*, 1994) that we find the fullest descriptions and the most interesting discussions for a sociological examination of the role played by rural credit in India. Neeladri

Bhattacharya, for example, has been able to demonstrate the inadequacies of analyses based on purely economic concepts, which do not take into account the fact that 'in the non-institutionalised money market in rural areas there is never one standard rate. Transactions are mediated by relationships of power, social, political, economic. Terms of exchange are defined by the relative strength of debtors and lenders' (Bhattacharya, 1994, p. 239).

Studies in economic history have certainly made possible a better understanding of the role played by the very diverse networks of financial and merchant middlemen in the global economy of the subcontinent (Bayly, 1983; Subrahmanyam, 1994). What has perhaps not yet been sufficiently emphasised, on the other hand, is how decisive an effect these middlemen have exercised on the basic structure of the rural economy. Their involvement did not take exclusively the form of draining off production towards the towns, and it was not only linked either to other phenomena such as the monetarisation of income from land, the forced commercialisation of agriculture, or the emergence of new agrarian relationships resulting from the development of a land-market. Sugata Bose (1994) has recently shown that historians specialising in the colonial period have tended to analyse the various forms of non-institutional credit too systematically in the light of the process of commercialisation of local economies and the changes in agrarian relationships which took place during that period. He notices also that it has taken more than thirty years for most economists and historians to be aware of the importance of an observation that had been very clearly stated in reports of Indian Government officials as early as the 1950s: 'The moneylender has different kinds and degrees of hold on those to whom he chooses to lend. Least important of all for him is the possibility of recourse to the law, and almost as unimportant is the possibility of acquiring his debtor's property' (AIRCS, 1955, pp. 62-3).

The obstacles encountered by social science research in this domain are, however, in a way indicative of the skill the merchants developed at carrying on their affairs at the most local level without apparently disrupting the dominant forms of behaviour or agrarian relationships. Nevertheless, their presence did profoundly shape existing patterns of consumption and production in the rural society.

The district of Sirohi in Rajasthan offers an interesting example in this perspective. Unlike most areas examined by historians, this is a district where up to the time of Independence there was neither any real land-market, nor any significant introduction of cash crops. I want to show that, contrary to common belief, the forms of credit practised by the Jain merchant community there did not lead to changes in existing social relations but, on the contrary, helped to perpetuate them. In places like Sirohi, where such merchant communities were long-standing residents, these practices formed an even more integral element in the existing order, because they played a crucial role in regulating mechanisms on which the economic viability of the life-styles of other communities depended.

Rural indebtedness in fact occurs within a social logic in which the behaviour of the various agents, and particularly their spending on consumption, are governed by socio-cultural constraints that do not necessarily conform to purely economic imperatives. In a system of this kind, contrary to the expectations of economists, expenditure on consumption cannot, and could never be, defined simply as a predictable reflection of available income. Of course there has to be some long-term correspondence between consumption and production, but this is rarely consciously perceived by the people involved in the economic process.

In Sirohi, the responsibility for regulating economic activity rested in practice upon one single sector of the society, the Jain merchant community, which combined the functions of merchants and moneylenders, while simultaneously acting as agents and managers for landowners. They were practically alone in having mastered the accounting techniques which enabled them to conceptualise a long-term system of equivalence between the consumption-expenditures and the incomes of the various sectors of the population. And it was indirectly that they imposed an economic rationality on the rest of the population. They were also practically the only people with sufficient knowledge of the social and economic conditions governing local production to be able to direct the economic activities of the various communities to their own profit, without however obliging them to modify behaviour-patterns in which economic considerations weighed little compared with all sorts of other imperatives. Until the advent of a new social or economic order, only a local merchant was able to turn these imperatives discretely and in the secrecy of his account-books towards new goals directed to his own profit. This means that the merchants' position depended on a dual monopoly of expertise: first, a monopoly over accounting and financing techniques, relative to the local population; but also, a monopoly over social information about this population, relative, this time, to merchants from outside the locality.

The Jains had no traditional right to a share of the harvests, and did not take any direct part in production. But because they supplied credit, and bought and sold all merchandise, they were in fact in control of the rhythm of all economic activity. Of course this situation favoured their enrichment at the expense of the other communities, although prevailing economic and social conditions also set some limit to their capacity to appropriate surpluses.

I should argue that some of the difficulties being experienced by rural India today are, paradoxically, linked to the skill with which the mercantile castes used to regulate the economic activity of local populations, not by imposing on them any general ideology about rural society, but rather by knowing how to make use of the specific socio-cultural features of each caste and community.

SIROHI DISTRICT

Bordered on the east by the Aravallis, the district of Sirohi is situated on the edge of the arid half of Rajasthan (Marwar). In 1981 the population was 541,000, living in 446 villages and 5 small towns of about 20,000 inhabitants each.[2] It has only a few insignificant rivers, and only 27.63 per cent of the land area is cultivated (net area sown) and 37 per cent of this land is irrigated. The main crops are: cereals (52 per cent), pulses (23 per cent), and oil seeds (13 per cent) which are of more recent introduction. Stock breeding (sheep and goats) is traditionally important in the area, while industry, with only a thousand registered jobs, is still undeveloped.

The district has taken the place of the former small kingdom of Sirohi, which was dissolved in 1949 when the State of Rajasthan was constituted. The sociological composition of the kingdom reflected a classical pattern in Rajasthan: at the summit of the social hierarchy stood the Rajputs, the Brahmins and the Jain merchant community. Various castes of artisans, farmers and stockbreeders, as well as some castes whose status was somewhat similar to that of Brahmins or Rajputs (Purohits, Bhats, Charans), constituted a middle position between that of the lower castes, while the tribal populations (Bhils, Minas, Girasia) had a special status.

Up to the time of Independence practically all land ownership—

which entailed the right to claim as much as half the produce—was in the hands of the ruler and his clan (the Deora Chauhans). Half of the villages lay within the sovereign's domain (Khalsa) and most of the remaining ones were connected with estates of Thakurs, who then shared the income from them with the ruler. The only lands partially exempted from land taxes were those which had been granted as religious donations to certain Brahmins or to temples, and those in tribal areas, some of which had retained a degree of local autonomy. On the Thakurs' estates (*jagirs*), ordinary peasants (*hali*), mainly from the lower castes, normally had only a provisional right to farm the land. Their position was slightly better if they were directly responsible for producing revenue in the villages within the sovereign's domain.

The Jain community represented approximately 10 per cent of the population.[3] They were the main traders in the kingdom. They were to be found in the bazaars of the small towns and in all the villages, where they combined the roles of merchants and of moneylenders. They also occupied most government posts and acted as stewards (*kamdar*) for local Thakurs. Since Independence and the financial reforms which followed it, a few of the Jains who used to live in the villages have acquired land which they get farmed for them; but most of them have shifted their businesses to the towns, or outside the district. However, they usually maintain their old homes, where their families sometimes still reside.

THE JAINS' HOLD OVER THE RURAL ECONOMY

In an article of 1983, J. Burghart pleaded the necessity for an intracultural approach towards the study of Indian society. Burghart was challenging a long-dominant tendency in the sociology of India, that gave too homogeneous a view of the prevalent ideology in Indian society. This recommendation is particularly called-for when we are investigating a community such as that of the Jains in Sirohi. They not only possess a distinctive ideology, but also a unique view of the rest of society. To give only one example, the Jains, who on the whole are puritan, very religious, vegetarian and non-violent, felt an equal disapproval for the life-styles both of the Thakurs and of most of the lower castes. This was not solely either a matter of economic status, of financial solvency or of social status—the Thakurs and the lower castes stood at opposite extremes of the social hierarchy—but an intricate combination of each of these factors which was at stake in their perception of others. Each individual and each caste or community was implicitly evaluated by the Jains according to a combination of moral and economic criteria directly linked to the Jains' own social and cultural ideals and patterns of life as well as to their specific position in the local society.

If the Jains were so concerned about details in the lives of members of other communities, this was nevertheless not so much for ethical reasons but may be, more decisively, as a direct result of the traditional position which they occupied for hundreds of years in the local economy. In fact, they were the first to benefit from other communities' attitudes towards consumption, on two counts: first, as merchants, they supplied the rest of the population with all articles of consumption not produced on the spot. And from this point of view, the Thakurs were certainly their best clients; especially so because from the seventeenth century onwards, local nobles led an increasingly expensive life-style in order to maintain their rank; secondly, as moneylenders, the Jains, like other Indian merchant castes, have always combined the buying and selling of merchandise with money lending. And the peasants did not borrow only in times of distress or for agricultural needs. The largest loans were taken to cover the various social and religious ceremonies which occur regularly in the life of every individual, family and community.

Here we encounter a special feature of Indian culture, the effect of which would be hard to exaggerate. In India the respective positions of debtor and creditor, and the relationship between the two, are viewed differently from the way they are considered in many other cultures. Lending money, as such, is not considered reprehensible—it has always been accepted and practised even by Brahmins; nor is being in debt perceived as a mark of failure. On the other hand, it is a serious failure to be unable to perform the social and religious expenditures required by one's status—and this is true at every level of society.

So we can see why it is impossible to apply economists' current standards of analysis, which are implicitly moulded by attitudes prevalent in Western society, to the examination of rural consumption in India. Even for the very poor, the scale of expenditure is still determined by the socio-cultural context, which defines for each community a minimum threshold of unavoidable social and religious expenses, below which a person and his family

Rural Credit and the Fabric of Society in Colonial India 93

run the risk of losing their social standing, and possibly even their identity. Only keeping this point constantly in mind can we begin to examine the way in which debt actually occurs in rural conditions.

The hold exercised during the colonial period by merchant castes over the country-side has almost always been explained, as we have seen, with reference to a progressive monetarisation of the rural economy. In this type of analysis, the need for a cash income, the increasing commercialisation of agriculture, and lastly the emergence of a land market, were seen as the determining factors of rural debt. But in Sirohi, none of these factors seems to have played any role at all throughout most of the colonial period. Only in the 1920s did the government of this princely state attempt to monetarise land-taxation to any significant extent. In 1949, when the kingdom was dissolved, this process had still not been completed. Until Independence there was almost no land market, and cash crops made hardly any appearance for a long time.

So in order to understand rural indebtedness, one has to look for explanations in the ways merchants took advantage of the structural inequalities in the rhythms of spending and income of the population. Two principal factors lie at its origin: first, the irregular nature of the social expenditures which the population as a whole had to face; and then the equally irregular nature of incomes, in a region where agriculture is totally dependent on the vagaries of the climate, and the only well-irrigated lands formed part of the domains held directly by the sovereign or by local Thakurs. In addition there was a very great instability in the prices of agricultural produce, which dropped considerably after the monsoon if there was a good harvest. Peasant communities, rendered especially vulnerable by irregular harvests, thus accumulated debts consisting of advances against the produce of future harvests, at high interest-rates.

How did the merchants recoup their advances? In this region, where agrarian relationships altered only very late compared with the rest of the country, harvests were distributed mainly according to the so-called '*jajmani* system' (*bhog batai* system). The apparent logic of this system, however, masked a different reality. The distribution between claimants remained largely virtual, because the merchants first took from each of them the advances they had been granted.

Since there were no suitable assets or property titles which could be used as surety, and given the very slow emergence of any civil legislation to which appeal could be made, only one constraint really limited the merchants' capacity to appropriate the harvests—but this was a fundamental one: their ability to effectively collect the advances they had provided to farmers and members of other communities. For this two conditions were essential: they had to command sufficient authority to obtain, without too much resistance, the share of the harvest due to them; and the agriculture had to be sufficiently productive for there to be anything to share.

In a society founded on relations of latent force, as has always been the case in rural India, if violence actually erupts, few choices exist: armed resistance or flight. In India, unlike other societies that are more homogeneous from this point of view, the legitimacy of recourse to violence depends essentially, for each individual, on his caste or community of origin. Only the 'warrior' castes would normally use force. In this region these were the Rajput landowners, the tribal groups, and to a lesser extent, the herding communities. On the other hand, Brahmins, Jains, and most cultivator castes did not ordinarily use violence to defend their interests. In cases of conflict, they had to find other methods of exerting pressure.

For Brahmins, their special status at the summit of the social and religious hierarchy gave them a kind of impunity. Driven to the last extremity, they would rather threaten to commit suicide, so that the culpability for their deaths would fall on their adversaries. This occurred in Sirohi as late as 1943. The only recourse of the other non-violent castes was to take flight. This was made easier by the fact that until the 1950s most of the population had no permanent rights over the land they cultivated, nor even to houses they built or wells they constructed. The procedure was quite formal. On a date chosen in advance by the traditional leaders of the community (their *panch*), the entire group would leave their settlement in the night and camp nearby (*uchala*). It was then up to the local authorities to negotiate conditions for the community's return (*manamana*). If this negotiation failed, the members of the community made a solemn vow, engraved on a stone (*gadatra*), never to return to the locality. This was still practised up to the 1950s. It was a formidable means of pressure, since it deprived the dominant castes of the resource that is still the most essential and difficult to obtain: a workforce.

In the case of the merchant castes, who were often in a state of latent conflict with their borrowers, and often isolated in the midst of more numerous communities, the problem took on a dual dimension. On the one hand, they had to avoid exploiting farming, artisan and tribal communities beyond the point where the latter would either resist with violence or take flight. Yet, on the other hand, they had to make themselves so indispensable to the landowning castes that they would be assured of protection, and would not be obliged in their turn to take flight themselves for fear of being dispossessed.

This dual constraint constituted the framework within which the Jain community, like other merchant castes, developed what we might call a 'sociological' view of the rural economy. We have seen that the farming castes, like those who had large incomes from land, were motivated less directly by the impulse to produce more than by the concern to maintain a scale of social and religious expenditure appropriate to their status. By providing them with this possibility, by means of ever-welcome advances, the merchants connected themselves to the rest of the population and made themselves part of the local economy. As long as they continued to supply on a regular basis the required advances, their position was hardly threatened. In the case of isolated conflicts, they turned to the traditional leaders of each community, and used diplomacy with the wealthy and powerful.

For this system to function, the merchants had to in fact, also find some kind of surety for the advances they provided, often more liberally than they would have wished. And if they took up management of the rural economy, this was also as a means of obtaining some medium-term adjustment between the consumption and the production of various communities they were dealing with. We have an indirect confirmation of this from another part of India: S. Guha (1987) has shown in great detail that only the emergence of a market in property-titles enabled local moneylenders in Maharashtra to withdraw from direct involvement in agricultural production, because they then had a new form of surety for the loans they made.

The merchants were in a strong position to exercise control on the rural economy, since they had a monopoly over the buying and the selling of all the people's goods, and were trading with practically their entire agricultural output. What they lacked was a guarantee that this output would be sufficient to provide them with a worthwhile profit. For this reason the merchants armed themselves with two additional advantages.

On the one hand, they took a direct hand in making the land productive as the following example will show. In this arid region, the usual form of irrigation was a 'Persian' well, with a pair of bullocks drawing the water up to ground-level. Constructing and maintaining this type of well was costly both in terms of labour and materials. But farmers felt even less inclined to make the necessary investment because until the 1950s the ownership of the well automatically reverted to the owner of the land. So it was the merchants who encouraged the farmers to ask permission from the Thakurs or the ruler to construct a new well. It was they who provided the entire cost, negotiating with the Thakurs to obtain a number of years (10 to 12). During this period the merchants would recover their advances from the portion of the harvest which would normally have gone, and which would subsequently go to the landowners. Up to the 1930s almost all wells were financed in this way.

On the other hand, the merchants acted as stewards and accountants at every level of the social structure. This responsibility automatically fell on them as far as their farmer-debtors were concerned. The relationship between a merchant and his debtors (*vohra-asami*) was thoroughly formalised, and most often hereditary. The merchant had both the responsibility and the obligation to furnish his *asami* with everything he needed, particularly at times of important ceremonies such as marriages, funerals, etc. In return, the *asami* relied upon the merchant who advanced him his seeds and sold his grain to establish, without any real degree of control on the farmer's part, the balance between what he had provided and what was due to him. In this process, practically no cash ever changed hands in these transactions between merchants and farmers. The Jains also fulfilled the same role, acting as financiers and managers (*kamdar*) for the landowners. And until 1920s they were also financiers to the ruler.

A study of this Jain community, therefore, shows how a merchant community could control practically the entire economy of a small Hindu kingdom. Within this kingdom, the community's practices were not aimed—as they might have been where they were outsiders—at immediately realising a maximum profit, with all the human and economic risks such an attitude would entail. At Sirohi, where their community was as old as the kingdom itself, Jains were to be found at every level of social organisation: in the villages, working for the Thakurs, and in the government of the kingdom. The latter position was the most sought-after, for the income it provided as much as for the prestige and security which accompanied it. But although they were in control of the local economy, the Jains were always in fact at the mercy of the other castes, first because they were dependent upon them economically, and then because their status was not sufficiently legitimised to totally protect them from the threat of violence from those around them.

The Jains occupied a key position in the rural economy because they both stimulated it and kept it in balance. That their vital role was recognised by other communities is revealed by the fact that in period of drought in the kingdom, people would blame neither the ruler nor the gods, but held the Jains, and especially their ascetics, directly responsible.

On the other hand, by basing a large part of their lending on the social and religious expenditure-needs of local groups in this way, the Jains made this form of consumption into an integral part of the overall economic process. In the system which developed under their direction, non-productive consumption paradoxically constituted an essential support of the dynamism of the rural economy. This form of consumption is not regulated by purely economic criteria; instead it is determined by the requirements of the specific status of each caste and community, and is rooted in the socio-cultural characteristics of each of them. One of the greatest difficulties confronting rural populations today derives precisely from the fact that the priority still accorded to this type of expenditure is not taken into account in the prevailing economic logic, and is often contradicted by it—as is shown, for example, by the innumerable problems which arise in connection with betrothal and marriage.

Thus the role played by merchant castes in the local economy had consequences which cannot be assessed until we take into account the way in which their presence gave its specific configuration to the cycles of production and consumption. In spite of the amounts they appropriated from available surplus, the hold of the merchant castes resulted in an overall increase in social and religious spending. For, let us repeat, it was by financing such expenses on credit that the merchants secured their claims upon future production.

In this case, the apparent absence of monetarisation in commercial transactions did not mean that production could not be economically or financially evaluated. In fact, this was a fully monetarised economy, the rationale of which was determined by the wish for profit of one category of non-productive middlemen, rather than by all the agents engaged in the process. Socio-economic conditions were such that monetarisation of the economy was essentially expressed by means of a credit logic which, paradoxically, was more akin to that regulating more highly developed economies. And this credit logic accustomed the population as a whole to maintaining a rhythm of expenditure that was relatively independent, at least in the short term, of the income immediately available to each individual. Such a system could neither arise nor be sustained without the participation of a group of people who had become indispensable because they assured a long-term settlement, if necessary drawing temporarily on resources outside the local market.

Although a detailed examination would lie beyond the scope of this essay, we have an indication 'a contrario' of this, in the way in which a local movement against the Jains (that of Anoop Das) developed from the 1920s onwards (Singhi, 1987; Vidal, 1995: ch. VI). This movement reached its climax in 1936, after the Jains resolved to stop all their activities in the kingdom in protest against a new legislation that was unfavourable to them (Vidal, 1995: ch. VIII). It is interesting to note the reproaches made against them at this time: they were accused not only—as we might expect—of exploiting the population, but were blamed perhaps even more for claiming the right to abrogate the implicit agreement on which this exploitation was based, by threatening, as they did, to stop all commerce and all credit in the kingdom.

THE JAINS' POSITION OF EXPERTISE

I began by describing the role played by Jains in the local economy and the effect their intervention had upon it, because no expert knowledge can be described except in connection with a position of expertise, by which I mean the general context which allows a form of expertise not only to be conceived but also to be exercised.

We have seen how the extension of credit throughout the entire society was based here on a set of behaviour-patterns in which the concept of status and the wish to preserve it very often took precedence over any strictly financial form of calculation. The tension which might have resulted from this, however, did not arise for the merchant castes: for them, on the contrary, wealth and prosperity were signs of their skill in pursuing their distinctive vocation within the order of *dharma*. Moreover, in this particular case, the Jain religion may have had the effect—though this hypothesis is difficult to verify (Cottam Ellis, 1991)—of reinforcing and giving additional legitimation to an ideology which was held more or less common by all merchant castes. This rested essentially, as C. Bayly (1983) has shown, on a cultural, social and economic evaluation of credit. In the eyes of a merchant, the value of an individual and his family is judged less on the basis of his status or apparent wealth, than on the moral and financial credit he commands in society.

However, unlike other elite groups in the kingdom such as the warrior castes who could legitimately resort to force, or the Brahmins who embodied the dominant ideology, the Jains, like other mercantile castes, lacked the means to impose their socio-religious ideas on the rest of society, or even to get their social and economic success acknowledged as legitimate. On the contrary, they had to develop skills in dealing with an environment that was often hostile to them, and whose values they did not fully share.

Thus, unlike castes associated with the functions of priesthood or rulership whose identity or social status were fully acknowledged by the dominant social values, merchant castes in general, and the Jains in particular, experienced a gap between their own motives and those of the society within which they were operating. On the one hand, they were putting into effect commercial, accounting and financial techniques familiar to any businessman. But on the other hand, they were using this expertise under conditions in which the transactions they negotiated with the local people seem always to be determined by other imperatives. Thus, as we have seen, the Jains' relations with their debtors were formalised in such a way that the flow of services and counter-services involved seemed to be dictated more directly by the social needs of their clients than by any strictly financial considerations.

Let us give another example. The Jains obtained some of the cash they might need through an itinerant pastoral caste, the Rebaris. These herders lived in Sirohi but they used to go and sell their animals in regional fairs and markets, sometimes several hundred miles away. Most Jains had among their clients a few Rebaris, who would entrust all their money and valuables to them, so as not to have to take them along when travelling with their flocks. This meant that the Jains had some useful cash at their disposal, which they could use for their own transactions. But the Rebaris had to pay them a fee in addition, for the service of keeping their belongings safe.

Only a residence on the spot and a detailed knowledge of the local population enabled the Jains to adjust complex social realities with financial considerations. Their only real monopoly consisted of this combination of knowledge which enabled them to operate on several levels at once. This is also why they were directly involved with so many different aspects of the rural economy. They could only be dispensed with when the old socio-economic order was replaced by a new one, based on new positions of expertise. And it was only towards the end of the nineteenth century that Western influences began to have any significant effect upon the economy of this kingdom in Rajasthan.

THE EMERGENCE OF A NEW FORM OF EXPERTISE

The 1823 treaty with the British prohibited any interference in the internal administration of the kingdom, in normal circumstances. Once the ruler had stated his intention—if not his capacity—to maintain civil order, and showed a minimum of ability in administering the kingdom, the British avoided direct intervention—or rather, the often decisive injunctions of the Political Resident were presented as pieces of friendly and respectful advice. The sovereign and his court were the only partners officially recognised by the British, and the task of gradually transforming a traditional Indian kingdom into a state with a modern form of government was entrusted solely to their care and supervision.

For this, one of the primary responsibilities of the ruler was to acquire sufficient revenue to establish and maintain an increasingly complex administration. Apart from taxes on merchandise, the revenue of the kingdom came from two main sources: on one hand, innumerable levies on all sorts of activities, economic or otherwise, engaged in by its subjects; and on the other, a large land revenue, which came in part directly from the Crown domains, and partly from a share levied on every harvest in the kingdom.

So far as the land revenue was concerned, an increase was

dependent not so much on an overall increase in productivity, which varied greatly from year to year, nor even on a nominal increase in the ruler's share. What was more significant, and there are parallels here with the Jain case, was the capacity of the administration to collect more effectively the share that was due to them. And every effort in this direction inevitably aroused resistance, often armed, from the subjects. Thus from 1823 up to 1950, the date when the kingdom of Sirohi was abolished, the primary concern of the administration was to increase land revenues, without, however, causing too much disturbance in the semblance of civil order which was achieved with some difficulty in the course of the nineteenth century, but which continued to rest on extremely fragile foundations.

This objective, not in itself very original, was however pursued by methods that were different compared with previous ones. In the system of dividing the harvests that was prevalent in Sirohi at the beginning of the nineteenth century, only the actual produce was taken into account. The landowning castes had an important place in the rural economy, but their direct participation was normally limited to claiming a share of the final product, rather than taking any active part in the process of production. Moreover, the amount of produce which went to the landowners varied immensely from year to year. And it was the Jains who, by extending credit, covered the difference between the expenses and the incomes of the property-owning castes, so that the ruler and the Thakurs were regularly in debt to them.

One of the first concerns of the British administration was that the government of the kingdom should balance its budget properly and avoid getting into debt. This presupposed that it could anticipate what revenue it would receive, in order to adjust current expenditures to it. So in addition to the wish to increase government revenue, there was a new requirement for advance knowledge of what amount the government could expect. Once the government needed to know in advance the revenue from production, and not merely seize a share of the final product, it was confronted with another problem familiar to the Jains: it had to supervise the production process much more closely. But the government did not have the means to influence the farmers as directly as the local merchants could; it had to find another approach.

According to the traditional concept of kingship, the ruler could claim first rights over everything that grew in the kingdom, whether men, plants or animals. This was the justification by which the ruler claimed his share of every harvest. And the government had to attempt to quantify the potential revenue corresponding to this right. This was a problem the merchant castes had never had to face. The success of their affairs was often uncertain, and also difficult to justify; but as we have seen, they always had first-hand knowledge of the resources at the disposal of their clients.

The task of formally quantifying not an amount of produce but the virtual potential represented by a particular territory, required a set of methods and skills which no one in the kingdom at that time possessed. And although estimates of this kind had often been made in India before (see Gordon, 1994), only colonial experience in the matter was taken seriously by the British. So colonial experts and their assistants were called in, and imposed their own approach to the rural economy. As far as the collection of land revenue was concerned, three main objectives were defined for the kingdom:

— making a survey of the land and registering all revenue-generating cultivators;
— setting a rate of taxation, no longer proportional to the actual year's harvest, but fixed for ten years on the basis of previous revenue and the presumed productivity of the land;
— a gradual shift towards payment of this land-tax in cash rather than in kind.

Not surprisingly, it was extremely difficult to enforce this system. Although it was started in 1911, the land survey was not completed before 1956, that is after Independence. And the transfer to a fixed rate of taxation and payment in cash could also be enforced only very slowly. However, it should be noted that even the partial introduction of this system led to a considerable increase in revenue. But apart from these results and the resistance aroused by this process, a radically different concept of the rural economy had been introduced.

Under the old system dominated by the merchant castes, the economic process had been rooted in a calculation of the consumption needs of all the different social categories who lived off the land or by animal-herding, whether they were productive or not, and whether they worked the land directly or not. The produce served primarily as a counterpart for this consumption, and the merchants, whose own interests were involved, played their part in the process by guaranteeing a minimum balance between the expenditures and incomes of nearly everyone in the kingdom.

Under the new system, production became increasingly defined as an autonomous process with its own logic. Attention focused more and more on the land itself, rather than on the people living on it, so that land came to be perceived as the key element in the rural economy as it came to be only defined as a productive potential whose primary function is to generate revenue. As a consequence, the access of the rural population to consumption is then regarded only as an indirect right, based purely on their capacity to earn an income. This new view of the problems of the rural economy rested therefore on a new basis: it obeyed an economic logic where individual spending was taken into account only in so far as it was directly related to production. This soon led to a reconsideration of the legitimacy of the claim to an income of the various sectors of the population to an income.

Viewed from this standpoint, Independence may be seen as only one stage in a general reshaping of the rural economy which is still continuing today. The new order was detrimental first to the trading castes, who after 1930 lost their dominant position in the local economy. Next it was the turn of the ruler, then of the small local aristocracy, and finally of all castes and communities not directly involved in the production process, to lose to a great extent their 'legitimate' rights to an income.

The consequences of this process varied greatly, however, depending on the adaptability of each community. Although today in Sirohi the former ruler has become a pure landowner, the Thakurs have, paradoxically, found a new economic and political status in the context of local democracy. As for the Jain community, its members have, with few exceptions, reoriented all their economic activities towards commercial and financial undertakings outside the district, whereas traditionally this was true of only a few of them.

Their economic success, as evidenced by their present prosperity, is not surprising. They were the only community whose values found a natural extension in the new socio-economic order. As an indication, we can take the tremendous success of the Marwaris (a term which refers to Rajasthani merchants in general) who, in 1963, according to some sources, owned 60 per cent of all India's industrial capital (Timberg, 1978). Their ideology always encouraged them not to make large expenditures, nor even to favour opportunities for immediate enrichment, but rather to convert their income into capital by continuously seeking fresh openings for investment, within a social order to which they adapted without necessarily sharing all its values, and without receiving any particular legitimation. It is paradoxical that although their traditional position in the local rural economy was contested and attacked by the British administration, their approach to economic reality, which up to then had been a minority view in Indian society, had now become the norm to which society as a whole had to adapt itself.

In the socio-economic order which is presently becoming more dominant everyday, the need for a strict equivalence between spending and income, between consumption and productivity, is no longer regulated, as it sometimes was by the Jains, by converting a social logic into an economic and financial one that was controlled by a minority who profited from it. Nowadays everyone is required to adapt strictly all their living conditions to their income. In this context, the persistence of traditional forms of rural indebtedness is increasingly perceived as the consequence of a dual 'ignorance' on the part of rural and tribal populations: ignorance first of the way they are being exploited by local moneylenders, but above all ignorance of the economic and monetary constraints they must learn to adapt to, in order to avoid this kind of debt.

Hence a statement by an economist, written in 1982, which perfectly reflects such an ideology:

Although the Indian peasant lives normally a most frugal and abstentious life, he is undoubtedly apt to carry on his expenditures to extravagant limits. The methods on which the peasant spends his money are extremely immethodical and baneful. He squanders his money extravagantly in unproductive consumption like social ceremonies, upon marriage, ornaments, funeral rites, *sradh* ceremonies of ancestors, etc., which is often beyond the means of the cultivator. The long series of seasonal feasts, religious observances as *kathas*, as well as caste dinners on auspicious occasions, have stimulated family extravagance. (Marmoria, 1982: p. 40)

Although this description borders on the caricature, it none the less demonstrates the huge gap between the logic of traditional practices of credit and present-day perceptions.

CONCLUSION

The types of spending which modern economists consider 'unproductive' are very often those on which the social identity of individuals and groups depended and still depend. Affirming one's status in the eyes of others may involve huge financial cost, as the merchants—who were also the first to benefit from it—knew very well. It is nevertheless the usual practice of individuals or a community for demonstrating (and for preserving or for increasing also) their social status in a way relatively independent of immediate economic constraints. Within the older prevailing social logic, the sums advanced by the Jains for social, not directly 'productive', ends represented the counterpart to the opportunity given to them to appropriate a large share of surplus produce. In these circumstances, the granting of credit could be formally expressed in financial terms, but it could never be reduced to purely financial considerations because the terms of its recovery depended as well on the balance of power existing between the Jains and the rest of the society. And this balance of power was affected by the status and identity of each individual, as much as by the resources each party had at his disposal. Thus the real negotiation which credit occasioned, far from being reducible to a purely economic record (advances granted, interest rates, etc.) reflected more generally the terms of the state of mutual interdependence between debtors and creditors—terms which varied considerably according to the relative power and status of the parties involved.

It would then be relevant to ask more generally whether rural credit practices have really changed so much in rural India as to make it justifiable to analyse them on a strictly economic basis. Given the trends which have been analysed by D. Rajasekhar and D. Vyasulu (1991) in their description of the banking formal sector in rural Rajasthan, one can't but express certain doubts about it. Not only do these authors show that apparently neither the granting nor the amount of capital loaned are related in any way to the rates of interest charged for the loans; they also insist that the ever-increasing number of bad loans is due mainly to political interference, rather than to strictly economic causes. As a result, even nationalised banks whose explicit objective is to contribute to local development, are thinking more and more seriously of closing their rural branches.

A study of this kind leads us to wonder which is the more urgent priority today: should economists remain content to restrict their questioning to the issue of knowing whether or not non-institutional forms of credit involve some form of 'economic logic'? Or should they rather reconsider their assumption that all spending that is aimed towards the existence of social life and even of social status in rural society is necessarily termed as 'unproductive' and should be considered as such by the people themselves? Until they give due attention to such factors, economists will never really understand either the real significance of rural credit or the preference of the people for the informal credit, whatever the degree of exploitation it is involving.

NOTES

1. The field-work for this study was carried out in Sirohi in 1988; it has been funded by the French Institute of Research for Development through cooperation (ORSTOM). I am especially grateful to Sohan Lal Patni, Pukhraj Singhi and all those who helped me gain a better understanding of the credit-practices of the Jains in this area. A first analysis of this material has appeared in French in G. Dupre ed., *Savoirs paysans et développement*, L'Harmattan, Paris, 1991.
2. In 1991 the population had increased to 654,029.
3. For a detailed analysis of the Jain community, see Singhi, 1987; 1992

REFERENCES

All India Rural Credit Survey: the General Report, Reserve Bank of India, Bombay.
Bayly, C.A., 1983, *Rulers, Townsmen and Bazaars*, Cambridge University Press, Cambridge, 1955.
Bhattacharya, N., 'Lenders and debtors: Punjab countryside 1880-1940' in Bose, S., ed., *Credit, Markets and the Agrarian Economy of Colonial India*, Oxford University Press, Delhi, 1994.
Bose, S., ed., *Credit, Markets and the Agrarian Economy of Colonial India*, Oxford University Press, Delhi, 1994.
Bouman, F.J.A., *Small, Short and Insecure: Informal Survey Finance in India*, Oxford University Press, Delhi, 1989.
Burghart, R., 'For a sociology of India: an intracultural approach to the study of "Hindu Society" ' in *Contributions to Indian Sociology*, 17.2.1983, Delhi, 1983.
Carrithers, M. and Humphrey, C., eds, *The Assembly of Listeners: Jains in Society*, Cambridge University Press, Cambridge, 1991.
Cottam Ellis, C.M., 'The Jain merchant castes of Rajasthan: some aspects of the management of social identity in a market town' in Carrithers, M. and Humphrey, C., eds, *The Assembly of Listeners: Jains in Society*, Cambridge University Press, Cambridge, 1991.

Chandra, D., *Rural Credit: Role of Informal Sector*, Segment Books, Delhi, 1993.
Cheesman, D., ' "The omnipresent bania": rural moneylenders in nineteenth century Sind' in *Modern Asian Studies*, vol. 16, pp. 445-63, 1982.
Darling, M., 'The Punjab peasant in debt and prosperity (1925)' in Bose, S., ed., *Credit, Markets and the Agrarian Economy of Colonial India*, Oxford University Press, Delhi, 1994.
Fuller, C., 'Misconceiving the grain heap' in Bloch, M. and Parry, J., eds., *Money and the Parity of Exchange*, Cambridge University Press, Cambridge, 1989.
Ghate, P., ed., *Informal Finance: Some Findings from Asia, Asian Development Bank*, Oxford University Press, 1992.
Galey, J.C., 'Le créancier, le roi, la mort: essai sur les relations de dépendance au Tehri-Garwhal' in *Purushartha 4*, EHESS, Paris, 1980.
Gordon, S.N., *Marathas, Marauders and State Formation in Nineteenth Century India*, Oxford University Press, Delhi, 1987.
Guha, S, 'Commodity and credit in upland Maharashtra, 1800, 1950' in *Economic & Political Weekly*, 26.12.1987, pp. 126-34, 1987.
Hardiman, D., *The Coming of the Devi*, Oxford University Press, Delhi, 1987.
Harris, B., 'Money and commodities, Monopoly and competition' in Howell, ed., *Borrowers and Lenders: Rural Financial Markets and Institutions in Developing Countries*, Overseas Development Institute, London, 1980.
Marmoria, C.B., *Rural Credit in India*, Kitab Mahal, Allahabad, 1982.
Mayer, P. 'The North Indian *jajmani* system' in *Modern Asian Studies*, 27.2.1993.
Padmanabhan, K.P., *Rural credit*, ITP, London, 1988.
Rajasekhar, D. and Vyasulu, D., 'The rural credit system: a study in Pali District of Rajasthan' in *Rural Credit: Issues of the Nineties*, Oxford & IBH, Jaipur, 1991.
Singhi, N.K., ed., *Ideal, ideology and Practice: Studies in Jainism*, Printwell, Jaipur, 1987.
———, 'A Study of Jains in a Rajasthan town' in Carrithers, M. and Humphrey, C., eds., *The Assembly of Listeners: Jains in Society*, Cambridge University Press, Cambridge, 1991.
Subrahmanyam, S. (ed.), in *Money and the Market in India: 1100-1700*, Oxford University Press, Oxford, 1994.
Timberg, T.A., *The Marwaris: from Traders to Industrialists*, Vikas, Delhi, 1978.
Vidal, D., 'Le savoir des marchands: comment prendre en compte les valeurs en jeu dans l'économie—Sirohi District, Rajasthan, Inde' in Dupré, G., ed., *Savoirs paysans et développement*, L'Harmattan, Paris, 1991.
———, 'Le prix de la confiance' in *Terrain 21: Liens de pouvoir ou le clientelisme révisité*, Paris, 1993.
———, *Vérités et violences: un royaume du Rajasthan face au pouvoir colonial*, EHESS, Paris, 1995.

The Role of Trade and Traders in Small-Scale Industrial Development: The Example of a Textile-Printing Centre in Gujarat

VÉRONIQUE DUPONT

INTRODUCTION

The primary role of merchant capital and merchant communities in indigenous industrial development is an acknowledged feature of the economic history of India. In the second half of the nineteenth century and the beginning of the twentieth century, national capitalist industrial enterprise clearly emerged from certain specific and limited sections of Indian society which had the common characteristic of belonging to religious communities or castes that were traditionally involved in trade and money lending, and therefore equipped with capital, business experience and contacts (Pouchepadass, 1975: 35). Thus the pioneer Indian industrialists—among the largest ones even today—hailed from the communities of Parsis, Jain and Vaishnava Banias from Gujarat, Marwaris, and Chettiars from south India. Gujarat in particular was famous for its enterprising class of traders, carrying on commerce with foreign countries from very ancient times, which played an important part in promoting industry on the basis of indigenous resources (Gadgil, 1971: 198).

However, the transition from merchant to industrial capital was initially hindered by a combination of several factors: the competition for limited capital resources between agriculture, commerce and industry; the inadequacy of industrial financing systems, and a lack of interest on the part of existing banks for financing industry; and the attractive high and quick profits offered by commerce and money lending as compared to the greater risks and longer term returns of investments in new manufacturing industry (Gadgil, 1971: 199).

The development of the textile industry in Ahmedabad from the opening of the first mill in 1861 up to 1933 illustrates the initial hesitancy of the Bania community to enter what was then a new industry, and their subsequent direct and decisive contribution to its rapid growth (Spodek, 1965, 1969). The first two mills were promoted by Gujarati entrepreneurs who were 'outsiders' from the traditional trading and banking community of the city.[1] However, from the beginning, Bania financial support remained a prerequisite of industrial expansion. From 1877 onwards Jain merchants and financiers or merchants from the Vaishnava Bania caste also started promoting their own mills and formed the predominant industrialists' force, despite the fact that new families were attracted by the success of this industry (especially from the Patel community, traditionally involved in farming).

More specifically, regarding small-scale industrialisation and the evolution of manufacturing industry out of handicrafts from the mid-eighteenth century up to Independence, the organisation of industry had been marked by the merchants' growing control over the producers and production, through the supply of raw materials, the system of cash advances, and the introduction of daily wages paid to the artisans (Raychaudhury, 1982: 22). Widening of markets and the introduction of outside competition also contributed to 'the divorce of the direct connection between the actual producer and the consumer' and 'strengthened the hand of the middleman' (Gadgil, 1971: 192). Gadgil further characterised traditional and small-scale industry prior to Independence by its 'lack of finance and of contacts with sources of raw material or markets, when they were not local', with the result of 'complete dependence on moneylenders and trader intermediaries' (1971: 334).

From the beginning of planning by the independent Government, the promotion of small-scale industry was given special attention, and was assigned a major role in achieving a well-balanced pattern of industrial development. One facet—and objective—of this industrial strategy was 'to stimulate the formation of an industrial middle-class which would act as a counter-force against the powerful industrialists in large cities' (Streefkerk, 1985: 41). The industrial estate programme launched in 1955 and the newly created state financing institutions aimed to provide for production space along with the necessary facilities and public utilities, as well as special financial and technical assistance to entrepreneurs. This programme was also expected to help artisans 'overcome their shortage of capital' and transform 'their artisan skills into entrepreneurial productivity' (Spodek, 1976: 87).

Despite special support accorded by the Indian Government to small-scale industry, as Streefkerk rightly underlined in the concluding remarks of his own research work and review on industrial transition, 'post-colonial development of small-scale industry also was largely based on the transition from trade to industrial capital' (1985: 256).

With reference to this general historical and socio-economic background, this article attempts to evaluate more thoroughly the effective role played by trade and traders in small-scale industrialisation in the context of a middle-sized town of Gujarat which specialises in textile dyeing and printing, Jetpur. This case study exemplifies mono-industrial development based on an ancient traditional craft, in a region acknowledged for the dynamism of its merchant communities.

This assessment is envisaged from different angles. From the historical angle, the conversion of an ancient textile-trade town into an industrial textile-printing centre is analysed in order to highlight the role of the 'merchant heritage' in the emergence of the contemporary urban economy. The relative place of the traditional merchant groups within the class of industrial entrepreneurs, as well as the significance of transfer of capital from trading activities to the printing industry are then appraised. In addition to the direct participation of the traditional trading communities in industrial investment and management, other forms of traders' control over the printing industry are also examined.

The findings presented in this paper are based on historical documentation and primary data collected through various surveys conducted in Jetpur from October 1987 to November 1989, as part of a research project on urban development, industrialisation and migration processes in middle-sized Indian towns.[2] The primary data analysed here refers more particularly to: a statistical survey of migration and employment covering 10 per cent of the households of the urban agglomeration and five nearby villages (namely a total sample of 14,412 residents with a sub-sample of 215 entrepreneurs in the textile industry); in-depth interviews with a sample of 50 entrepreneurs; as well as various interviews with leaders of industrial and commercial associations, bank managers, officials and local dignitaries. In addition, the research area was revisited in August 1992, in order to update our observations.

THE TEXTILE TRADE IN JETPUR AND ITS REGION AT THE TIME OF THE PRINCELY STATES

THE REGIONAL CONTEXT: SAURASHTRA

Jetpur is located in Saurashtra, the western peninsula of Gujarat, which was known as Kathiawar from the eighteenth century until Independence. The region was then a conglomeration of princely states, small principalities and estates (or *giras*) with varying territories and jurisdictions, and as many as 222 of these were enumerated on the eve of Independence. Their rulers, designated as *Rajas, Talukdars, Darbars* or *Girasdars*—depending on the importance and type of the possessions—belonged to the Kshatriya warrior castes of Rajput and Kathi, and the latter gave their name to the whole peninsula.

The peculiar location of Saurashtra, with a coastline of 829 kilometres stretching out into the Arabian sea, explains the historical integration of the region in seaborne trade with the countries of the Arabian Gulf, East Africa and East Asia, as well as with other parts of the Indian subcontinent. During the nineteenth century, cotton developed as the leading commercial crop of the regional economy and supported a flourishing trade. It was sent to Bombay and constituted the chief item of export from the peninsula. The merchants involved in this trade belonged mainly to the castes of Vaniyas (the Gujarati Banias), Bhatias and Lohanas, and to the Muslim communities of Memons and Khojas. Till the second half of the nineteenth century, cotton was exported in loose bales, without any processing. The first ginning and pressing factory was established in 1866 at Wadhwan, and the first spinning and weaving mill a few years later at Bhavnagar in 1873. The availability of raw material from the region itself, viz., cotton, greatly influenced the development of the textile industry. This became the most important industry in Saurashtra, from the viewpoint of both employment and investment, until at least the early fifties (Vakil *et al.*, 1953).

The merchant classes formed one of the leading groups in Saurashtran urban life, but their interests could come into conflict with those of their rulers. As shown by Spodek (1975), this traditional conflict increased under British rule which strengthened both merchants and princes. On one hand, the cotton trade was favoured by British policy, while the construction of new transportation and communication systems encouraged commerce and business. On the other hand, the princely states were politically better protected under the British rule, while economic competition between them pushed their rulers to take isolationist measures, restricting the merchants' activities. As a result, the frustrated professional and merchant classes, which already had a long tradition of spatial mobility in search of better opportunities, responded by increased out-migration from the peninsula, especially to Bombay.

THE DEVELOPMENT OF JETPUR AS A TRADING CENTRE

Within the regional context of a cotton-trade oriented economy, the town of Jetpur developed as a prosperous trading centre during the nineteenth century and the first half of the twentieth century. The historical roots of the economic dynamics of the town can be grasped through the reports made by a British political agent of that time, Colonel Walker (1808), and later developed in the *Kathiawar Gazetteer* (1884: 185-6). At the time of the princely states, Jetpur was ruled by Kathis. When Colonel Walker entered the peninsula in 1807 in order to pacify it, 'the country was in a state of chronic disorder and desolation'[3] (Wilberforce-Bell, 1980: 179). In marked contrast to the Kathis' predatory habits and very poor state of prosperity, Colonel Walker pointed to the orderly and flourishing estates of Jetpur and Chital (a neighbouring town), under the sway of what he designated 'Reformed Khatis'. The protection that those rulers provided to merchants and artisans attracted others, and allowed these towns to develop as prosperous trading centres.

The insertion of Jetpur into the communication network further fostered the commercial activities of the town. As long ago as the twelfth century, Jetpur was a fortified stage along the military road constructed by the Solanki of Anhilvada (1094-143) to link their capital Patan with Junagadh. Trade followed this route for many years, and subsequently this direct link between the mainland and the peninsula supplanted the more circuitous coastal road, except for religious pilgrims (*Rajkot District Gazetteer*, 1965: 29). In 1865 the then Political Agent in Kathiawar, Colonel Keatinge, began systematic construction of roads, several of which passed through

Jetpur, in particular the Rajkot-Junagadh road which was later improved into a bridged and metalled road. The bridge over the Bhadar river at Jetpur, built of stone masonry, which was opened in 1877, is mentioned in the *Kathiawar Gazetteer* as one of 'the chief bridges in the province' (1884: 222). Jetpur has also been well connected by rail since the construction of the first railway lines in the peninsula in December 1880: a branch line passing through Jetpur was opened in January 1881, and in 1893 a new line passing through Navagadh, a village on the outskirts of Jetpur town.

By the end of the nineteenth century, Jetpur was a town with a population of 13,085 (1881 census), which is described in the *Kathiawar Gazetteer* (1884: 242) as one of the chief trade centres of the province:

The leading merchants in these trade centres are among Hindus, Vanias, Bhatias, and Lohanas, and among Musalmans, Vohoras, Memans, and Khojas. Some of the traders of the seaports and of Wadhwan, Jetpur, and Dhoraji own capital up to £ 100,000 (Rs 10,00,000). They trade direct with Bombay and other larger markets, sending cotton, grain, clarified butter and other local produce, and bringing cloth, timber, groceries, and metals.

One specific factor gave an impetus to the commercial development of Jetpur: in this former Kathi state no duty was levied on goods imported into the town, which attracted traders and artisans. Jetpur especially emerged as an important centre of trade in textiles, as cloth was also exempted from octroi. As reported by Trivedi:

This concession made it profitable for the traders of Jetpur to import cloth from Japan and western countries and sell it in other parts of the country. . . . It is reported that in the past cloth merchants of Jetpur had brought cloth from Japan by chartered steamers. Bosky and satin-duck imported at Jetpur from Japan had acquired a market all over India at one time. (1970: 38)

During the three decades preceding Independence, a Muslim community of traders, the Memons, also played a particularly important role in the development of the town. Many Halai Memons from Saurashtra had started migrating to Burma around 1850-5, and prospered in business there (Engineer, 1989: 173). For the Jetpur Memons, however, the event which triggered off migration occurred in 1885. Following a clash between the Muslim and Hindu communities on the occasion of the Moharram festival that year,

Memons were prosecuted for rioting. Subsequently, they escaped to Burma, while maintaining their wives and families in the place. Initially, the Jetpur Memons were rather petty traders. They built their fortunes on trade in Burma, especially during the First World War, and eventually reinvested their savings in Jetpur in the construction of spacious houses. Some entire sections along the main streets of the bazaar and in the heart of the town were built by the Memons at that time. Their prosperity had side-effects on the economic life of Jetpur, as well as on its social development, through charitable institutions, and the construction of a hospital and a high-school, both free and eventually open to all communities. The most famous and richest Memon of Jetpur was Sir Admji Haji Daud, who started a jute business in Burma and later in Calcutta where he owned and ran a large jute mill. He is the founder of the above-mentioned hospital in Jetpur, and in 1928 he was knighted by the British.

RADICAL CHANGES BROUGHT ABOUT BY INDEPENDENCE

The advent of Independence radically altered the political and economic background in which the commercial development of Jetpur was rooted. Independence put an end to the state of political fragmentation which characterised the peninsula. In 1948, the formation of the United States of Saurashtra led to the dissolution of the princely states and their integration into one political entity tied into the national structure of the Indian Union.[4] The integration of the former princely states gave shape to a new unified regional economic space, integrated with the national one and open to competition. Following a better harmonisation of the regulations concerning sales taxes and octroi all over the country, Jetpur lost its comparative advantage in the cloth trade, which affected its commercial prosperity.

In addition, the disturbances which accompanied the Partition of the country undermined the development of Jetpur. The town was subject to communal riots in 1948 and 1949. The neighbouring state of Junagadh, to which was attached a village adjoining Jetpur, Navagadh, was previously under a Muslim ruler who was eager to merge with Pakistan. Jetpur was used as a military base for the army sent to crush the rebellion, and eventually the Nawab of Junagadh escaped to Pakistan. The Memon community of Jetpur had financially supported the Muslim League and its leader Mohammad Ali Jinnah, the founder of Pakistan, whose family hailed from Saurashtra.[5] Following these events, a large part of the Muslim community of Jetpur, especially the Memons, also migrated to Pakistan. The group migration of this prosperous community led to an economic depression, which was further aggravated by the successive departure of other sections of the population. Many artisans left the town, and most of the Vaniya traders migrated to Bombay, which had been for long an out-migration destination for Gujarati traders. As a result, the population of Jetpur diminished dramatically in the years following Independence: according to estimates provided by the Municipality, the decrease was approximately 15,000 people. The census data also reflect a dramatic inversion in the population trend of the town. Between 1921 and 1941 the population of Jetpur increased at a decennial growth rate of about 23 per cent, to reach 28,406 inhabitants in 1941. A decade later the population was at almost the same level: 28,444 inhabitants in 1951. This apparent stagnation in fact masks a continuation of the demographic growth of the town up to 1947, followed by considerable out-migration.

While the development of dyeing and printing crafts in Jetpur under the Kathi *Darbars* followed the general expansion of the town as an important trading centre, after the political events which put an end to the commercial prosperity of Jetpur in 1947-9, the printing industry took over and gradually emerged as the leading economic sector in the town. The merchant economy had however laid foundations on which industrialisation could rely. This transition is examined in the following section.

TRANSITION TO DYEING AND PRINTING INDUSTRY

ORIGIN AND DEVELOPMENT OF DYEING AND BLOCK-PRINTING IN JETPUR

Dyeing and printing of textiles was a traditional craft in the Saurashtra region, and its origin in Jetpur could be traced to the beginning of the nineteenth century (Sampatram, 1868). The counsellor of the then ruler of Jetpur[6] called upon various artisans as well as traders from different places in Saurashtra in order to promote the economic expansion of the town. Around 1813 the first families belonging to the Khatri community were called from Kalavad in Jamnagar district to develop dyeing and printing crafts and trade in Jetpur. Some were traders in dyed cloth, and others skilled craftsmen working for the former. They were followed by other Khatri artisans coming from textile-printing centres located in the neighbouring districts of Junagadh and Amreli (such as Kuthiana, Bhesan, Majevdi, Bagasara, etc.). Hence, from its beginnings the textile dyeing and printing craft in Jetpur was linked with the cloth trade, and artisans were to a certain extent already dependent on traders.

The development of dyeing and printing of cotton cloth in Jetpur progressed along with the expansion of the textile trade, as the two activities maintained close links. The dealers in cloth supplied the main raw material to the artisans, and the marketing of the finished products went through the cloth traders. In some cases artisans were entirely dependent on cloth traders, when the latter gave out the raw material and paid a piecework wage to the artisans for the dyeing and printing work. This shows the craftsmen's loss of independence to the benefit of the dealers, as occurred generally in the early stage of the industrialisation process.

According to Trivedi's monograph (1970: 38), around 1915 nearly 100 artisans were engaged in dyeing and printing craft in Jetpur. Then textile hand-printing is reported to have received a considerable impetus during the Second World War. In 1947, the technique of screen-printing was introduced in Jetpur and gradually supplanted block-printing, while the new mode of printing and further improvement in the technique allowed the expansion of the industry on a larger scale.

DEVELOPMENT OF THE SCREEN-PRINTING INDUSTRY SINCE 1947

As explained earlier, the economy of Jetpur was undergoing a serious depression following Partition when the introduction of a new technology for the printing of textiles, screen-printing, marked the beginning of a new era of industrial development for the town.

The screen-printing industry in Jetpur was pioneered and developed by Shri Gordhandas Karsanji Bosamia, popularly known as Bachubhai, who started the group 'Jagdish Textile Dyeing and Printing Works' in 1947-8. Bachubhai was a direct descendant of Manji Parsottan Bosamia, a trader in dyed cloth from Kalavad, who was the first Khatri called to Jetpur to develop dyeing and printing craft at the beginning of the nineteenth century. At the time of Independence, Bachubhai was involved in the cloth trade in

Ahmedabad. His foresight and business acumen enabled him to visualise Jetpur as an ideal place for the development of the printing industry, while the slackness and unemployment which prevailed in Jetpur after the sizeable out-migration of traders and artisans also prompted him to return to his native place and try to give a new impetus to its economy. In addition to block-printing, Bachubhai started screen-printing on a very small scale. This technique, though already known in western India, had not yet been introduced in Saurashtra. The method of screen-printing originated from the Japanese *Yuzen* style, which was carried out with screens made from specially prepared rice-paper cut in stencil form (Trivedi, 1970). In 1954, Bachubhai went to Japan to improve his knowledge of screen-printing and other modern techniques of dyeing, bleaching and printing. This brought a new outlook into his industrial group, which progressively expanded in Jetpur itself, as well as in Ahmedabad, along with the setting up of trading companies in Bombay, Delhi, Madras and Indore.

Following the establishment of the first screen-printing factory in Jetpur, other printing factories gradually changed over from block-printing to screen-printing in the fifties and early sixties, while traders and entrepreneurs of the Khatri caste came to settle in Jetpur. Later the prospects of the printing industry attracted many entrepreneurs from other communities, in particular Vaniya traders and Kanbis.

As a result of this industrial redeployment from block-printing to screen-printing, the number of screen-printing factories set up in Jetpur has shown a continuous and rapid growth. In 1964, Trivedi (1970) reported 110 screen-printing units. The maximum number of units was reached around 1985, with 1,200 units, and since then it has been fluctuating between 1,100 and 1,200.[7] All of these belong to the small-scale sector[8] and specialise in the printing of cotton saris for the lower and lower-middle classes.

The development of the screen-printing industry in Jetpur also promoted several ancillary manufacturing and servicing activities: about 200-300 small units manufacturing screens, about 100 small units engaged in finishing processes, and about 20 to 30 factories manufacturing dyes or other chemicals used in the printing process (gum powder, silicate, etc.) located in the town and nearby villages. Along with manufacturing activities, trade (in cloth, dyes and chemicals, packaging materials, and other accessories) as well as transport (from handcart to truck) related to the textile-printing industry also expanded.

The dyeing and printing industry in Jetpur has become the leading sector of the urban economy, and has had an appreciable impact on the economy of the surrounding villages through the supply of large employment opportunities to the rural population. According to the industrial association's estimates, the maximum employment capacity of this industrial sector, including its ancillary activities, would be around 40,000 jobs. The considerable expansion of the printing industry has also resulted in fast population growth. The urban and industrial spread of Jetpur has given shape to an urban agglomeration with a total population of about 114,000 inhabitants in 1988.[9]

FACTORS OF INDUSTRIAL GROWTH AND CONCENTRATION IN JETPUR

The industrial development in Jetpur corresponds to a case of endogenous dynamics which did not benefit from any exclusive governmental programme. Nevertheless, Jetpur's entrepreneurs proved capable of taking advantage of the government's general industrial policy, and in particular of the measures aimed at promoting small-scale industry and favouring industrial decentralisation away from metropolitan areas. At the time of Independence, in the general context of the country's underdevelopment, Saurashtra was moreover a relatively backward region industrially; the government of the time recognised the importance of state aid and encouragement to promote industrialisation and took various policy measures to this end. Altogether, this created radically new conditions for industrial development (Vakil *et al.*, 1953). In order to provide an adequate infrastructure, the State Government developed roads and road transport, power generation which was—and still is—an important bottleneck, communications, and the banking system through the State Bank of Saurashtra created in 1950. The thrust of the new economic policy was toward small-scale industrialisation, through the establishment of several supporting institutions[10] and the implementation of an industrial estate programme.[11] Industrial development gathered further impetus with the formation of the Gujarat State in 1960, and new specialised institutions were created to channel state assistance.[12]

Within this general context, several specific factors played an important role in the concentration and growth of the screen-printing industry in Jetpur.

After Partition the emigration of the prosperous trading community of Memons, on the one hand, ruined the economy of the town, and on the other turned out to be a favourable factor for the establishment of new industries in Jetpur. The Memons left behind all their properties, spacious houses and vast buildings, which were sold at very low prices. Some Khatri artisans, the first entrepreneurs in Jetpur, took advantage of this situation, and converted the properties evacuated by the Memons into printing factories. At the same time there was an influx of Sindhi refugees from Pakistan to Gujarat and to Jetpur, among them Sindhi Khatris who belonged to the traditional dyeing and printing community of Sind. Taking advantage of the Custodian property system, under which the refugees of India and Pakistan could, by mutual agreement, exchange their properties, the Sindhi Khatris acquired spacious buildings, which they gradually turned into printing units.

Some administrative measures taken in 1963 by the Municipality of Jetpur also gave a major impetus to the development of the local industry. In 1950, Jetpur got the status of Municipality, and its trade thus became subject to high octroi taxes. That constituted an additional force of dissuasion for trade and commerce in the context of an already depressed economy. The Municipality, aware of such a hindrance, managed to lower the classification of Jetpur for the purpose of octroi collection, which resulted in a reduction of 25 per cent octroi. A modification in the rules governing the octroi system was further introduced. In the initial system, the merchants importing goods (like cloth) had 15 days to pay the octroi tax. The Municipality of Jetpur extended this period up to 60 days, which created a unique situation among all the towns in Saurashtra. This comparative advantage allowed the printing industry, which was entirely dependent on cloth coming from outside, to flourish.

The rapid expansion of the screen-printing industry can be explained by its economic characteristics. To start with, it is not a capital intensive industry: it does not require high initial investment, nor specific machinery or sophisticated technology. Easily obtainable bank credit facilities for plant and equipment up to 1983 was an additional favourable factor.[13] Raw materials were also available on credit, and cotton cloth supply was abundant. As the entire process of dyeing and printing is manual and the main equipment consists of printing tables and screen plates, this enabled the entrepreneurs to start their concerns on a small scale, even in rented premises which were sometimes already equipped, and to expand it progressively. Moreover the system by which the entrepreneurs undertake printing work on subcontract, according to orders placed by traders, allowed the entrepreneurs to minimise expenses as well as risks, since the traders both provide them with the cloth, and market the finished products. About 75 to 80 per cent of the printing factories in Jetpur today function under this system, locally known as 'job-work'.

The concentration of printing factories in Jetpur induced further industrial growth and concentration as the new entrepreneurs were assured of finding appropriate conditions and infrastructure to start their concerns: factory premises on a rental basis, skilled labour and a network of traders. As long as the level of demand for Jetpur's printed cotton saris was high, this industry offered good and fast profits, with a minimum of economic and technological constraints. This explains why it attracted many entrepreneurs, who did not necessarily belong to the traditional communities of craftsmen or traders (see later).

Good infrastructure facilities also contributed to the promotion of trade and industry in Jetpur. This town is situated on the National Highway from Rajkot to Porbandar. State Transport buses regularly pass through it and connect it with the main towns in Gujarat. In addition, it is linked by rail to major cities of the state and the country. The town is also equipped with the administrative infrastructure of a *taluka* headquarters, and with good banking facilities (eight main regional or national banks have local branches in Jetpur).

What should, however, be underlined to conclude this panorama of Jetpur's economic evolution is the significance of the merchant heritage in endowing the urban economy with favourable factors for further industrial development, and the close links between the cloth trade and the textile-printing industry. The town has long been connected with trading routes and networks; cloth merchants and dealers in printed textiles have always played a strategic role in supplying raw material to craftsmen, later to entrepreneurs, and in marketing their finished products. The prevalence of subcontracting (the 'job-work' system) in the Jetpur dyeing and printing industry, which shows a high degree of dependence of entrepreneurs on traders, nevertheless contributed to attract new generations of entrepreneurs into this industry.

FROM MERCHANTS AND MERCHANT CAPITAL TO INDUSTRIALISTS AND INDUSTRIAL INVESTMENT

This section deals with the direct participation and contribution of the traditional trading communities to entrepreneurship and investment in the Jetpur dyeing and printing industry.

TRADITIONAL MERCHANT GROUPS IN THE CLASS
OF INDUSTRIAL ENTREPRENEURS

The Khatris, who were the original craftsmen and the first entrepreneurs to develop the dyeing and printing industry in Jetpur, still constitute the majority group of entrepreneurs running printing factories (44 per cent in 1988), followed by the Kanbis (also locally called Patels), traditionally a caste of agriculturists who have gradually entered this industry in increasing numbers, especially from the 1970s onwards (34 per cent of the concerned entrepreneurs) (see Table 1). The Vaniyas, who form the traditional Gujarati caste cluster of merchants (the Gujarati Banias), represent a significant though minor group among the entrepreneurs running printing factories: 11 per cent, which is significantly higher than their demographic share in the population of the Jetpur urban agglomeration (5 per cent). These are essentially Hindu Vaniyas, Vaishnava or Modh Vaniyas, whereas the Jain community is negligible among the entrepreneurs as well as among the total population of the town (less than 2 per cent). The Vaniya entrepreneurs have not, however, penetrated the ancillary industry—screen manufacturing and sari finishing units—which is dominated by the Kanbis (67 per cent of the entrepreneurs of this ancillary sector). Another traditional Gujarati trading caste which has entered the textile-printing industry, though only marginally, also deserves mention: the Lohanas, who account for 5 per cent of the entrepreneurs. Only a very few Marwari entrepreneurs from Rajasthan or previously settled in Calcutta are acknowledged in Jetpur.

In order to correctly appraise the relative place of the traditional trading communities in the formation of the contemporary class of industrialists, the role of some of the Khatri entrepreneurs, those who hail from families involved in cloth or printed textile trade for generations, should also be taken into account. This group of Khatri entrepreneurs is numerically less important than those coming from families of artisans engaged in traditional cloth dyeing and block-

TABLE 1: PERCENTAGE DISTRIBUTION OF ENTREPRENEURS
IN THE JETPUR DYEING AND PRINTING INDUSTRY BY CASTE
AND TYPE OF ESTABLISHMENT IN 1988

Caste	Entrepreneurs by type of establishment			Population of Jetpur urban agglomeration
	Sari-printing factories	Ancillary units	All establishments	
Kanbi	33.5	66.6	42.3	22.0
Khatri	43.7	8.8	34.4	7.1
Vaniya	11.4	0.0	8.4	4.9
Lohana	5.7	1.8	4.7	5.9
Brahmin	0.6	12.3	3.7	5.5
Others (not BC or SC)	3.8	3.5	3.7	16.0
Other Backward Classes	1.3	3.5	1.9	32.7
Scheduled Castes	0.0	3.5	0.9	5.9
Total	100.0	100.0	100.0	100.0
No. of observations	158	57	215	11 925

BC = Backward classes; SC = Scheduled castes
Source: The 10 per cent household survey, 1988

printing; however, textile trade and printing work are two activities that are economically linked, and the combination of both is—and was—not rare among Khatri families. The pioneer entrepreneur in the screen-printing industry in Jetpur provides a famous illustration of this strategy of diversification (see earlier section).

Considering now the first 25 leading industrial groups in Jetpur, the competition seems most keen between the traditional artisan and merchant communities on the one hand, and newcomers from agriculturist families on the other: 12 groups, including the biggest one in Jetpur, are run by Khatris, 10 by Kanbis, 2 by Vaniyas and 1 by Lohanas.[14]

The evolution of the competing forces within the class of entrepreneurs reflects the major changes which marked the social sphere of Saurashtra in terms of politico-economic dominant groups in the post-Independence period. The integration of the principalities in 1948 meant for the former princes, *girasdars* and *jagirdars* of the Rajput and Kathi castes, the loss of their political and economic power. Other leading urban groups, the Brahmin and Bania professional and business classes, came to dominate the region's politics during the construction of the new Saurashtra State. The peaceful revolution brought about by integration 'replaced the "*Bhom Raj*", based on aristocratic landlord values, with "*Bania Raj*", based on merchant values' (Spodek, 1977: 64). The political dominance of the Brahmin and Bania urban elite in Saurashtra was however put to an end by the mid-sixties by the competition of a newly rising group, the Kanbis. The Kanbis form a majority caste of agriculturists who were tenants-at-will of the former landlords and gained full occupancy rights and ownership of land following the integration of Saurashtra and the land reforms of 1951-5. Their entrepreneurial capabilities as cultivators made them contribute to and benefit from the transformation in agriculture—namely the development of commercial crops, especially groundnut which supplanted cotton as the main cash crop, and progress in irrigation facilities. The nationalisation of banks in 1969 further provided them easy access to financial facilities. The shift in favour of cash crops in particular enabled them to draw surplus from agricultural incomes, which they invested in agro-based industries and other industries and businesses. The rise of the Kanbis' economic power has been accompanied by their growing political influence, reinforced in the democratic system by their numerical strength.[15]

MERCHANT ENTREPRENEURS' LIFE HISTORIES AND INVESTMENT STRATEGIES

The contribution of the traditional merchant communities to the formation of the contemporary class of industrial entrepreneurs goes beyond their demographic strength, which remains relatively modest in the case of the Jetpur printing industry. Their contribution should also be appraised in terms of capital transferred from trade to industry.

The entrepreneurs from merchant communities (Vaniyas, Lohanas and some Khatris) belong more specifically to families of merchants specialising in the textile or sari trade. They extended their familial trading activity to the sari-printing industry. Before running their own printing unit, these entrepreneurs had previous work experience in the familial trade, or—among Khatris especially—an experience of management in a printing unit started by parents or relatives.

These merchant-entrepreneurs raised their initial capital to invest in industry from profits earned in familial trading activities, in Jetpur itself or, for some in-migrant entrepreneurs, in other places before settling down in Jetpur. If necessary, familial savings were supplemented by bank or GSFC loans. This transfer of capital often allowed these entrepreneurs to start their first printing factory on a larger scale, compared to artisans who converted from traditional textile dyeing or block-printing to screen-printing, starting on a very small scale and operating on a familial basis, with a gradual extension of the enterprise by reinvestment of the profits earned. Moreover, a personal or familial experience in the cloth or sari trade also equipped merchant-entrepreneurs with the necessary contacts and thus made it easier for them to turn to the textile-printing industry. They often started as traders, placing orders with Jetpur factories to get saris printed, and subsequently decided to set up their own printing factories when they realised the possible return. This was generally a diversification of the familial business rather than a reconversion. The combination of sari trade and printing industry allows the traders a better control over the quality of the prints, and enables them to develop their own lines of products, and increase their profits.

Compared with the large majority of Jetpur's entrepreneurs, who undertake printing work under subcontract according to traders' orders (the 'job-work' system described earlier), the entrepreneurs from merchant communities generally purchase the cloth to be printed themselves and then market their finished products, hence working as independent manufacturers. This last mode of business involves more risk and requires more capital, but can yield better returns.

Some entrepreneurs' life histories illustrate more concretely the passage from trade to industry, and the transfer of capital from one sector to the other.[16]

Jamnadas' story is typical of Khatri families which have combined craft and trading activities for generations.

Jamnadas, over 60 years old, is still very active in running the family commercial and industrial enterprise along with his two sons. They are Khatri by caste and their family hails from Bagasara, another nearby town of Saurashtra which was also famous for its ancient tradition of textile dyeing and printing craft. Jamnadas' grandfather was an independent craftsman who bought raw cotton, got it spun and woven by specialised artisans, then dyed the cloth and sold it himself, going around from village to village. Around 1920, part of the family, including Jamnadas' father, migrated for better business prospects to Visavadar, a centre for textile trade in a neighbouring district. There they opened a retail cloth store while pursuing the dyeing craft, and traded both in mill-cloth and traditional printed cloth. In 1949 Jamnadas came to Jetpur along with his maternal uncle in order to start a business in mill-cloth, purchased from Bombay and Ahmedabad. Ten years later, as Jetpur had lost its importance as a cloth trade centre whereas the printing industry developed, they changed over to the sari trade. They placed orders to get saris printed in Jetpur factories, and marketed the printed saris in various parts of the country. Meanwhile Jamnadas' younger brothers had also migrated from Visavadar to join the family business in Jetpur. They realised that they could increase their profits and ensure a better quality of print if they manufactured the saris themselves. Future prospects for the sari-printing industry were bright at that time, and land was cheap. Hence, in 1963, they decided to establish their own printing business. They purchased at a very low price a residential house abandoned by a Memon family and transformed it into a small factory. The required capital was raised with savings from trade, supplemented by a loan from a private money-lender. The ownership and management were shared between five familial partners: Jamnadas, three of his brothers, and his uncle. The manufacturing activities gradually expanded (though the joint-family ownership eventually broke up), new factories were set up covering 15 printing units under six different industrial groups, the total processing capacity increased by more than ten times, and their market sales extended all over India. New investment was financed with the profits made in sari trading and printing factories, as well as bank loans.*

Girishbhai exemplifies the case of printing factory owners belonging to well-established Bania families of textile traders.

Girishbhai is a Jain Vaniya, whose family belongs to Jetpur and had for generations traded in mill-cloth. His grandfather's commercial establishment was well-known in the place. His father found a new business opportunity with the development of the printing industry: he started to work as a commission agent to supply bleached cotton cloth to the manufacturers. In the early sixties he was the sole broker in grey cloth in Jetpur; since then many more agents have entered this business. Later Girishbhai's father also started in the sari trade and placed orders with printing factories. Thus, in 1984, when Girishbhai and his three brothers started their own printing factory in partnership, they had previously acquired long years of experience in the familial trade and were equipped with the right network of contacts in the sari business. They invested capital raised from trade and got a loan from the GSFC for the construction of plant and machinery. They work as independent manufacturers and run their printing factory in close association with their father's cloth and sari trade.

Mansuklal's story illustrates the career of a member of a merchant family with a lower initial profile.

Mansuklal belongs to the Vaishnava Vaniya community, and hails from a village in Ahmedabad district. His father, who had a provision store in his native place, migrated to Jetpur in 1970, attracted by the better trading prospects provided by the sari-printing industry. Though Mansuklal's father had no relative in Jetpur, he relied on members of his community to help him start a new business. In fact he started a sari trade—semi-wholesale—with partners from his caste. Mansuklal joined his fathers' trade in 1976 after leaving secondary school and worked as a commercial traveller. After ten years of this job he wanted a more settled life and decided to set up a printing factory, while the saris would be marketed through his father's trade. They also thought that running their own manufacturing unit would enable them to get better quality of prints for sale. Mansuklal started his printing factory in rented premises. He raised the initial capital with his own savings from trade and with the help of his maternal uncle who joined the business as a financial partner. He recently got a bank loan for the extension of the factory. Interestingly, Mansuklal thought that his previous experience in the sari trade was not sufficient to ensure the success of his sari-printing enterprise; he felt his lack of knowledge in dyeing was a handicap as he could not properly control the work of the dyer, who occupies the most strategic position in the printing process. Following an unfortunate precedent with his first dyer, he summoned his younger brother, who was a student in law, and placed him as an apprentice with a master dyer, so that he could learn all the skills of this job and later work in the family factory.

Lalitbhai's career provides one of the most spectacular success stories among the Jetpur entrepreneurs.

Lalitbhai was born in 1902 in a small village of Jetpur taluka, and was a Lohana by caste. His father was however a simple cultivator, and the family lived poorly. At the age of 15 he left for Bombay to earn a living. He did not know anybody there, and at the beginning slept on the pavement outside the shops of Mulji Jetha Market, the biggest textile market in Bombay, where he could find jobs as a casual loader. Then he worked as an assistant and later a salesman in the same sari shop for eighteen years, starting with a monthly salary of 15 rupees. In addition, he worked on a commission basis for three more years with the firm. Equipped with 21 years of experience and wide contacts, he started his own shop in the same market, gradually developed his business and became a prominent dealer in hand-printed saris. He placed orders to get saris printed with factories in Bombay, Ahmedabad, Rajkot and Jetpur. After more than 20 years in the sari trade, in order to be able to meet the growing demand for Jetpur-style printed saris, he decided to manufacture his own products and in 1953 started his own printing factory at Jetpur, where he already had some business contacts. He bought the land and built the factory with savings set aside from his trade in Bombay. This first printing unit started on a very small scale, with a processing capacity of only 10 saris at a time. He gradually established new factories and when he died in 1983 he bequeathed one of the biggest industrial groups in Jetpur. Today this includes 16 companies, with a total processing capacity of 1,700 saris at a time, and an employment capacity of almost one thousand workers. Now the family business is run by Lalitbhai's two elder sons, who successfully continue to develop their sari trading company in Bombay and the manufacturing activities in Jetpur.

These few cases of entrepreneurs' life histories clearly indicate the advantages of the merchant communities in penetrating this industry: the traders, and more specifically the textile and sari dealers, have financial capital to invest, as well as experience in business and the right network of connections, relying on caste solidarity and professional contacts. These examples also illustrate the opportunities for upward socio-economic mobility that the development of the dyeing and printing industry has provided.

THE TEXTILE TRADE AS A SPRINGBOARD TO ENTER THE SARI-PRINTING INDUSTRY

The favourable position held by cloth and sari traders for entering the sari-printing industry is further highlighted by the strategies of some entrepreneurs who belong to neither traditional artisan nor merchant communities. In particular among Kanbis, whose familial agricultural background did not equip them with specific training and contacts to enter this new business, it is not rare to find entrepreneurs who previously worked as employees in the sari trade, as salesmen, or sometimes as partners. This experience enabled them not only to acquire some skills in business management, but also to become familiar with the trading networks and to establish personal contacts in the sari business, which is also a strategic asset in starting and successfully running a printing factory. Entrepreneurs working under subcontract are entirely dependent on the traders for regular orders, so good relations with them prove fundamental.

THE TRADERS' EXTERNAL CONTROL OVER THE JETPUR PRINTING INDUSTRY

INCREASING HOLD OF SARI TRADERS ALONG WITH WIDENING OF THE MARKET FOR JETPUR PRINTS

In addition to their direct entrepreneurial and financial participation in the printing industry, the cloth and sari traders exert an external control over the entrepreneurs and their production. As mentioned above, about 75 to 80 per cent of the factories in Jetpur undertake printing work on subcontract; their operations are thus determined by orders provided by sari traders.

Local cloth and sari traders, belonging mainly to the Vaniya and Khatri castes, in fact form a minority group amongst traders, stockists, and wholesalers dealing with the Jetpur printing industry. Most of these dealers are based in the major markets for Jetpur prints (Bombay, Ahmedabad, Delhi, Kanpur, Calcutta, Madras, etc.); they visit establishments in Jetpur and place orders. To better understand the increasing hold of the traders over the Jetpur printing industry, a preliminary presentation of the finished products and the development of the market for them is necessary.

The main product of the textile-printing industry in Jetpur is cotton saris for the lower and lower-middle classes, with selling prices ranging from Rs 35 to 50 in 1988-9 (Rs 45 to 60 in 1992). In the early stage of this industry, Saurashtra and the rest of Gujarat constituted the major market. Since then the development of the industry has been associated with an extension of the market, and gradually Jetpur saris have come to be sold all over India. Today Gujarat represents only a very small part of the entire consumer market, and the Saurashtra part is almost insignificant. West Bengal, Uttar Pradesh, and Bihar as well as south India have become major markets for Jetpur saris. Large quantities of saris are also sent to Bangladesh through Calcutta, and some to Nepal, Sri Lanka, and Mauritius. Length, colours and designs of the printed saris are prepared to fit the specific customs and tastes of customers from different parts of India and abroad. In addition, a few factories in Jetpur also print *khangas* and *mishars* (that is, pieces of cloth worn by African and Arab women) which are exported to East Africa and West Asia. Bed sheets, dress-material and scarves, though minor in the total production, require mention. Dress material is printed for export houses of ready-made garments, and along with printed scarves they are sent to Europe and North America. Establishments printing textiles for foreign markets work on subcontract for export houses. Only a couple of industrial groups in Jetpur have direct contacts with these countries and export themselves, which involves high risks.

The follow-up visit to the area in August 1992 confirmed a trend toward diversification of products, in relation with a significant increase in exports. It seems that the new economic policy implemented since 1991, with its marked emphasis on fostering liberalisation and integration in the international market, has given a boost to exports: despite the abolition of cash subsidies for exports, other measures, such as in particular the devaluation of the rupee, the establishment of its partial convertibility[17] and the simplification of export procedures, have had a positive direct or indirect impact on exports. It has created altogether a favourable psychological climate, as is acknowledged by entrepreneurs in Jetpur. Although at the level of Jetpur's total production, the share of exports remains low compared to that of the internal market, the entrepreneurs already engaged in exports have strengthened this orientation, and many others have also entered the export market through export houses.

The widening of the market for Jetpur prints, from Saurashtra and the rest of Gujarat first to the rest of India and then abroad, increased the distance between the actual producers and the consumers, and further strengthened the role of dealer-intermediaries. This corresponds to a classic type of development, commonly observed in the history of cottage and small-scale industries, extended today by integration into the international market. The high degree of dependence upon the sari traders nourishes today a shared resentment among entrepreneurs working under subcontract. They often complain that the traders impose their own conditions of payment, and they feel that the fruits of their work are being partly appropriated by the traders, who make profits at their expense. The extent of the tension existing between the entrepreneurs and the sari traders is further indicated by the first objective which was assigned to the Jetpur Dyeing and Printing Industries Association, namely the safeguard of the entrepreneurs' interests vis-à-vis those of the sari traders. In order to face the problem of traders not paying in time, or even refusing to accept saris printed according to their orders, the industrial association blacklisted and boycotted such traders.

THE ROLE OF OTHER MERCHANTS

Dye and chemical merchants, as well as the cloth merchants and brokers who supply cotton cloth to independent manufacturers, also have a share of control over the printing industry, through the credit granted to the entrepreneurs for the purchase of raw materials. Interestingly, these traders have formed their own association too, in order to defend their own interests faced with the manufacturers. The dye and chemical merchants of Jetpur founded an association in 1969, which counted about 110 members in 1988-9: it aimed to tackle the problems of non-payment of credit by the entrepreneurs. The cloth brokers, about a score in Jetpur, work as intermediaries between grey-cloth traders in Bombay and sari traders and independent manufacturers in Jetpur, for whom they get the cloth bleached and mercerised. The brokers' association is more recent; it was created in 1986 in order to face problems of non-payment by Jetpur traders and manufacturers. Though a small one, this association is noteworthy, as it seems rather exceptional in this type of trade. For example there is no association of cloth and sari traders, each trader running his business independently and confidentially.

The existence of these professional associations and their specific objectives reveal some of the problems faced by the Jetpur dyeing and printing industry, as well as the tensions existing between suppliers and customers, entrepreneurs and traders, at stages preceding and following the printing process.

TRADERS AS CREDITORS AND DEBTORS, AND THE FINANCIAL CONSTRAINTS IMPOSED ON ENTREPRENEURS

Some entrepreneurs may end up financially trapped between two types of traders' intervention: as creditors to merchants supplying raw-materials and as debtors for sari traders buying the finished products. Problems arise for entrepreneurs who want to increase their production without a sufficient initial capital base, and who do not implement a strict financial management. In particular the balance between the creditors and the debtors is often not maintained. On the creditor's side, the entrepreneur has to pay interest charges to the dye and chemical merchants and cloth traders for the purchase of raw materials, and to the bank for the financing of working capital. On the debtor's side, the finished products are sold to the traders on a credit basis, with the period of credit ranging from 30 to 180 days, which creates liquidity constraints for the printing unit and curtails its quantum of working capital. Realisation of sales determines the entire working capital cycle of the manufacturing unit, and any disparity between the creditors' side and the debtors' side has a direct impact on the health of the unit. Attracted by mass production on the one hand and pressured by traders on the other, many entrepreneurs tend to allow sari-traders credit facilities which go beyond their financial capacity, resulting in over-indebtedness. Under such conditions, the traders' double-sided financial control over the enterprise may become a factor of financial crisis for the industry.

SUMMARY OF MAIN FINDINGS

This case study of Jetpur has given us a better grasp at a micro level of the various facets of the role played by trade and traders in industrial transition. The expansion of the town as an important trading centre, especially known for its textile market from the end of the nineteenth century till Independence, prepared the ground for the emergence of the textile-printing industry. Since its origin in Jetpur the dyeing and printing craft had been closely associated with the cloth trade, and the insertion of the town into commercial routes and networks constituted an asset for further industrial development. Cloth merchants and dealers in printed textiles have always exerted some control over manufacturing activities, through supply of raw materials and marketing of finished products. This system of contract, which is a common feature in the history of cottage and small-scale industry, still prevails today in the Jetpur printing industry. This reveals the high degree of dependence of the entrepreneurs upon traders, but it has also proved to be a factor in the expansion of this industry as it attracted a large number of entrepreneurs without a substantial capital base.

Cloth and sari traders have also directly contributed to industrial investment through the transfer of capital from trade to printing factories. This economic strategy corresponds to a diversification of established familial businesses and ensures a better control over production and commercialisation processes as a whole. Not only do the traders have the financial capital to invest, but also the right network of connections to establish industrial concerns. As a result, the economic position of the merchant entrepreneurs was stronger than that of the large majority of entrepreneurs: those working under subcontract for traders. The strategic position held by the cloth and sari trade has been rightly appreciated by some new entrepreneurs who used their work-experience in this sector as a springboard to penetrate the sari-printing industry.

The demographic weight of the traditional trading communities in the formation of the contemporary class of entrepreneurs, though notable, is still relatively modest, and the industrial transition in Jetpur cannot be reduced to a mere transition from trade to industry. Industrialisation in Jetpur was at the outset the result of a gradual transition in capital accumulation from family craft to industrial production by castes of artisans traditionally specialising in dyeing and printing work. More recently, especially from the 1970s onwards, this industry has been increasingly penetrated by a new generation of entrepreneurs with an agricultural background, and the urban industry has benefited from a transfer of capital from agriculture. Yet external control by traders over the Jetpur printing industry has remained unabated, and has even been strengthened along with the widening of the market.

NOTES

1. The first industrialist was Nagar Brahmin by caste, and the second a Patel from the Kadwa community of Ahmedabad.
2. See Dupont (1995). This project was financed by ORSTOM, the French Institute of Scientific Research for Development through Cooperation (Paris, France), where the author is a research fellow. To conduct her research in India, she was a visiting scholar from July 1987 to June 1990 at the Gujarat Institute of Area Planning in Ahmedabad (renamed Gujarat Institute of Development Research since 1992).
3. This state was primarily the outcome of annual Maratha expeditions to collect tribute from Kathiawar chiefs for the Gaekwar of Baroda, as well as of continuous feuds between the local chiefs. Following the alliance of the Gaekwar and the British Government in 1805, Colonel Walker was sent to Kathiawar in order to establish the permanent settlement of the tribute from Kathiawar chieftains. 'In addition, a number of chiefs, which included ... the Kathis of Chital, Jetpur and Kundla, had applied to the British for assistance against their more powerful oppressors' (Wilberforce-Bell, 1980: 178).
4. However, the State of Saurashtra ceased to exist as a separate entity in 1956 when it was merged into the bilingual Bombay State comprising all Gujarati and Marathi-speaking areas. Lastly, with the formation of Gujarat State on 1 May 1960, the region of Saurashtra was integrated into Gujarat. As an administrative unit, the Saurashtra region covers an area of 64,338 square kilometres, which includes six districts (Rajkot, Bhavnagar, Jamnagar, Amreli, Junagadh, Surendranagar) and accounted for 11.23 million inhabitants in 1991.
5. Jinnah, however, belonged to another Muslim Gujarati community, the Shia Isna-Ashari Khojas.
6. Namely Shardul Vala, whose counsellor was Gopalji Chatrabhuj Kamdar.
7. However, due to the industrialists' common practice of dividing their concerns into small-size units, in order to avoid extra taxes and to escape labour legislation, these 1,100 to 1,200 small-scale units correspond to only about 500 distinct individual enterprises or family industrial groups.
8. According to the official criteria applied from 1986 until May 1990, an industrial undertaking belongs to the category of 'small-scale industry' if it is: 'an undertaking having investment in plant and machinery, whether held on ownership basis or by lease or by hire purchase, not exceeding 3.5 million rupees', or an ancillary unit which is an 'undertaking having investment in fixed assets in plant and machinery whether held on ownership basis or by hire purchase not exceeding 4.5 million rupees'. In May 1990 the thresholds were raised to 6 million and 7.5 million, respectively.
9. This estimate is based on the 10 per cent household survey conducted in January-April 1988. It covers the population of Jetpur town itself and the population of the adjoining ex-village of Navagadh, including the populations of their outgrowths.
10. The Saurashtra Cottage Industry Board in 1949, the Saurashtra Small-Scale Industries and Handicraft Board in 1953, supplemented by the Saurashtra Small Industries Bank in 1956, and the Saurashtra Industrial Finance Corporation.
11. Since the establishment at Rajkot in 1955 of the first industrial estate built in India under the Central Government scheme, the number of industrial estates

developed by the Gujarat Industrial Development Corporation in Saurashtra reached 44 in 1989-90 (out of 145 for all Gujarat).
12. Such as the Gujarat State Financial Corporation in 1960 (GSFC), the Gujarat Industrial Development Corporation in 1962 (GIDC), the Gujarat Industrial Investment Corporation in 1968 (GIIC).
13. Following acute water pollution problems due to industrial effluents loaded with dyes and other chemicals, from 1983 the Gujarat State Water Pollution Control Board stopped issuing 'No Objection Certificates' for the construction of new printing factories, except for those setting up in the GIDC industrial estate. This official ban 'theoretically' prevented the entrepreneurs from obtaining loans from public credit institutions and the Gujarat State Financial Corporation. Some industrialists managed, however, to avoid the ban.
14. Source: *Mamladar* Office, Jetpur.
15. 'The emergence of the Kanbi cultivators as a dominant middle order caste in Saurashtra' has been analysed by Joshi (1989).
16. The names mentioned in the entrepreneurs' accounts have been changed in order to respect the anonymity of the individuals.
17. The total convertibility of the rupee on trade accounts (that is, for the purpose of import and export payments) was established one year later, in March 1993.

REFERENCES

Ashraf, M.S., *Economics of Cloth Printing in the Decentralised Sector: a Study of Hand Printing in Jetpur (Gujarat)*, Giri Institute of Development Studies, Lucknow, 1985.

Divekar, V.D., 'Regional Economy (1757-1857), 3—Western India', in *The Cambridge Economic History of India*, ed. Dharma Kumar, Cambridge University Press, vol. 2, pp. 332-52, 1982.

Dupont, V., *Decentralized Industrialization and Urban Dynamics: the Case of Jetpur in West India*, Sage, New Delhi, 1995.

Engineer, A., *The Muslim Communities of Gujarat: an Exploratory Study of Bhoras, Khojas and Memons*, Ajanta Publications, Delhi, 1989.

Enthoven, R.E., *The Tribes and Castes of Bombay Presidency*, Government Central Press, Bombay, 3 vols., 1922.

Gadgil, D.R., *The Industrial Evolution of India in Recent Times: 1860-1939*, 5th edn, Oxford University Press, Delhi, 1971.

Joshi, V.H, 'Modern politico-economic change and rural social transformation: a case study of Saurashtra', Paper presented at the National Seminar on Rural Social Transformation, University of Jodhpur, Jodhpur, 7-10 March, 1989.

Joshi, V.H., Joshi, B.H., and Parmar, B.D., *Changing Pattern of Sectoral Behaviour in a Regional Economy*, B.R. Publishing Corporation, Delhi, 1988.

Kumar, D. (ed.), *The Cambridge Economic History of India*, Cambridge University Press, 1982.

Gazetteer of Bombay Presidency, vol. 8, *Kathiawar Gazetteer*, Government Central Press, Bombay, 1884.

Gazetteer of India, Gujarat State, Rajkot District, Government of Gujarat, Ahmedabad, 1965.

Pouchepadass, J., *L'Inde au XXe siècle*, Presses Universitaires de France, Paris, 1975.

Raychaudhury, T., 'The mid-eigheenth-century background', in *The Cambridge Economic History of India*, ed. Dharma Kumar, Cambridge University Press, vol. 2, pp. 3-35, 1982.

Sampatram, Bhagvanlal, *Saurashtra Deshnio Itihass*, Ganpat Krishnajina Chhapana, Bombay, 1868.

Spodek, H., 'The "Manchesterisation" of Ahmedabad', *Economic and Political Weekly*, 13 March, pp. 483-90, 1965.

———, 'Traditional culture and entrepreneurship: a case study of Ahmedabad', *Economic and Political Weekly*, February, Review of Management, pp. M-27-31, 1969.

———, *Urban-Rural Integration in Regional Development*, University of Chicago, Chicago, Dept. of Geography, Research Paper No. 171, 1976.

Streefkerk, H., *Industrial Transition in Rural India: Artisans, Traders and Tribals in South Gujarat*, Popular Prakashan, Bombay, 1985.

Trivedi, R.K., *Block and Screen Printing in Jetpur*, Census of India 1961, vol. V, pt VII-A, *Selected Crafts of Gujarat*, No. 20, Central Government Publication, New Delhi, 1970.

Vakil, C.N., Lakdawala, D.T., and Desai, M.B., *Economic Survey of Saurashtra*, School of Economics and Sociology, University of Bombay, Bombay, 1953.

Walker, A., 'Report on the District of Sorath in the Province of Kathiawar, Submitted to Government on the 12th January, 1808'; 'Report on the District of Kathiawar proper in the Province of Kathiawar, Submitted to Government on the 7th February 1808'; 'Review of the proceedings (up to the month of May 1808) on the Honorable East India Company's Government in the western peninsula of Gujarat, accompanied by miscellaneous information connected with the Province of Kathiawar, Submitted to the Government on the 15th May, 1808'; in *Selections from the Records of the Bombay Government*, no. XXXVII (in two pts)—New Series, Reprinted at the Government Central Press, 1893, Bombay, pt I, pp. 119-38, 163-78, 179-200.

Wilberforce-Bell, H., *The History of Kathiawar from the Earliest Times*, Ajay Book Service, New Delhi, 1980.

The Part Played by Merchant Castes in the Contemporary Indian Economy: The Case of the Jains in a Small Town in Rajasthan

PHILIPPE CADÈNE

There are not many sociological studies of commercial activity in India, particularly for towns. The ways in which merchant communities have adapted to the large-scale changes that have taken place in India since Independence, for example, have only rarely been discussed.[1] And yet these communities play an essential part in the nation's economy, and development in most regions of India depends largely upon their ability to adapt to a modern economy.

This theme is approached here by way of a study of families belonging to the Jain community in a small town in Rajasthan. Jains traditionally dominate commercial activity in this area, and are distinguished from other communities by their religious practices. This article aims to give a brief account of the results of this study, dealing with the social situation of the members of these families, their occupation, and their place in the present-day society and economy. This work forms part of an ongoing investigation into the social processes of economic development in the small towns of south Rajasthan, processes in which members of merchant communities play an essential part.

The information on which this article is based was acquired in the course of several visits to the town concerned.[2] In addition to information gathered during qualitative investigation, or drawn from the daily life of the inhabitants, the study makes use of data concerning Jain families drawn from an investigation questionnaire carried out at the end of 1986 amongst practically every household in the town, about 5,200 families.[3]

This work is based on the hypothesis that members of this community are, parallel to or along with the Government and other social groups, the agents of a progressive integration of local societies and areas with the national social system, which itself could be viewed as the concrete system at the level of which global movements, of an international type, crystallise. The present article does not aim to describe the various processes involved in this integration; it limits itself to showing, by analysing the economic activity of Jain families in the small town where we made our investigations, the special role which the members of this community have played in the development of a modern economy since Independence.

The integration of the small town into national society and economy depends above all on external factors. Two stages can be distinguished, during which members of the local Jain community have played different roles.

The first stage began in the 1960s with the setting up of a modern local government; but it corresponds essentially to the 1970s and the establishment of a large tyre factory, which was accompanied by the arrival of workers from outside and the strengthening of governmental structures. Jain families, whose most dynamic sons used to emigrate and establish themselves in business in Bombay, or occasionally in one of the large cities of Gujarat, seized the opportunity to extend their commercial activities within the town, in response to the various needs of a rapidly increasing population with a much higher average standard of living than before. In this process of creating new types of business, the Jains face competition from members of other communities. But they stood out in this attempt by their economic success, which was possibly due to their long commercial tradition and their investment capacities. The Jains remained dominant in the local economy and are actively participating in its growth.

The second stage began in the 1980s with the country-wide expansion of the marble market. Here too, local Jains were among the first to take advantage of the opportunity offered by the existence of marble in the neighbourhood. They opened quarries, started small factories for cutting mosaic pieces, acted as agents in commercial transactions, and provided numerous services which were started by outside investors, among whom were many Jains; on the other, some local members of other communities were successful in setting up flourishing businesses.

At the end of the 1980s, members of Jain families from Rajasthan still held an important position in the local economy. They now view this small town as a place where opportunities to remain and be successful exist. Moreover relations who have emigrated, invest locally profits they have gained outside. But their special characteristics as members of a merchant caste are getting diluted within a local social system which is growing more industrialised, where Jains coming from outside are not connected with the bazaar, and where some families belonging to other communities have grown much wealthier. Jains are still among the most important agents linking this locality to the national economy. They have a great advantage as a result of their past position of dominance over the rural economy. They seem to have a great capacity to adapt to a modern type of economy. But a challenge from other local groups to this privileged situation seems possible, and no doubt constitutes an important factor in the social and political processes of south Rajasthan, and probably even throughout the state as a whole.

THE JAINS IN THE TOWN

RAJSAMAND, A SMALL TOWN IN SOUTH RAJASTHAN

Situated in the south of Rajasthan, the town of Rajsamand is the outcome of a complex history. It is in fact the result of the expansion of several nuclear settlements which were established towards the end of the seventeenth century, following the excavation of a lake at the foot of the Eastern slope of the Aravalli hills which was initiated by the Maharana of Udaipur with the aim of irrigating this part of the plain of Mewar and increasing the value of its agricultural lands. First a small town, named Rajnagar, was placed under the direct administration of the king, to enable him to control the irrigated lands. His authority extended to 123 villages around the shore of the lake. A second small town, named Kankroli, was built on lands gifted by the Maharana to the leaders of a Hindu sect.[4] Through its temple, this became a pilgrimage centre that is well-known throughout north-west India.

The present town of Rajsamand, which has been given the name of the lake, is the outcome of the unification of these two centres and several nearby villages within a new urban area which was created by governmental fiat between 1949 and 1953. Until the

RAJSAMAND URBAN AREA

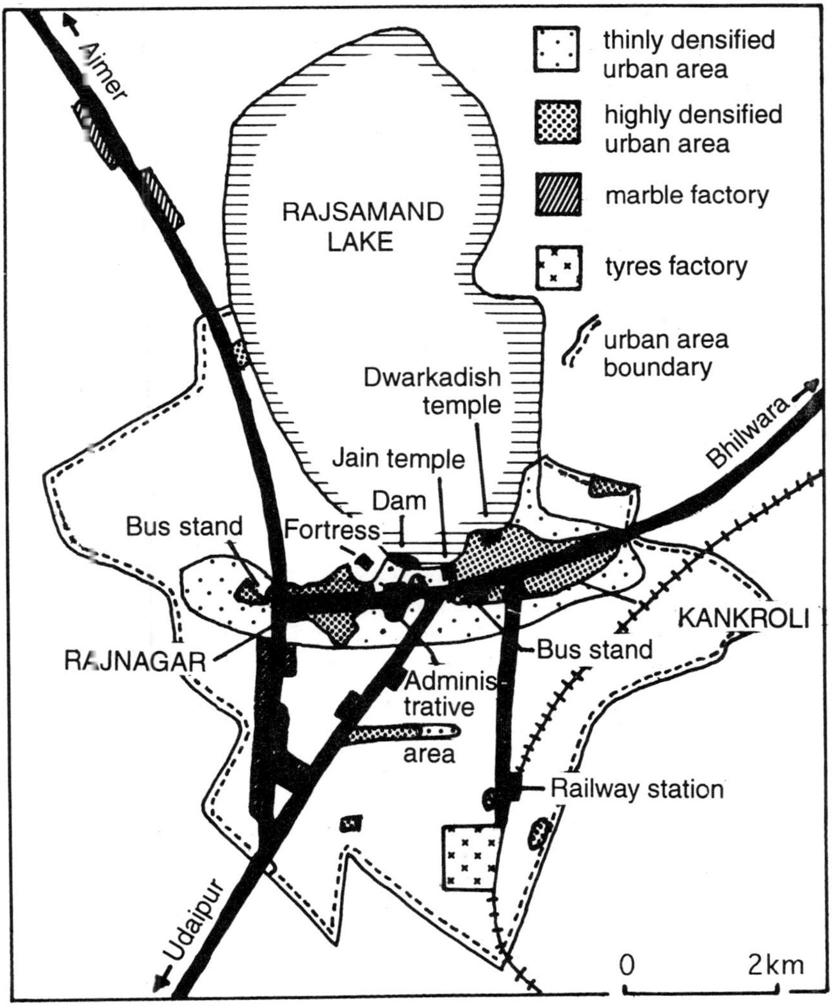

middle of the 1970s local life was hardly affected by this change. The population increased at quite a rapid rate, but one similar to that of neighbouring towns. For example it grew from 11,000 to 14,000 between 1961 and 1971, the first two censuses in which the town was counted in its present form. Local government services were increased, creating new jobs, but nothing changed significantly in the economy.

The most visible changes took place after 1972, as a result of the establishment of a tyre-factory with about 2,000 employees to the south of the urban area, near the railway. To make up for insufficiently skilled local labour, many workers came from neighbouring districts, and many even came from north Rajasthan or other Indian states. So the population of the urban area increased considerably. By the time of the 1981 census the town had 27,500 inhabitants, while new buildings had started to spread beyond the partly-conserved walls, engulfing two villages within the built-up area, and almost covering the two kilometres separating the two original centres. Finally, within the last few years, the *tehsil*[5] of which Rajsamand is now the headquarters, together with adjacent *tehsils*, has become a centre for the extraction and cutting of marble for construction purposes. Quarries are springing up in the uninhabited areas on the slopes of the Aravallis, and many small marble-cutting factories have been started on the outskirts of the town and along the Ahmedabad–Ajmer national highway, built since Independence, which crosses the town to the west. In 1991, the new census shows the continuation of the development with a population of 39,000 inhabitants. Some hundred marble cutting factories opened within ten years; this activity, after tyre manufacture, has become the main focus of local development. Many businesses have expanded or have been started in the course of these years in response to the needs of a population which has not only increased but, to a large extent, grown richer.

THE IMPORTANCE OF JAINS IN THE TOWN OF RAJSAMAND

The Jain population we are concerned with has evidently been established in the area since the creation of the two original small towns. These families supported themselves mainly by trading and moneylending, depending on a clientele of small peasants and artisans living in nearby villages. A wonderful temple, built on one of the two hills overlooking the towns, testifies to this long-standing Jain presence, and to their relative economic power in the course of history.

In fact Rajsamand lies in the heart of the area where the Jain minority is most numerous within the Indian population.[6] Although Jains are an extremely small minority in most parts of India, the area included since Independence in the states of Gujarat and Rajasthan is an exception. Here the proportion of Jains within the total population sometimes exceeds 6 per cent. Usually involved in commercial activities, Jains populate the bazaars of small and large towns, and are also present in market centres and villages, where in many cases they maintain a practical monopoly over trading and moneylending.[7] This dominant position in the rural economy led to them becoming, in these areas where the Indian princes remained in power right up to Independence, stewards and managers for the big landowners. They were almost alone in mastering the techniques of accounting and profit-making, and inevitably became intermediaries between the peasants and the princes or Thakurs,[8] as well as linking the rural areas with the royal capitals and certain business centres throughout the sub-continent.[9]

In the past, however, it is unlikely that their power extended beyond the economic domain. The lands controlled by the burg of Rajnagar belonged to the crown. The ruler's interests were represented locally by Rajput warriors whose authority was unchallenged. Drinking alcohol and eating meat, easily aroused to violence, they still evoked a rather fearful respect in most country people. Kankroli and its dependent villages were governed by Brahmins of the temple sect under the authority of their leader, who bore the title of Maharaj. They owned all the land and made their own laws. Participating today not only in government but also in business, they still consider themselves the leaders of local society, as indeed they are in many respects.[10]

There have been changes in the situation since Independence however. Land is now privately owned, and today many Jains are officially landowners. Their power has increased. In the political domain, they make use of their privileged position at the peak of client-networks to gain control of the Panchayat Samiti, or to direct the local organisations of the main political parties. On the social level, they play a major role in associations where local industrialists, wealthy businessmen and some high officials meet. On the symbolic plane, they are constructing new religious edifices; over the last fifteen years they have been building luxurious houses in the open area between the two original centres, and they are buying cars.

The example provided by some members of the Jain population, however, does not justify generalised conclusions about their increased wealth or their control over the local or regional social system as a whole. On the one hand, austere principles and prudently self-effacing habits are far from dead, and make it impossible to assess by observation alone the real weight of the Jain community within the local community. On the other obvious social disparities exist within the community. Finally, although the community has visibly succeeded in adapting to the upheavals following Independence and to economic changes, it seems difficult to evaluate whether, in comparison with their past situation, the present one is advantageous to them.

At the end of 1986, when the data on which this work is essentially based was being collected by means of questionnaires, out of the 5,200 families questioned, representing practically all the households[11] living in the urban area, 358 heads of household stated that they were members of the Jain community. The total number of Jains therefore probably amounts to about 2,000 people.

The information provided by the questionnaires concerns the heads of household, their fathers and their children, as well as their respective spouses if any. The questions enquired especially into communal origins, occupations, and places of origin, as well as land and property owned. Only a small part of the information collected about each family is used in the present article.

THE PART PLAYED BY JAINS IN THE ECONOMY

THE PREPONDERANCE OF JAINS IN THE BAZAAR

A preliminary analysis of the occupations of heads of household by general category of activities does not enable us to deduce the existence of significant changes in the economic position held by members of the Jain population within the town. Today, just as in the past, the majority of them are either shopkeepers or engaged in activities closely connected with the world of business and the handling of money.

In fact, shopkeepers make up half of the 345 heads of household whose answers about their occupation could be used. This would represent a reduction of about 15 per cent in this sector activity compared with the situation at the beginning of this century, if we accept the evidence about economic activities at that time provided by analysis of the occupations of fathers of heads of household aged over 60.

However, calculations based on figures involving only heads of household who were born within the town show that the proportion of traders among the latter is much higher, reaching 61 per cent. If the calculations include both commercial and craft sectors,[12] the proportion of Jains in the bazaar, at 67 per cent, is very close to the 71 per cent which indicates the importance which trading had in the activities of local Jain families at the beginning of the century. Only 2 per cent of the Jains fall within the industrial sector, and 21 per cent of them are employed in public services. These two figures together come close to that of 23 per cent for people classed in the agricultural sector at the beginning of the century, which today includes only 3 per cent of the Jain heads of household.

A WIDENING RANGE OF COMMERCIAL ACTIVITIES

Change since the beginning of the century, and particularly over the last 20 years, is however much greater than these general figures by sector of activity would indicate. Comparison of the number of Jain households working in various types of business in the two centres of Rajnagar and Kankroli with the number of shops belonging to the various types existing within the two bazaars shows an increase in the types of business in which Jains are now involved. They have obviously been able to adapt their activities to the increasing penetration of rural India by the market economy.

Groceries, cloth shops and clothing shops remain the principle activities of 56 per cent of the family heads occupied in the commercial sector, with 31 per cent grocers and 25 per cent merchants. Investigations in the two bazaars of Rajnagar and Kankroli showed that the vast majority of grocery stores belong to Jain families (39 Jain heads of household own groceries, while 55 grocery shops were counted). The same applies to shops selling cloth or clothing (35 Jain heads of household own cloth shops, while 55 shops of this kind were counted). The proportion of Jains engaged in these two categories of business is actually even higher, since some shopkeepers' sons, not counted here, remain in the same type of business as their fathers, but leave the paternal shop to open a second one in the same bazaar. Jains also have a local monopoly over the supply of seeds, although there are only 6 shops of this type. Similarly real-estate transactions seem to be mainly in the hands of two Jain businessmen. While the 8 proprietors of general stores,[13] 8 vendors of kitchen utensils, 6 moneylenders do not have a monopoly over these activities, they too are engaged in types of business which in south Rajasthan have commonly been carried on by Jains, and are further evidence of the major role which members of this community played in the past and still play today in the economies of towns and villages in this part of India.

Commercial activities are not the only manifestations of a rural and agricultural economy. Over the last twenty years, or even more, new kinds of shops have been opening in the bazaars, reflecting the increasing penetration of rural India by the industrial economy. A new middle class has appeared in the towns, and even in villages, as a result of the westernisation and modernisation of the economic and social system and the increasing appearance within rural society of the consumer habits connected with it. This phenomenon is largely a consequence of the green revolution, whose effects have been experienced to a greater or lesser extent practically everywhere, enriching quite a few, as well as providing opportunities for children to study further and obtain the new qualifications required in a modernising society. In Rajsamand, for example, new shops are opening up in the old bazaars, and new streets are appearing lined with shops on the ground floor of residential buildings. One of the most striking symbols of this recent development is definitely the shop selling televisions sets[14] which appeared in 1985 at the time when Rajsamand, along with the rest of Rajasthan, became capable of receiving television transmissions.

The Jains have shown a great ability to take advantage of these new commercial opportunities. They are involved in almost all the new activities, although in each of them their numbers are quite limited. Among all the family heads questioned, for example, out of 16 people selling machine parts only 4 were Jains, as were 2 watch sellers out of 20, 2 owners of cycle-shops out of 27, one person selling electronic equipment out of 21, and one supplier of electric appliances out of 23.

The Part Played by Merchant Castes

In each case however, these are businesses requiring large-scale investment. Neither in Rajnagar nor in Kankroli is any Jain involved in activities which do not require a large capital but where profits on the other hand are limited, such as for example the shops which supply only one type of article: gas stoves, small gas bottles, motor oil, rope. And the Jains often seem to be among the leading and most enterprising traders in their field. This situation is clearly illustrated by the family-heads who are the owners of two other types of business in which Rajsamand Jains were not formerly represented: a restaurant and a cafe. Both own the most luxurious places in the town, frequented by well-to-do clients who are often on business trips, or stopping over while travelling, or who come in from nearby villages. The tea-shop[15] offers the best cakes in town in a pleasantly decorated room, and is the only one in Rajasthan to supply ice-cream. The restaurant is connected to a small hotel where commercial travellers and businessmen stay.

Jain family-heads whose occupations might, in a Western context, be included in the crafts sector also show this tendency to spread from traditional activities to new ones. But there are not many of them.

In the cases observed, they are small bosses in charge of a few workmen, who themselves did not take part in the production process. We did not get to know the Jain pastry cooks, but the 4 jewellers and the clothier[16] whom we met seemed in fact really to be shopkeepers. These are not new activities in the bazaar, and although only a few Jains are involved in them, they seem to have been so for long time. Others, however, are small bosses in occupations that are new to Jains, such as the one motor-mechanic, 3 printers (out of 4 in the town as a whole) or the 2 cabinet-makers— who are mainly furniture suppliers, and exercise only partial control over the manufacture of the furniture they sell.

EVER-INCREASING PARTICIPATION OF JAINS IN NON-COMMERCIAL ACTIVITIES

Although they are still connected with the bazaar, many Jains now have jobs in non-commercial sectors. But an examination of their activities in these areas shows that the positions they occupy often remain close to those held by Jains before Independence in royal households or with Thakurs or other landlords in the kingdom of Mewar. The opportunities presented by a modern economy thus allow them to make use of a long-standing expertise, supplemented by a school or even university education, and, as in the past, to put these skills at the service of the community or the state, while gaining certain advantages for themselves, their family or their relatives.

Jain household heads who are not engaged in commerce are mostly employed in the public sector. This is hardly astonishing when we consider the large number of public sector positions available in most small Indian towns.[17] Thus, 78 of them are employed in various government offices, more than one fifth of all the Jain household heads are one third of those not engaged in a commercial or craft occupation.

Ten of them occupy senior positions in the state civil service, and thus control some crucial workings of the client networks without which no project can be realised within the Indian social system.

Less powerful but equally necessary for the working of this system are officials in various government services. Several family-heads who were questioned, occupy positions of secondary power at this level, in areas that are not surprising. Apart from one police officer and one local official of the State bus company, these are in fact essentially either patwaris[18] or tax officers. The patwaris, five in number, represent the State government in the villages (four) and in the urban area (one), and their main duties are connected with the collection of property taxes and interest on state loans. There are three tax officers. Two of them work in the town, one being a native, the other coming from a neighbouring *tehsil*; the third was born in Rajsamand but works in an adjacent *tehsil*. Like all government employees above a certain rank, they are frequently reposted, because the administration tries in this way to limit corruption. But, as we have shown in another article,[19] such people are only relatively independent in the exercise of their office in the face of pressure brought to bear by certain local groups, and community loyalties are bound to come into play.

A further ten heads of households are clerks in government offices, seven of them within the town, and three in nearby *tehsils*. These jobs are relatively poorly paid and carry little formal authority. They are nevertheless sought-after on account of the advantages they confer from the point of view of security of tenure and the social benefits to which they entitle the employee's family as a whole. But the strategic significance of certain government office jobs should not be overlooked: knowledge of the regulations, the possibility to expedite or block movement of a file, etc., all this, without any doubt, is of advantage to members of the officials' families and their relatives.

Within the public service sector we should also include Jains working in nationalised banks. There are three such offices in Rajsamand. Nine of the household heads we questioned work there (three managers and six clerks). The small number of them is even surprising, if we consider that 34.5 per cent of all bank employees in Udaipur are Jains;[20] even more so, in that of the three managers appearing in our sample, only one is actually employed in Rajsamand itself (the two others work in Amet, the headquarters of an adjacent *tehsil*). The explanation may lie in the fact that the banks in Rajsamand are public ones, which will not allow a single community to be over-represented on their staff—as opposed to the private banks, one of which, in Udaipur, is owned by Jains and employs only members of that community. In addition, the manager of the local office of the Life Insurance Corporation is also a Jain head of household, and this very wealthy public organisation is one of the main investors in industry.

Four doctors in Rajsamand hospital, one university lecturer in Udaipur and eighteen secondary-school teachers also appear among the household-heads we questioned. This is certainly indicative of the high level of education provided by Jain families.

These positions are valued for the security they carry, as well as for their flexible working hours, which sometimes even permit a certain degree of absenteeism. While benefiting from an administrative post acquired through family connections but also by scholastic qualifications, it is also possible to keep an eye on family affairs or to develop a sideline of one's own which will also benefit from the knowledge and connections derived from a position within a government office, or, for example, a State Bank.

Not many Jain family heads are involved in private sector services, and from many points of view they can be grouped with the government employees. Their activities are even more closely linked to the business sector, and thus not very far removed from trading.

Lawyers especially play an important role in business life. There were nine of them among the family heads we questioned; all of them work in the town itself, and five of them were born there.

The cases of three accountants are also similar. They are very useful to shop owners above a certain size, guiding them through the arcane regulations imposed by the bureaucracy, and in the complex combinations which some traders elaborate in order to spread their profits.

One Jain astrologer also appeared among the family heads questioned, and another who is a land broker practices astrology as a second occupation. This service seems to be a very important one in the daily life of many Indians. According to the astrologers in Rajsamand Bazaar, the occupations of people in the private services sector are very similar to their own.

Finally, three family heads are involved in transportation, and form a link between commerce and industry. These are small businessmen with one or several lorries, usually in a rather poor condition. They work for shopkeepers in and around the town, or for marble-factory owners or agents who use them to transport blocks and sheets of marble from quarry to factory or from one factory to another.

Participation in the industrial sector by members of the local Jain population is obviously new. Movement of merchant communities into industry is however a long-standing phenomenon. From the management of craft activities in the villages to the establishment of industrial workshops was only a small step for Jains to take, and those who could accumulate enough capital took it, long before Independence, already in the case of some rich merchants in the large cities.[21]

Until recently, Jain traders who wanted to go into industry were obliged to leave the town. Since about ten years it has been possible for them to go into industry in Rajsamand, as a result of the recent development of the marble industry.[22]

The first factory was started in 1975 by a member of the local Muslim community, one group of which is specialised in the extraction and working of marble, and has been engaged in this activity as a craft ever since the seventeenth century. Local Jain businessmen were not slow to notice the opportunity provided by the existence of marble quarries, and in 1976, the son of a rich local family started the second factory cutting blocks of local marble.

In 1986, when we carried out our first enquiries, it was difficult to ascertain the number of Jains involved in marble extraction, because the quarries are on the slopes of the Aravallis, and this work usually requires the presence of several associates including people living in nearby villages. But one thing is certain, that many Jains are involved in quarrying the stone. It is less difficult to count the factories, although the small size and short existence of some of them prevents an exact count. Including all sizes, there were about 70 of them in 1986, and our enquiries at the factories showed that more than a quarter of them belonged to Jain families. Members of this community also own 6 of the 13 factories that can cut marble blocks, where the investment required is incomparably greater than that needed to open a factory that simply cuts mosaic pieces out of marble sheets obtained from larger factories.

The Jain industrialists we met had, for the most part, gone into this line from a commercial activity which they were careful not to relinquish. Moreover they often own marble quarries as well. If we count not factories but the number of Jains who were in charge of marble industries in 1986 when we carried out our enquiries, 17 were born in Rajsamand; 3 came from nearby villages; and 5 from the adjacent *tehsils* of Amet and Bhim; 12 had come from further away to invest in this industry: 9 from Delhi and 3 from Bombay. Many of these industrialists still live in their native place, which is the focal point of most of their business. The Jains from the large cities still live there, where they often own sales outlets or construction firms. Those who live within Rajsamand *tehsil* continue to take care of businesses, usually grain or cloth shops. So only 6 of the family heads investigated described themselves as marble-factory owners, for although their factory may be an increasingly profitable activity, they remain primarily merchants. In addition, these small factories employ very few office staff. In the urban area, only 4 Jain heads of household held this position.

In spite of the close connections in many respects between commercial and industrial activities, the growth of the marble industry seems to be the phenomenon that has most effect on the structure of the local Jain community. Probably for the first time since Independence, its most enterprising members can find an occupation locally. Their success has considerably accentuated the social differences between the families. This has necessarily lead to significant modifications in the economic and social relations between the bazaar shopkeepers, although at this level the secrecy which surrounds commercial transactions and intra-communal relationships prevents the signs from being apparent. Moreover there now exists an open rivalry between the Jains and members of other local communities, in particular with some Brahmin families who can rely on their own networks of relationship and alliance to get ahead.

Finally, the entry of external investors, many of whom are Jains, is affecting the balance of power between local members of the community and between Jain families and others in the town's population. These newcomers do often have business connections with local families—but not always. And above all, they often own the machines for cutting marble blocks, and are thus in control of the entire process of production, often forcing local factory-owners to buy marble sheets from them in order to cut them up further in their own factories to produce mosaic pieces. Members of some local Jain families who today possess a large degree of economic and political importance cannot in future avoid taking into account in their policies the existence of these powerful outside industrialists, a few of whom have actually come to settle in the town and have built themselves houses there.

Heavy industry, present in Rajsamand since the creation in 1972 of the factory to manufacture tyres, does not seem to attract members of Jain families: of the heads of household questioned, only 5 managers and 25 employees or labourers work in the factory,[23] and most of these had come from outside.

The small number of Jains in the tyre factory seems indicative of the role played by the followers of this religion in Rajsamand and the ways in which they have adapted to a modern economy. Since the creation of the first settlements on the shores of the lake, Jains have controlled and organised the rural economy, while taking great care not to transgress the strict regulation of life enjoined by religion, which forbids them, in particular, to endanger by their activities any form of life, however microscopic. Obliged to adapt to the modern economy, they have managed to maintain control or at least a presence in most productive or commercial sectors and the services, while not disregarding the benefits offered by certain posts in government service. Today, as in the past, they are able to combine different activities, and they have learned to strategically extend the skills of their family members. The jobs held by most of them are never very far removed from the business world, and they have not lost their habit of delegating work which is impure to them. This is true in the area of crafts, just as for agriculture, in which 161 Jains are involved, but which remains, except for 13 of them,[24] a secondary activity, which is often left to the care of their wives.[25] This is obviously also the case for the extraction and working of marble, activities where the Jain proprietors deal only with clients and agents,

The Part Played by Merchant Castes

delegating the running and maintenance of machinery to a foreman, and frequently leaving the hiring of workers to a labour contractor or the agents.[26]

OCCUPATIONAL DYNAMICS OVER THREE GENERATIONS

LOCAL JAINS, MAJOR AGENTS OF THE OCCUPATIONAL CHANGE IN THE COMMUNITY

Examination of the occupation of family-heads by generation provides valuable details about the type of change that has taken place in the occupational situation of Rajsamand Jains. This analysis excludes Jains who have come from elsewhere. But a detailed examination of the activities of heads of household who have come from other regions of Rajasthan, and even from other states, indicates that the latter are not agents of change in commercial activity. The appearance of new types of shops was not connected with the moving into the town of 34 Jain merchants, 27 of whom were less than 50 years old. Only 5 of the latter are in fact engaged in modern types: 2 marble merchants, one supplier of spare parts for mechanical tools, one supplier of electronic appliances, one of spare parts for cars. The agents of change in the two bazaars of Rajnagar and Kankroli are Jain merchants of local origin. A study of the types of occupation followed by the fathers and sons of these household heads thus seems indispensable for understanding the mechanics of these changes.

Occupations of fathers of household heads

Like the heads of household themselves, their fathers seem to have been firmly rooted in trading and agriculture, this latter activity generally combined with moneylending; they are absent from industry, and only sparsely represented under services, especially in the case of members of families native to the settlements now included in the urban area. For the most part engaged in activities connected with a rural and agricultural economic system, they present above all a picture of stability. It is true that the fathers of the heads of households we questioned all belonged to generations predating the changes of the last 20 years.

We can, therefore, obtain a picture of recent developments by comparing the activities of the fathers with those of their sons, the present heads of family. Here too, it is necessary to go into detail, for a mere account of mobility by sector shows no more than a state of stability over the generations. In fact, for three quarters of the fathers who were shopkeepers or craftsmen their son is occupied in one of these two sectors. Similarly, half of the fathers working in the public or private service sectors have a son in the same sectors. This proportion is small only in the case of agriculturist fathers, half of whose sons, born within the urban area, have become shopkeepers—which is probably an indication of the close connection between commerce and agricultural activity amongst Jains.

A more detailed examination of the categories of occupation, however, throws a new light, and gives us some understanding of the processes of change.

Certainly, stability is evident, and in an even more detailed way, as the major phenomenon: more than 60 per cent of the grocers and cloth merchants are carrying on the same occupation as their fathers—to mention only the two most representative occupations for shopkeeping Jains. However, not all the shopkeeper heads of family whose fathers were in either shopkeeping or the crafts sector are following the same occupation as their fathers. Over the last few decades at least, in each generation some new form of commerce has been started. The son of a grocer becomes a cloth-merchant or opens a general store. So when mechanisation and electricity began to spread in rural India, and then a demand for modern manufactured goods developed, it was relatively easy for the children of shopkeepers to set up these new types of business. They possessed the necessary know-how, the social networks in which their families participated, and they were assured of financial help from their relations. This was true even for activities in which Jains were not traditionally involved, such as for example shops selling electric or electronic appliances, or catering and hotel management.

Moreover, not every son remained in the same economic sector as his father: passages from one sector to another appear quite often between two generations. But our enquiry shows that with the exception of agriculturists, whose sons, as we have seen, have often become shopkeepers, it is very rare for those who have not been born into shopkeeping to go in for it. And this is even more so for those coming from outside the town. Shopkeepers, however, move readily into all the other sectors: government service, private service, and even industry. On the other hands, heads of family whose father is or was employed in private or public service have generally remained within these two sectors. Only exceptionally do they become traders, and they seem not to be attracted by industry. In any case there are not many of them, and no firm conclusion can be drawn from analysis of an insufficient number of cases.

Occupations of sons of family heads

Examination of the occupations followed by sons of family heads enables us to gain more knowledge about the ways in which members of the Jain community have adapted to economic development. Not only do the recent occupational changes of Rajsamand Jains emerge more clearly, but also, since there are many children, the family policies underlying these changes can be taken into account. The picture presented above gets significantly modified.

Migration appears as a fundamental phenomenon. More than half the sons are working outside the town or the *tehsil* of which it is the headquarters: 22 in other *tehsils* in Udaipur district, including 13 in Udaipur itself; 6 in other districts of Rajasthan; and 154 outside Rajasthan, mainly in Bombay (123) or in Gujarat (25), especially in the two cities of Ahmedabad and Surat.

Most of the sons who leave Rajsamand take up some commercial activity. But the categories of shop preferred are no longer the same as in Rajsamand: away from the rural economy, the Jains usually start cloth or jewellery shops, and, to a lesser extent, shops selling kitchen equipment (these three occupations account for more than 40 per cent of the shop kept); they also take up modern types of commerce, either similar to those started in Rajsamand (spare parts of machinery, electric or electronic appliances), or different ones (selling petrol, shoes, construction materials).

The public and private services are rarely taken up, nor are jobs in industry: one accountant, 4 bank employees, 2 civil servants and 5 teachers, including one at the University of Udaipur. Similarly for industry, in which only one son is involved, working as a labourer, or more probably as a clerk, in the state of Madhya Pradesh.

The sons of family heads who remain and work within the urban area or in villages of the same *tehsil* thus constitute the other half of the working sons. In general, their occupation differ very little from those of their parents. Three-quarters of them are engaged in trading or crafts sector activities identical to those encountered amongst the household-heads.

A detailed analysis of types of shops kept, however, does reveal some significant features. Very few of the working sons remain in their father's shops: many of them have a shop of their own in the same bazaar, even though most of them continue to live in the parental home, whether they are already married or not. They rarely take up the same type of business as their father's, but often engage in a closely related activity: the grocer's son opens a general store, or devotes himself exclusively to lending money; the son of a cloth merchant opens a clothing shop. Only a few of them (5 in all) have taken up commercial activities of a modern kind such as the sale of machinery, electric goods. Some of the sons in the families we investigated have however found a path that has only been open a few years, one that offers an opportunity for profitable activity: 13 of them are working full-time in the marble trade, and 8 in the mosaic-cutting industry. Others, we are certain, although engaged in other occupations, are also involved in this fast-growing field.

Apart from commercial activities, out of all the sons only four accountants and two lawyers represent the neglected private service sector. Twenty-nine are in government service, but still these make up just over 8 per cent of all the working sons. Five of these work in banks, but the largest group consists of twenty-one secondary-school teachers.

ECONOMIC SHIFT, MIGRATION AND SOCIAL STABILITY

Interpretation of these findings is not easy. The occupation situation of sons of family-heads seems to be a reflection of changes in the local economy, and to a certain extent in the country as a whole. It also illustrates significant social differences within the Jain population.

The 1970s were typified in Rajsamand by state intervention (establishment of a governmental development agency, creation of a large factory) and by movement towards an industrial type of market economy (modernisation of agriculture as a result of the green revolution, improved transport, appearance of new manufactured products). Many Jains now in their 1940s and 1950s were able to adapt to these changes. They gained a degree of control over the new institutions, from which they benefited in various ways. They extended their presence in the bazaar by investing in modern activities. Half of them also had to leave the area, to join an uncle or a cousin in one of a few large cities, especially Bombay, and take their chance there in their turn. According to our findings, the latter are far from appearing the most dynamic members of their community. Of course they have agreed to leave their home-town to take employment or start some activity in a big city. But the vast majority of them have invested in the traditional activities of their community. Innovation has come from those who remained in Rajsamand, who were able to adapt to economic and social changes and take up new activities.

In the 1980s departures of the new generation remained numerous, and the same places occupied by the precedent generation, now become fathers of families and heads of households, were taken up again, whether in the bazaar, in the services or the government. Certainly the consumer needs and wishes of the population are immense, and the purchasing power of most families has increased somewhat, but to go on opening more shops supplying electronic appliances, which requires a heavy investment, does not seem a very promising line. On the other hand, a new industry is developing around the marble quarries. Those who have something to invest, and who know how to get hold of the subsidies offered by the local government, find a chance here to prosper. In this way young school leavers can avoid going away—which in other times would have been practically unavoidable. Others will benefit from the secondary effects of industrial growth (the tyre factory expanded its staff in the early 1980s) by taking up an activity that Indian merchants are very good at: adding to the number of small shops selling items of everyday use in the bazaar which is now spreading beyond the ancient walls of the original centres.

Finally, an assessment of the sons' situations shows a diversification of occupations within families which corresponds to quite deliberate policies. The average number of children per family is 3.5. More than one third of those over 40 have at least 3 sons, some of whom are married and working. In 60 of the 87 families with more than 3 sons, at least one of them has left to work elsewhere, usually in a big city. Those who remain are encouraged to set up a shop in the bazaar, often in a trade not far removed from that of the father, or one sufficiently well known to Jains to present little risk. Occasionally a new type of commerce is attempted, in the hope that the high investment required will bring in proportionate profits. When possible, a place in government service is taken by one of the sons, whose family will benefit from its status; in this case, the teaching profession is particularly valued, because there are many jobs, and plenty of free time. And of course, succeeding the father is always a possibility for one of the sons, if necessary.

In these ways members of the Jain community in the small town of Rajsamand have been able to adapt to economic changes without overthrowing either their long-standing economic foundations in the town, or the forms of social organisation typical of the merchant castes to which they belong, or even the ideology which is characteristic of their religion—a mixture of austerity, self-control and pugnacity. The Jains today seem to be, just as they were in the past, dominant in the local economy, most of whose processes they control. But the context has changed: they are no longer working to gain a share in the wealth produced by an agricultural economy within which they used to play a clear-cut role; nowadays many of them are engaged in activities that generally remain connected to the members of other local communities, with whom at the same time they obviously maintain close connections and even a degree of collaboration. The latter could however, in the future, come to play a part as great as that held by the Jains today in connecting this town with the economy of India as a whole.

NOTES

1. Among existing studies cf. M. Singer, *When a Great Tradition Modernises*, Preager, New York, 1972 and the article by H. Stern 'L'Edification d'un secteur économique moderne: l'exemple d'une caste marchande du Rajasthan', in *Purusartha 6*, Paris, 1982.
2. Many visits were made in the town from 1983. The longest, for one year in 1986, was financed by M.S.H., Paris, and the Romain Rolland Foundation.
3. This is only a partial exploration, for a particular group of information contained in these questionnaires, which is still being analysed. Cf. also Philippe Cadène 'Réseaux Economiques et territoires de l'identité: les migrations de travail et les relations de mariage d'une communauté marchande dans une petite ville indienne', in *Cahiers de l'ORSTOM*, vol. 29, nos 2-3, 1993.
4. The Krishna-worshipping sect of Vallabhacharyas originates from the Mathura region, some of its followers arrived in the seventeenth century, fleeing from the Mughal Emperor Aurangzeb. This sect recognises seven seats, seven temples, each of which has an image of the child Krishna. One of these is still in Mathura, but the main seat is at Nathdwara, a small town next to Rajsamand. The temple of Sri Nathji at Nathdwara has made this town prosperous through the large number of pilgrims arriving every day, most of them from the neighbouring state of Gujarat and belonging to wealthy merchant castes. The followers of the sect at Rajsamand consider their own temple of Dwarkadhish, situated in the old market centre of Kankroli and attracting only a limited

The Part Played by Merchant Castes

number of pilgrims, to be the second seat, and are often critical of the commercial exploitation carried on at Nathdwara around the temple of Sri Na hji.

5. The *tehsil* is the administrative unit between the 'village' at the base of the system, and the 'sub-division' and the 'district', this latter being the main administrative level in the states constituting the Union of India. In the headquarters of the *tehsil* resides the *tehsildar,* the local representative of the 'district magistrate', who is the chief administrative officer of the 'district'.
6. Originating about six centuries before the Christian era, Jainism is the religion of about four per cent of the 844 million inhabitants making up the Indian population in 1991. The Jains constitute in many areas of north-west India quite a significant social grouping. On the Jain community, cf. V.A. Sangave, *Jaina Community: A Social Survey,* Popular Book Depot, Bombay, 1957. On the role of Rajasthani merchants in the Indian economy, cf. T.A. Timberg, *The Marwaris: From Traders to Industrialists,* Vikas, New Delhi, 1978.
7. One should not overlook the competition currently presented to the Jains by rich peasants and agricultural credit organisations set up by the Government.
8. The Thakurs were a local class of minor aristocracy who shared with the ruler the revenue from lands granted to them as *jagir.*
9. Cf. article of Denis Vidal in the present volume.
10. Cf. P. Cadène, 'Etat et société dans une petite ville du Sud du Rajasthan', in *Purusartha 13,* EHESS, Paris, 1991.
11. It seems that about 5,600 families live within the urban area of Rajsamand, including those residing inside the tyre-factory compound and in a nearby small peasant village, where we were unable to work.
12. This is entirely justified in this particular case, as will be shown.
13. The term 'general store' is used to describe a shop which sells all kinds of objects and utensils, and sometimes also foodstuffs.
14. The appliances sold are mostly assembled in Udaipur from parts manufactured in the main industrial centres of the country.
15. The term 'tea-shop' is justified in this case by the high standard of the place.
16. However it is interesting to note the existence of a Jain clothier at Rajsamand at the beginning of the century.
17. Cf. P. Cadène, 'État et société dans une petite ville de l'Inde du Nord', cited earlier.
18. The patwaris represent the government in villages or municipal divisions. They form the base of the administrative system.
19. C. P. Cadène, op. cit.
20. Cf. A.K. Paksha, Department of Geography, Sukadia University, cyclostyled, M. Phil., 'Jains in Udaipur', Udaipur, 1976.
21. Cf. T.A. Timberg, op. cit.
22. For more details on this passage, cf. P. Cadène, 'Development in a backward area as a result of general development: a case study of the marble industry in a Tehsil of South Rajasthan', in D. Rothermund, S. Saha (eds) *Regional Disparities in India: Rural and Industrial Dimensions,* Manohar, Delhi, 1991.
23. There may be other Jains among the managers and workers living inside the factory compound who could not be questioned, but there cannot be many of them.

24. The people who stated that they were occupied solely in agriculture live mostly at Dooda, one of the large villages within the urban area, where they must certainly be the village moneylenders.
25. Forty-two wives of heads of families were stated to be working. Among them, there were six dressmakers, one bank employee, seven teachers (these were wives of government employees or tyre-factory staff). The remaining twenty-eight were taking care of agricultural land. Most of the shopkeepers' wives remain at home and are probably not very educated. This attitude towards women is however changing, and young Jain girls are increasingly being encouraged to study, with the idea of enhancing their marriage chances.
26. Small industrialists with limited funds often hire machinery from agents, who then take care of the entire production process according to their client's requirements.

REFERENCES

Cadène, P., 'Etat et société dans une petite ville du Sud du Rajasthan', in *Purusartha 13*, EHESS, Paris, 1991.

———, 'Development in a backward area as a result of general development: a case study of the marble industry in a Tehsil of South Rajasthan', in D. Rothermund, S. Saha (eds) *Regional Disparities in India; Rural and Industrial Dimensions*, Manohar, Delhi, 1991.

———, 'Réseaux économiques et territoires de l'identité: les migrations de travail et les relations de mariage d'une communauté marchande dans une petite ville indienne', in *Cahiers de l'ORSTOM*, vol. 29, nos 2-3, 1993.

Paksha, A.K., Department of Geography, Sukadia University, cyclostyled, M. Phil., 'Jains in Udaipur', Udaipur, 1976.

Rosin, R.T., 'Quarry and field: source of continuity and change in a Rajasthan village', in P. Hockings (ed.), *Festschrift in Honour of David Mandelbaum*, 1985.

Sangave, V.A., *Jaina Community: A Social Survey*, Popular Book Depot, Bombay, 1957.

Singer, M., *When a Great Tradition Modernizes*, Preager, New York, 1972.

Stern, H., 'L'édification d'un secteur économique moderne: l'exemple d'une caste marchande du Rajasthan', in *Purusartha 6*, Paris, 1982.

Timberg, T.A., *The Marwaris: From Traders to Industrialists*, Vikas, New Delhi, 1978.

Grocers and the Grocery Trade in Ratlam: Madhya Pradesh

FREDERIQUE BOURGEOIS

As in most third world towns, in India too it can be observed that a growing urban population, and the employment problems which this entails, have led to the development of many small businesses, offering either goods or services. These occupy an important position in towns on account of their numbers, the quantity of jobs provided, the amount of finance involved, their impact upon the urban space, and their tendency to proliferate.

Amongst these activities, the grocery sector is distinguished by the very large number of shops, situated in all urban quarters, and by the everyday nature of the contact between shopkeepers and customers. Moreover, this type of trade, far from disappearing as a result of current economic changes, is on the contrary rapidly expanding. These shops, known in north India as 'general stores', 'provision stores' or *kirana*, provide both foodstuffs and other supplies. They may be built of bricks or of concrete, or may be temporary stalls, so-called semi-*pucca* or *kutcha* structures, that are more or less sturdy and liable to disappear at any time, but have fixed locations in the towns.

In the town of Ratlam, where we carried out the fieldwork on which this essay is based, the grocery sector dominates local trade, representing 27 per cent of all sales outlets in the town—that is, one business in four. And yet this town of 160,000 inhabitants in the west of Madhya Pradesh, on the Malwa plateau, bordering Rajasthan and Gujarat, possesses commercial facilities that are both numerous (2513 sales outlets were counted in the course of our investigations) and varied. They offer the inhabitants of the town and the surrounding area some less commonly-used items such as electric mixers and furnishings, without however providing the more complete and varied range available in Indore or Bhopal, the two nearest large cities.

Ratlam is a regionally important centre, whose wealth is based on a particularly fertile agricultural region (opium and then cotton). Its growth too is largely dependent upon its capacity to supply and stimulate trade, the key-factor in urban growth.

Taking Ratlam as an example, this article attempts to show the importance of the grocery sector in medium-sized Indian towns, and lays emphasis upon the social origins of the shopkeepers, the economic structure of the sector, and the spatial distribution of the stores in various areas of the town. It presents the findings of a field study carried out in 1984, when we performed a virtually exhaustive survey of the grocery stores in the town (668) as well as a detailed investigation into a sample of 328 groceries (50 per cent of the total number), selected according to precise methodological criteria.[1]

WHAT KIND OF PEOPLE ARE THE GROCERS IN RATLAM?

First of all, it should be mentioned that grocers in Ratlam are normally male. We found only five women amongst the 328 grocers investigated. This very low figure reflects a social and economic reality which is far from unique to this town. Many of the shopkeepers are young: 39 per cent of them were aged between 20 and 30. In each succeeding age group, the percentage of grocers becomes significantly lower. This situation should not be surprising in a country where the age-structure of the population is dominated by the young. It is none the less important to note that the management of more than a third of the groceries in Ratlam is in the hands of young men of under 30. These grocers had rarely originated from another town. Only 15 per cent of them were born outside Ratlam. This low figure is in accord with the situation found in the town as a whole, for Ratlam is little affected by migratory movements. Most of the non-native grocers had come from Madhya Pradesh or its neighbouring states (Gujarat, Rajasthan). And this immigration has been relatively recent: 64 per cent of them had settled there less than 10 years before, and more than 50 per cent had moved to Ratlam in the hope of finding work.

Half of the grocers we questioned had always been involved in some kind of commercial activity. More than a quarter of them had never been in any other occupation, having taken up grocery immediately after leaving school. Many of them are sons of

Grocers and the Grocery Trade in Ratlam

TABLE 1: RELIGIOUS BACKGROUND OF GROCERS

Religions	Grocers in Ratlam (%)	Total population of Ratlam (%)
Hindu	58	68
Muslim	15	21
Jain	27	8.5
Christian	0	2
Sikh	0	0.5
Total	100	100

Source: Field work, 1984.

shopkeepers who have inherited a family business. This feature should be seen in relation to the large proportion of members of merchant castes amongst the grocers interviewed. Members of the Jain community, belonging to a minority religion close to Hinduism, constituted 27 per cent of the grocers—although Jains form only 8.5 per cent of the total population of the town. This situation is not surprising if we consider that a large part of the business community of central India, especially the Malwa plateau, is comprised of adherents of this religion. Of the 58 per cent of Hindu grocers, one third stated that they belonged to merchant castes; these were mainly Maheshwaris and Agrawals, very well-known merchant communities, especially in north and west India. Lastly, among the 15 per cent of Muslim grocers—a proportion less than that of Muslims in the total population of the town—half were members of the Bohra community, which may be considered equivalent to a mercantile caste. These Muslims originate from western India—to be more precise, from Gujarat. In the nineteenth century, they specialised in the spice trade and were given preferential treatment by European dealers. The Bohras profited greatly from these deals, prospered, and are at present one of the richest merchant communities in India. No grocers were Christian or Sikh, and in fact these communities constitute a tiny minority amongst the residents of the town.

ECONOMIC HIERARCHY IN THE GROCERY SECTOR

The starting point for our investigation of the structure of this branch of activity was the hypothesis of an economic hierarchy based on the amount of stock held. As this indicator seemed in fact to be the most reliable, after the first on the spot investigations, we made a classification on this basis, using several types of products sold in groceries: wheat, tea, soap, padlocks, and cooking fuels. These were chosen according to the following criteria: products used daily by all levels of the population, involving varied forms of production and distribution; foodstuffs and other produce; local and external products. Next we established a classification into three groups, distributed as follows: small groceries (48 outlets), medium-sized groceries (223) and large ones (57).[2] Our work then consisted of analysing the validity and consistency of this classification by comparing it with other indicators.

In the first summary table (Table 2), for each column we have related the figures for these indicators to the total number of groceries in each category, so as to get a more accurate picture. In particular, this makes it possible, for each indicator, to compare the observed figures with the average (last row of the table).

In order to understand how and why the grocery stores were set up, we first of all focused on their age. We noted that although the percentage of recently created shops is quite high (37 per cent are

TABLE 2 : ECONOMIC HIERARCHY OF GROCERY STORES IN RATLAM
(findings in percentages)

Type	Number	Age of Stores				Inherited	Vehicle
		<1 year	2-4	5-19	>20		
Small	15	21	25	23	12	31	2
Medium	68	16	20	29	22	33	4
Large	17	9	19	33	23	40	12
Total	100						
Average	16	21	29	20	34	5	

Type	Suppliers			Credit	Asso-ciation	Non-Native	Staff
	Wholesale	Retail	Agent				
Small	63	36	1	21	4	21	21
Medium	78	16	6	35	16	14	29
Large	86	8	6	53	25	14	39
Total							
Average	77	18	5	36	15	15	29

Source: Field work, 1984.

less than 5 years old), some groceries are also remarkably old, 20 per cent of them having been in existence for more than 20 years. If we add to this the fact that the closure rate is low, it is easy to conclude that one does not readily shut up shop in India. In addition, there are significant variations according to the type of outlet. The age of the establishments increases with the size of the shop. The small outlets are mostly newly established, whereas the large ones are, on the contrary, old. This may seem logical, since people who are just setting up in business rarely have all the economic advantages enjoyed by those who have been in business a long time. Moreover, while it is possible to start a business with few resources (low levels of equipment and stock), achieving a higher level demands capital and time.

To 24 per cent of the grocers questioned, this trade seems to have been a kind of 'hereditary right': material assets and trading tradition are passed from father to son. The idea that starting a grocery shop is a way of creating an occupation for oneself is not very widespread. Only 14 per cent of the members of the sample mentioned it. Employment problems are certainly as crucial in Ratlam as elsewhere in India, but this motive was not in the forefront of the minds of the people interviewed. In fact, the most common replies were formulated in terms of income: the grocers used a formula such as 'in order to earn my living' (35 per cent) or referred to the possibility of an improvement in social standing offered by this activity (8 per cent). Many Indian merchants, especially the smallest ones, think that with luck they may become a lakhpati, a millionaire. Commerce seems to be a sector which allows scope for every hope of success. Among small grocers, this hope certainly forms a part of their motivation. However, this type of response makes no distinction between different trades, and has not been included in our table.

As a rule, these shopkeepers said that they worked alone, without the help of any employees. The information obtained about the workforce involved in this trade is certainly inaccurate. On the one hand, it is very usual for several members of the family to work in the shops. And on the other, if there are any employees, these are rarely officially declared, or work only part-time. In fact 96 grocers (29 per cent of the sample) stated that they had some paid assistance. The great mistrust of the investigator shown in this matter however does not prevent the emergence of the essential point: the rate of activity increases in proportion to the level of development of this type of trade (from 21 per cent to 39 per cent).

Investigation of the ownership status relative to fixed assets, on the other hand, made it possible to go deeper into the conditions under which the groceries were established. Of the shopkeepers 52 per cent own the premises where they work, while 48 per cent are tenants (we found no cases where the person interviewed was a manager or partner, at least officially). Although family ownership of the grocery shop is often the rule, this was never mentioned as such. The owner-grocers whom we questioned stated that they were sole proprietors of their shops.

As for the modes of acquiring the business, the responses of owners were as follows: purchase, 53; inheritance, 113; other, 5. One major fact emerges from these figures: the high proportion of businesses acquired by inheritance (66 per cent of all answers). This factor is extremely important for understanding the processes involved in the perpetuation of commercial activities. It also indicates a certain stability in the commercial establishment of Indian towns. But on this level, we may note some significant differences between the categories of grocery stores; the percentage of inherited businesses was only 31 per cent in the smallest group, but reached 40 per cent for the biggest ones.

Another important factor: 31 per cent of the grocers had purchased their business. About the origin of the capital used for this, the responses were: personal savings, 41; loans from relations or friends, 6; loans from banks, 1. In 78 per cent of the cases, the shopkeepers' own personal savings formed the starting capital. Shopkeepers with some capital prefer to reinvest it in trade, and do so by acquiring new outlets—rarely by enlarging or modernising their existing shops. The extended family then provides the key-staff of these new establishments. It is probable that former tenant shopkeepers, after amassing a small capital, invest it in acquiring a business which they both own and manage. When a grocer has to borrow money in order to set up shop, he does not go to a bank. There are several kinds of reason for this, two of which are most important. First, even though the interest rates charged by banks are low compared with those required by traditional moneylenders, the bank asks for all sorts of guarantees which the shopkeeper may not be able to provide. Then the procedures are often long drawn out, and the trader, weary of official complications, often chooses to turn to other sources. This means that the preferred sources of loans are close friends and other shopkeepers.

Closely connected with the question of ownership of the store is that of how well-equipped it is. For purposes of our research we took three variables into consideration in order to assess the level of equipment of the businesses: basic facilities (water, electricity, fan, telephone); secondary facilities (scales, safe, shelving, calculator); and means of transport. The differences in means of transport turned out to be the most revealing in indicating distinctions between the different types of grocery store. The data shown in Table 2 shows an increase in vehicles proportional to the level of development of the stores.

An analysis of the role of suppliers and supply-circuits seems as significant as that of ownership. It enables us to evaluate the dependency of the grocers upon suppliers, and, by inference, the conditions under which this type of sales outlet can be established and kept running. In the table we have distinguished three types of suppliers: wholesale, retail and agent. It should be pointed out that 15 per cent of the shopkeepers had several suppliers, the most common combination being that of obtaining supplies from both wholesalers and retailers. And we should also mention the difficulty of distinguishing a wholesaler from a retail supplier, because wholesalers usually also provide retail supplies. Agents or representatives are middlemen between wholesale establishments in Ratlam or elsewhere, and grocers. Using leaflets and orders, they take responsibility for delivering merchandise. The figures shown in the table reveal significant correlations between types of store and types of suppliers. A decrease in reliance upon retail suppliers appears proportional to the level of economic development of the grocery, from 36 per cent for the smallest stores, to 8 per cent for the largest. Inversely, use of wholesalers increases with the size of the grocery store: 63 per cent for the small ones and 86 per cent for the big ones. Agents play only a minor role in the groceries' supply system, especially for the smallest ones.

Next we took a look at credit practices between shopkeepers; 118 grocers, 36 per cent of our sample, were involved. The most modest traders do not benefit from this—only 21 per cent of the small grocers, as against 53 per cent of the bigger ones. This is a consequence of the precarious position of the smallest shopkeepers, and their increasing insolvency. It is not surprising to discover that people only lend to the wealthy. A wholesaler or pawnbroker does not grant credit without some guarantees. These are affected by social relationships. Both religion and caste enter into consideration, but not in any systematic way. Economic criteria are decisive. The creditor considers the grocer's prosperity, and his reputation for punctually honouring his debts. In this connection, a remark of T.A. Timberg, an author who has done much work on the merchant communities of north-west India, about the criteria used by a businessman in selecting debtors, very clearly illustrates the situation in this domain: 'All his clients were children and grandchildren of businessmen with whom he and his father and grandfather had done business.'[3] These findings demonstrate that special relationships grow between grocers and their suppliers, particularly by the extension of credit, the conditions imposed, and the dependencies it leads to. Relationships between suppliers and grocers, which are long-term ones, are a significant factor in explaining the how grocery stores are set up and maintained.

Finally, through our investigations, we were able to observe what an important role is played by associations in relationships within the trading community. Associations, formerly guilds, exist in all Indian towns. They are strictly urban in origin or else are attached to federal organisations. But in all cases they are particularly influential at the local level. Like the old guilds, they are based upon some occupational speciality. In Ratlam we found, among others, an association for grain dealers, and another for cloth merchants. These associations normally act on two levels. On one hand they exercise some control over the prices, quantity and quality of products promoted, and the frequency of supplies. On the other hand, they act as mediators in any conflicts which may arise, either between shopkeepers, or between a shopkeeper and the government. We should point out that these associations are entirely independent of the state organisations, and that at least in Ratlam, they are often in opposition to the government authorities. Belonging to an association provides an advantageous position in the business world. For example, when deals are being made, the parties involved consider membership an additional guarantee, sometimes even sufficient in itself, of professional probity.

In the course of our enquiry, we counted 51 grocers (15 per cent of the sample) who belonged to some association, distributed as follows: grain-dealers' association, 18; shopkeepers' association, 15;

grocers' association, 9; others, 9. In Ratlam the grain-dealers' association is the most influential one. Its members belong to the traditional merchant community of the town. Their social influence extends far beyond the framework of their association. The shopkeepers' association consists mainly of Hindu grocers, while the grocers' association is monopolised by Muslim merchants. The figures in Table 2 show that membership of an association increases with the economic level of development of the stores, and this reinforces the idea that merchants' associations are bodies reserved for an elite, intended to provide them with social, and sometimes economic, support within the merchant community as a whole.

SPATIAL DISTRIBUTION OF GROCERIES IN THE URBAN AREA

Analysis of the distribution of trade within the urban area of Ratlam reveals a differentiation into four sectors: the town centre, the area around the railway station, the pericentral areas around the centre, and the outskirts. The town centre was identified on the basis of the density and diversity of trades, the population density (above 750 inhabitants per hectare) and the number of shops in permanent premises. The centre zone covers an area of 40 hectares, houses 17,700 inhabitants, and 34 per cent of the town's grocery stores. The building of the railway station at the beginning of the century led to an increase in commercial activity limited to two streets (Free Ganj Road and Station Road) meeting at a commercial cross-roads known as Do Batti; together, these form the railway quarter. In this zone are to be found 12 per cent of the grocery stores. For the rest of the town, we have considered separately the pericentral areas, south of the railway, and the outskirts to the north. This classification enabled us to include all the grocery stores in the town.

On the map, we have shown in proportional circles the percentage of each type of store in each of the four geographical sectors defined above. It appears that the pericentral areas and the outskirts have a proportionally higher concentration of small groceries, and that inversely, the town centre and the railway area have the bigger ones.

This is logically explained by the fact that the town centre and the area around the station are the town's 'shop-windows' where the most varied and 'luxurious' sales outlets (in all types of businesses)

TABLE 3 : SPATIAL HIERARCHY OF GROCERY STORES IN RATLAM
(in percentages)

Type	Shops	Age of Shops				Inherited	Purchased
		<1 year	2-4	5-19	>20		
Centre	34	11	12	27	38	54	3
Station	12	10	18	35	20	23	13
Pericentral	45	19	28	31	11	27	26
Outskirts	9	21	21	22	4	14	21
Total	100						
Average	16	21	29	20	34	16	

Zone	Rent in Rs			Water	Religion			Asso-ciation	Migrants
	<50	50-200	>200		Hindu	Islam	Jain		
Centre	12	60	26	54	61	13	26	20	15
Station	9	63	28	24	46	21	32	33	4
Pericentral	17	66	10	72	66	13	21	4	21
Outskirts	18	78	5	82	57	4	39	0	21
Total									
Average	14	66	17	54	58	15	27	15	15

Source: Field work, Ratlam, 1984.

are to be found. This higher standard also applies to grocery stores, which take full advantage of a position in the town centre. There, competition is greater (businesses stimulate each other) and the number of customers is higher. In addition they enjoy certain undeniable social and economic privileges in the business life of Ratlam which are reinforced by their central location.

Analysis of the correlation between the age of the groceries and their location in the town (Table 3) confirms this phenomenon, and reveals situations that conform to the economic and spatial logic: 38 per cent of the groceries in the town centre have been in existence for more than 20 years; 35 per cent of the grocery stores around the railway station have been there between 5 and 20 years; 47 per cent of the stores in the pericentral areas, and 42 per cent of those on the outskirts, are less than 5 years old. Similarly, while 34 per cent of the stores we investigated in detail were situated in the central area, 54 per cent of the inherited businesses were among them. This underlines the more traditional character of the town centre. As for businesses which had been purchased, most were in the pericentral areas, and to a lesser extent on the outskirts. In the town centre and around the railway station, businesses are rarely for sale. Only away from these traditional centres can one be acquired.

In the centre, the proportion of tenant shopkeepers is lower than in the rest of the town: 34 per cent of the groceries investigated were situated in this central area, and only 29 per cent of all the tenants were among them. Studying the correlation between amount of rent paid and location, the average rate is found to be higher near the centre and the station. Rates are less in the other two zones. This corresponds to the relative commercial and financial importance of each of the zones. While the average monthly rent for a shop in Ratlam is Rs 120, the variations extend from Rs 5 to Rs 700: two exceptional cases which should be seen in the light of the fact that three-quarters of the rents for grocery-stores lay between Rs 50 and Rs 200.

The same phenomenon of spatial differentiation can be observed in connection with the religious or community origins of the shopkeepers. Jain grocers have a privileged position in the centre of the town (32 per cent). Among the significant number of Jains who have established themselves in the outlying areas (39 per cent), many are members of families long-established in the centre who have created or purchased businesses in order to extend the family activities in the town. Muslim grocers belonging to the Bohra community are all located in the centre of the town. There they constitute a very influential social group. Hindu shopkeepers, on the other hand, do not seem to be restricted to any particular part of the town—they are found equally throughout all the commercial areas.

The associations, on the other hand, are active mainly in the centre of the town. Only one third of the grocers we investigated had their businesses in the centre, but almost two-thirds of the members of associations were located there. The pericentral zone included 45 per cent of the sales outlets, but only 12 per cent of association-members. In the outskirts, we found no grocer who was a member of any association. This means that the associations are dominated by the traditional trading community established in the central area.

Finally, and there is nothing surprising about this, grocers who are not native to Ratlam are comparatively poorly represented in the town centre: only 4 per cent of all the grocers there. On the other hand, they are relatively numerous in other parts of the town, especially in the outlying zones. It is clear that families belonging to the traditional merchant classes of Ratlam monopolise the trade in the centre of the town, and restrict merchants from outside from establishing themselves there.[4]

CONCLUSION

The main finding of this study of grocery stores in Ratlam lies in the observation of the homogeneity and stability of this economic sector, both from the standpoint of the social origin of the shopkeepers who run them and the economic structure of the sector, and of the spatial distribution of the shops in different parts of the town, in spite of a certain degree of openness which makes this line of business one of those which is most accessible for newcomers. Indeed it seems that grocery is a commercial sector which requires neither a major initial investment, nor any great degree of commercial skill, thus allowing people on the lookout for an occupation to try their hand.

But the fact that there is a hierarchy of marketplaces in Ratlam, revealed by investigation into commercial activities in the town in general as much as by our analysis of the grocery sector, means that not everyone who would like to open a shop of this kind can do so in the centre or around the railway station, the two main shopping centres of the town. In these areas, shops are rarely put up for sale, and prices are extremely high. Very few people from outside these locations, even if they have sufficient capital to enter these two marketplaces, in fact do so. It is clear that a cohesive group of traders, consisting of members of a few particular communities, maintains some sort of control over this activity in the long-established shopping areas. These are the merchant communities which have been running bazaars in the towns and villages of this region for hundreds of years: Jains, Bohras and Agrawals. These are the groups with the greatest economic influence. Their members are also the most active in the traders' associations. Few outsiders are in a position to compete with them in these marketplaces. This is especially the case in the old centre of the town, where the structure of the grocery sector seems to be most traditional. This area contains most of the large grocery stores, which are also the oldest and the wealthiest, and it houses most of the members of traditional merchant castes. The outskirts of the town have a greater concentration of grocery stores with the opposite features: few large or long-established stores, and a low percentage of members of merchant castes.

It is clear that here we are again confronted with the centre vs. periphery model, which has so often been described by geographers in connection with the location of production or service activities providing one or several products directly to the consumer. This is evidence for the validity of the theory of central places for the analysis of intra-urban spaces. This observation is not surprising, if we remember that the geographer Christaller and the economist Losch who in 1933 and 1940 respectively laid the foundations of this theory on the basis of an analysis of the spatial distribution of towns in south Germany and in the United States, viewed the town as an agglomeration of producers of manufactured goods for the benefit of the consumers living in the region encircling the town.

The validity of this centre-periphery model for the organisation of trade in intra-urban spaces in India has been established by the work of several geographers. Although most of the researchers interested in this sector of activity, following the example of the inventors of the theory of central places, have concentrated on analysing regional urban hierarchies, several publications have demonstrated the existence of a hierarchy between different business areas within towns. A.K. Dutt in Calcutta (1969), J.P. Singh in Shillong (1980), K.M. Kulkarni in Nasik (1980), and H. Mondal in Nagpur (1985), for example, describe towns where mercantile activity is concentrated in several hierarchised commercial centres. As in the case of Ratlam, a long-established centre usually heads the hierarchy because of the number and variety of stores offering the best services to consumers, whereas more recently-created secondary centres are also important, sometimes succeeding in supplanting the old centre as far as a certain type of shop is concerned. Different researchers in different places have proceeded to distinguish several other levels of commercial centre. In all these cases, even if this is not the main concern of the various authors, the existence of a certain rivalry between the various centres appears from their analysis, indicating the existence of dynamics capable of challenging existing hierarchies. Urban development is reflected by changes in business activities.

Analysis of the grocery sector in particular is more revealing than others about the general process of change that commercial activities in Indian towns have been undergoing over the last few decades.

Grocery stores, which are the most numerous and widespread type of shop in urban areas, also form the core of commercial centres, along with cloth shops, jewellery and household-utensil stores. But their status as sales outlets for articles of everyday use, that are ubiquitous and offer articles affordable by almost everyone, gives them a double character. On the one hand, they are most representative of the stability of urban commercial structures, both as shops which rarely close down or get sold, and as constituents of commercial centres, where their number and size are generally typical of the hierarchy. On the other they share fully in the general dynamism of commercial activities: they become relatively less numerous in the centres that are highest in the hierarchy, giving way to new activities in response to the modernisation of consumer-requirements; their features in less-privileged areas, where many shopkeepers are newcomers, show that they are one of the preferred forms of entry into business for people from outside this line.

The example of Ratlam thus seems specially representative of the structure of commercial activities in a medium-sized Indian town that still remains relatively little affected by industrial development and internationalisation of the economy. Comparison with the most recent investigations carried out in large cities, which reveal an increase in large commercial complexes on the western model, called in India 'market complexes', and those performed in villages, like those of Shuichi Nakayama in Karnataka (1984), showing a rapid growth in stores over the last twenty-five years, indicates that the dynamic we have mentioned leads to a relative weakening of the position of grocery stores in the largest cities, and in the largest shopping centres of such cities, and a strengthening of their role in smaller urban shopping centres and small rural settlements. Despite an obvious stability, this suggests a two-sided prospect for the future of the grocery sector. Nevertheless, it seems that grocers in India can still look forward to good days ahead.

NOTES

1. F. Bourgeois, 'Les activités commerciales dans une ville moyenne indienne: Ratlam (Madhya Pradesh)', Thesis submitted to Paris University 1, 1989.
2. For more detailed information cf. F. Bourgeois, op. cit., pp. 416-18.
3. T.A. Timberg and C.V. Aiyar, 'Informal credit markets in India', *Economic Development and Culture Change*, no. 33, 1984, p. 45.
4. It should be noted that this does not apply (or applies differently) to street traders.

REFERENCES

Dikshit, N.G., 'Development of commercial establishment in Gandhinagar, Gujarat', in *The Indian Geographical Journal 66 (1)*, June 1991.

Dixit, R.S. and Verma, D.N., 'An Inventory of bibliographies on geography of marketing and commercial activities in India', in *Geographical Review of India 50 (1)*, March 1988.

Dutt, A.K., 'Intra-city hierarchy of central places: Calcutta as a case study', in *Professional Geographer*, vol. 21, 1969.

Kulkarni, K.M., 'Shopping pattern in Nasik city', in *Geographical Review of India 42 (1)*, March 1980.

Mondal, H., 'Growth of market centres in Nagpur city', in *Geographical Review of India 47 (1)*, March 1985.

Nakayama, Shuichi, 'Recent growth of commercial activities in Naravi', in Fujiwara, Kenzo (ed.), *Geographical Field Research in South India 1982*, Dept. of Geography, University of Hiroshima, March 1984.

Sami A., 'The Geography of retailing: a conceptual review', in Mandal, R.B. and Sinha, V.N.P. (eds), *Recent Trends in Concepts of Geography*, vol. II, Concept Publishing Co., New Delhi, 1980.

Saxena, H.M., 'Marketing geography: a review', in *The Deccan Geographer 15 (1)*, 1977.

Singh J.P., 'Commercial structure of Shillong', in *Geographical Review of India 42 (1)*, March 1980.

Timberg, T.A. and Aiyar, C.V., 'Informal credit markets in India', *Economic Development and Culture Change*, no. 33, 1984.

Changing Aspects of Merchants, Markets, Moneylending and Migration: Reflections Based on Field Notes from a Village in Rajasthan

K.L. SHARMA

The main focus of this paper is on changing aspects of merchanthood, markets, money lending and migration, based on insights from a village in the Sikar district of the Shekhawati region of Rajasthan. Macro structural changes and their effects on the village community have to be kept in mind while analysing these aspects in terms of the emergence of new patterns of 'networks' and the 'country-town nexus'. Four factors, the *jagirdari* system, mercantile activities, village exogamy, and literary and priestly endeavours, formerly ensured a distinctive pattern of interaction between the rural masses and the outside world. In the post-Independence period, with drastic changes in these traditional mechanisms of social relationships, rural-urban connections and social networks have not only acquired a new form and character, but have also become more widespread and intense.

THE IMPORTANCE OF MERCHANT CASTES IN INDIAN SOCIETY

MERCHANTS IN ANCIENT INDIA

In ancient Indian society, different social strata were related to agricultural production and property, especially land.[1] The village community had an order of ranks based on the ties the people had with the resources. Institutions such as the guild (*sreni*), caste (*jati*), devotion (*bhakti*), etc., developed in course of time, but the order of ranks (*varnasaramadharma*) remained the ideological basis for the organisation of society.[2] Merchants had a distinct place in the structure and organisation of the rural economy. It would not be an exaggeration to state that the entire trade and commerce revolved around agriculture and its allied economic undertakings.

It would not be correct to accept that the village community was stationary. Two major aspects, namely, the functioning of social groups and their mobility in Indian society, speak of the flexible character of social structures.[3] A more settled agrarian economy and an emerging commercial urban economy are referred to by Romila Thapar as social evidences of flexibility in ancient India.[4] She also observes that 'changes at the level of elite groups were most obviously brought about by foreign invasions and migrations',[5] and that 'the migrations affected status relationships in as much as the rules of endogamy had to be adjusted to allow for hypergamy'.[6] One more observation by Thapar is relevant to an understanding of the dynamics of the merchant tradition. She reports that in early India in most areas a clear distinction was maintained between land and trade as sources of income, and that land was regarded as superior.[7] This is also reflected in the proverbial expression which says that agriculture is the best, business is at the medium level, service is low, and begging is condemnable. However, the hiatus between this dictum and its practice has become not only immense but also complex and varied over the centuries. 'Revenue from land was invested in trade by *grihapatis*, various royal families and the Buddhist Sangha.'[8] The importance of *grihapatis* as a new class was clearly evident in the Buddhist period. O.P. Verma states that the expression *grihapati* is exactly equivalent to the word 'vaishya'. Etymologically, it means a householder, the head of a household, and denotes a landowner or merchant prince of high birth and wealth.[9] The *gahapatis* represented the gentry of the land—the lower landowning nobility.[10] Verma visualises the *grihapatis* as a distinct social category, different from the great mass of the population.[11] There are references to the social position and wealth of the *grihapatis*, on the basis of which they 'played a significant part in the imperial court and were a regular feature in the retinue of the king'.[12] *Grihapatis* were generally of the Vaishya caste and were engaged in professions such as finance, trade and farming or carpentry.[13] Uma Chakravarti's study of Buddhist sources also refers to *grihapatis* as Vaishyas who had command over the economy, just as the domains of power and ritual were controlled by Kshatriyas and Brahmins, respectively.[14] They were always endowed with wealth and social prestige. The *grihapati* class was known as *shethi* or *shreshthi*. The words *seth, sahukar* or *mahajan*, commonly used for Vaishyas, referred to their social position and wealth. Even today these words are used for people who are engaged in trade, commerce and moneylending on the traditional basis. Metaphorically, the word *seth* is used for a newly-rich person whose style of life indicates his supremacy in terms of wealth and property.

However, two observations by Helen B. Lamb[15] regarding the Indian merchant are quite pertinent here. She notes that the great empires were sometimes inimical to business interests as their rulers were jealous of the merchant's wealth and hence attempted to restrict his activities, imposing heavy taxes and regulations, and sometimes indulging in outright confiscation. Secondly, the Brahmin tradition disparaged traders and merchants and accorded them a subordinate position in the caste hierarchy. However, Lamb herself qualifies these observations, finding a remarkable gulf between the theory and the practice of caste. Wealth and prosperity have always been important factors in enhancement of social status.

This is particularly true of the Vaishyas (including Jains) of north-west Rajasthan (including the Shekhawati region). As the Jains are predominantly a trading community, they too are referred to as 'Banias', like other Vaishyas who are traditionally merchants and shopkeepers. As long as feudalism was the predominant mode of social formation, the traditional hierarchy of Brahmins, Kshatriyas and Vaishyas remained mainly a theoretical construct, because in practice the Kshatriyas, as the rulers, dictated terms to both Brahmins and Vaishyas. Vaishyas, due to their economic superiority over Brahmins, in reality enjoyed a higher social status, although Brahmins continued to be ritually superior to both Kshatriyas and Vaishyas. In fact there were three distinct domains of power: priestly, political, and economic, vested in the Brahmins, Kshatriyas and Vaishyas, respectively, and a hierarchy of groups in the corresponding order; but there was no necessary correspondence between the three domains, and a given domain was both independent of and subordinate to the others in certain respects. Ritual power was above the other two domains, at least theoretically, but in reality political power subordinated both ritual and economic power. Economic power also exhibited its superiority at least over ritual power, if not over political power.

SPECIFIC CHARACTERISTICS OF INDIAN MERCHANTS

Why are there such marked contrasts in the position of the merchant in different parts of India and during different historical epochs? Why are some business families and some business communities more highly regarded than others? Is it that some groups have also become more successful than others due to their cultural heritage? What underlying factors make for an improved status of a trader?

In response to these questions Lamb writes:

My speculations have run something like this: Originally there was some kind of equilibrium when traders were both economically weak and looked down upon. This balance was subsequently destroyed by the growth of trade and wealth, which have always been explosive solvents of a hierarchical, theocratic and materially poor society. The importance of the trader's function is, of course, an overriding consideration in the determination of the position of Indian business. This new situation set in motion forces which tended further to improve the status of business.[16]

Merchants never constituted a monolithic and homogeneous entity anywhere in India. There have always been hierarchical distinctions as, for example, the one existing between *jagatseth, nagarseth* and local trader. Similarly, in most *jagirs* and *thikanas*, distinctions were made between *modis* (official suppliers) and ordinary traders and merchants. S. Nurul Hasan observes that in pre-British India business communities were numerous and trade was flourishing.[17] A 'constellation of forces' including religion, caste, psychological traits, state support and infrastructure facilities contributed to the emergence of various business communities in India, such as Banias, Parsis, Loharans, Jains, Khatris, Chettiars, Marwaris, Ramgarhias, Mahishyas, etc.[18] But in general it can be said that external trade formed a very small part of this flourishing trade and commerce in India.

These businessmen performed four main functions: (1) to stand surety for the payment of revenue, (2) to extend agricultural credit, (3) to take *ijara* or revenue farming, and (4) to run the grain trade, which they continued to do till recently on a large scale.[19] These functions performed by the business communities made them economically and culturally distinct from other groups or communities. Common business interests amongst various members of an extended family bound them together, discouraging bifurcation and the division of property, resources and manpower. A kind of traditionalism has been reported among such business families and groups.[20] Distinctive values and norms have encouraged them to undertake various measures for mutual social help and economic support, as well as welfare activities for their fellow businessmen and community. Renowned for their calculation, thrift and innovation, these 'Marwaris' have acquired considerable social acceptability and respect in spite of often being reproached for harsh commercial practices.[21]

MARWARI MIGRATION

The use of the word 'Marwari' to refer to the merchants of Rajasthan dates back to the establishment of Marwari business houses outside Rajasthan, particularly in Bengal, Bihar and Orissa. These early Rajasthani traders, who were then known as modis and potedars, in addition to supporting the Rajput army in eastern India, also engaged in private business, trade and money lending. Since these emigrant traders came from the Marwar region of Rajasthan they were known as Marwaris. The term was later extended to refer to all traders from Rajasthan. Once Marwaris settled outside Rajasthan, the chain of subsequent emigration became easier as they developed business networks between their places of origin and their places of work.

The early traders would often return to their native villages after working for one or two years in other states, and then, after spending a couple of months with their families, would go back again. Thus repetitive migration became a common feature in the Marwar region, particularly among Banias and Brahmins. Such migration was locally referred to as *musafari*, or *barwasi*, which meant undertaking a trip to a far-off place for a period of one or two years in order to earn one's livelihood. Those who settled permanently outside Rajasthan, besides being involved in trade and commerce, were also engaged in moneylending and other allied economic activities. G.D. Sharma observes that the Marwaris established their credibility in commercial enterprise and emerged as the leading merchants and traders wherever they were settled. Friends and relatives would then join them to help open new firms.[22] The migration of Marwari traders was motivated by two types of factors: on one hand, economic and political difficulties encountered in their place of origin; and on the other hand, the hope of achieving economic betterment and well-being by migrating.

James Tod recorded 128 merchant castes in Rajasthan, of whom the Agarwals, Maheshwaris, Oswals, Khandelwals, and Porwals were the most numerous.[23] In local parlance, Jains too are considered both as Banias and Marwaris. According to the 1921 Census, Banias comprise about 6 per cent of Rajasthan's population. However, due to migration over the past 200 years, it is difficult to ascertain the exact number of Marwari traders outside Rajasthan, as well as the number of trading groups and communities living in Rajasthan.

The significance of Marwaris in trade and industry is evident from the report of the Monopolies Inquiry Commission in the 1960s.[24] Out of 37 very big firms, 10 were owned and controlled by Marwaris; assets held by Marwaris amounted to 7,5 billion rupees out of a total of 15,6 billion. The 147 large enterprises owned by Marwari groups included 23 jute mills, 34 cotton textile mills, 11 sugar mills and 8 cement factories.[25] According to another estimate, 60 per cent of the assets in Indian industry were controlled by Marwaris.[26] A large number of these big Marwari merchants were Banias from the Shekhawati and Bikaner regions of Rajasthan. The Marus, Sahujains, Chamariyas, Podars, Ruias, Sheksarias, Birlas, Taparias, Bajajs and Goyankas all come from the Shekhawati area of Rajasthan.

The Marwaris emerged as traders, entrepreneurs and industrialists gradually over a period of time in far-off regions like Bengal, Assam, Bihar, Gujarat, Tamil Nadu, Maharashtra, etc., and in places like Guwahati, Calcutta, Patna, Ranchi, Kanpur, Ahmedabad, Bombay, Madras, Hyderabad and Kohima. Three factors in the spread of their mercantile activities have been noted by Ashim Dasgupta:[27] (1) the economic network of trade; (2) the social organisation within which the merchants function; and (3) the relationship between the merchant and the state.

These factors were not only relevant for the merchants in the pre-British period; they seem to be significant even today. Timberg's study of the Marwaris[28] shows that they are far behind various other social groups in the fields of education, professions and politics. They are socially more conservative. But they are ahead of other groups in trade and industry. Several studies have found that such factors as the joint family, caste, and religion have contributed to the success of business and industry in the case of many communities in India.[29] Timberg aptly remarks that the 'little tradition' of the trading castes is enshrined in the institutions, attitudes, 'resource groups' and skills which these groups have developed in the pursuit of trade.[30]

Marwari traders have migrated to different parts of India from both villages and towns.[31] But migrants from villages have been more numerous than those from towns, where employment opportunities were greater. It may also be pointed out that there has been a perceptible decline in the rate of migration by Marwaris in the post-Independence period, as more white-collar jobs are now available to the uppercastes Marwaris than before. Today, migrants are mainly those who have been unsuccessful in getting reasonably good jobs, either because they have not succeeded in competitions or are school or college drop-outs, or simply because they lack the necessary networks. Earlier the Marwaris were mainly Banias and sometimes Brahmins who had little more than a minimum education. The migrants had high aspirations of becoming economically prosperous, and also had the required orientation and acumen for business and entrepreneurship. Today, the Marwaris migrating to other parts of India come from a number of different castes and communities. Some of them have taken up new economic activities such as the construction of buildings and roads, or the ownership and management of restaurants. Earlier, the Marwari Banias and Brahmins who were a little educated and knew *Mahajani* accounting would invariably begin as *munims*. Today, the very nature of the job of a *munim* has changed. A person employed in a shop or firm starts as an assistant or salesman rather than as a *munim*. Earlier a Bania *munim* would graduate to the status of a partner in a shop or firm, and then would become an independent entrepreneur, wholesaler, or industrialist, while a Brahmin *munim* might remain a *munim* almost his entire life. A Marwari trader as a rule was more innovative and creative in his entrepreneurial endeavours. He also amply reflected the necessary orientation towards achievement[32] in trade and commerce.

Traditionally, particularly in north-west Rajasthan, Banias would not consider taking up any occupation other than trade and commerce. As a result of such a value-oriented economic socialisation, they tended to devalue formal higher education. They generally believe that if they are aiming to go into trade and commerce, higher education will not be of much use to them.

However, some formal education is considered desirable for boys, especially for attracting good marriage-partners. Even some education for girls is beginning to be valued for the same reason. Business, however, is the traditional occupation of the Banias and Jains, and is what they value most. Because of this, Banias have been in the habit of migrating to far-off places in search of untapped areas which may harbour a rich potential for trade and commerce. Once an emigrant becomes an established businessman, he attracts other members of his family, kin-group, caste and community. These subsequent migrants, after getting initial help, work for a couple of years as *munims*, and later go on to establish their own independent businesses.

THE MERCHANTS OF ROOPGARH, A VILLAGE IN SIKAR DISTRICT

THE SITUATION BEFORE MIGRATION

Roopgarh, a medium-sized village in the Sikar district of the Shekhawati region of Rajasthan, is an ideal locale to explore these changing aspects of merchanthood, markets, moneylending and migration.[33]

About 70 years ago, a Jain migrated from Roopgarh to Kanpur as he did not have any occupation in his own village. After working as a *munim* for some time, he entered the world of speculation. Later on, two of his sons migrated and joined him in his new economic enterprise. None of these three had formal education even up to the fifth standard. However they knew *Mahajani* (the indigenous Rajasthani method of accountancy). The life-styles of the father and his two sons did not change much. They did not wear western dress, and their women-folk were illiterate.

This businessman kept in contact with his kinsmen and other villagers in Roopgarh. He constructed a *dharamshala* (inn) in the village. Whenever he visited Roopgarh, he would give some money to Brahmins in the form of dakshina (*dan*), and the Brahmins always expected to receive some gift in cash or in kind from him. In this way he maintained the life-style of the traditional economic elite. But his sons did not follow in his footsteps, and practically severed contact with Roopgarh after his death.

Today one of his grandsons, who is highly educated and has taken up a western style of life, is engaged in the shares business. Besides owning a factory, he is also involved in the activities of the Kanpur Chamber of Commerce and Industry, and the Rotary Club of Kanpur. He was even once elected President of the local Chamber of Commerce and Industry. Neither he nor any other members of his family have visited Roopgarh during the last two decades or so. Two nephews of the elder *seth* (businessman) also joined him in business, but they have not been as successful as he and his grandson. The nephews are also uneducated. Another close relative was helped by the *seth* to get into the transport business, but, after initial problems, shifted to the iron and steel trade, establishing his own independent business at Raipur in Madhya Pradesh.

Another family of Jains used to be very prominent in trade and commerce in Roopgarh. This family consisted of two brothers, their wives, their mother, and their young sons and daughters. These two brothers (in fact, step-brothers) were considered an example of ideal brotherhood because they lived as a successful joint family, and had a joint business which included shopkeeping, moneylending, trade in food grains, and the supply of goods and services to the *jagir* of Khoor, of which Roopgarh was the second largest revenue village. They were *modis* (official suppliers for the *jagir*), and hence also enjoyed the patronage and protection of the royal clan. They became a very well-off and well-known family, living in the vicinity of the *jagir* of Khoor. Three sons and two daughters of the elder *seth* were married while the family was still in the native village. On the occasion of his eldest son's marriage, the *seth* hosted a lavish feast for all the villagers of the Roopgarh Panchayat, and served delicacies prepared in pure ghee.

Roopgarh used to have a market consisting of a square with shops on all four sides and an open space in the centre. The open space was used for public functions and gatherings. People would gather to discuss and decide community affairs at the marketplace. Day-to-day matters were talked about at the *dukans* of the *Banias*. Today, the marketplace still exists, but none of the shops are in operation. At that time the Jain family mentioned above controlled the small market of Roopgarh. They owned a big shop and used to trade in almost all the essential goods and commodities required by the lower and intermediate peasantry in particular. Besides owning this shop, the family practically had a monopoly over the local trade in food grains. Lending money, food grains, and even fodder, was another source of income. Most of the local peasants, artisans and other families were *dhurias* (regular borrowers) of this family. The *seth* was a popular figure, and the time when he organised his son's lavish wedding was the peak of his glory. The conspicuous expenditure incurred on the feast, ornaments, and on the guests, remained a memorable event for a long time. This was interpreted by an awakened section of the Roopgarh populace as a clever device on the part of the *seth* to keep his *dhurias* in a good humour.

Another Jain family in Roopgarh consisted of two brothers; the younger one died at an early age, and the elder did not have any children. The business of this family was similar to that outlined in the previous example, but on a smaller scale. Despite being rival of the previous family, this second family could not become a serious threat to the monopoly and prosperity of the first family. The deceased brother had two sons, and the elder of these emigrated to start an independent business of his own, while the younger one remained in Roopgarh. He is still there, engaged mainly in the foodgrains trade with some moneylending on a very moderate scale. His elder brother is educated up to Intermediate level, and is now engaged in the salt trade.

None of the younger members of the Jain families of Roopgarh are educated beyond graduation level, and only two are graduates, in commerce. Technical education remains a dream for them. Competition in Civil Services examinations also remains beyond their aspirations. In the third generation no one from these two families is educated up to graduation level.

There was also a family which belonged to the Brahmin caste and did not engage in the foodgrains trade or in moneylending. This family owned a small shop in the village. But the two Jain families did not like a Brahmin entering into shopkeeping and business. The Brahmin family could never prosper, partly due to the intense rivalry expressed by the two Jains, and partly due to the younger members' preference for white-collar government jobs.

Today no member of any of these families, apart from one Jain, is engaged in trade and commerce in Roopgarh. From the first Jain family, there is no one living in the village. No Jain family in Roopgarh is engaged in shopkeeping and moneylending as they were engaged nearly three decades ago. Most of the Brahmins have migrated away from Roopgarh to take up white-collar jobs elsewhere. In one extended Brahmin family alone can be found civil servants (in the Indian Forest Service, Indian Revenue Service,

Rajasthan Administrative Service), a university professor, lecturers, senior engineers, a senior bank manager, a chief cashier, school teachers, clerks, vaidyas, book-sellers, a wholesale foodgrains trader, and others employed in a host of different middle-level white-collar government jobs. Members of this extended family are working in Sikar, Jaipur, Delhi, Ranchi, Bhagalpur and in various towns of Rajasthan.

Some other Brahmin families have members working in towns in and beyond Rajasthan at the lower and middle levels of white-collar jobs. Some individuals are also employed in private firms and organisations. Most of the people in the latter category are school or college drop-outs who have not succeeded in getting government jobs locally and have been unable to establish their own businesses. They have migrated to places like Calcutta, Ranchi, Patna, Guwahati, Rangia, Purulia, Kanpur, Lucknow, Delhi, Jaipur, Jodhpur, Sikar, Ahmedabad, Bombay, Nizamabad, Raipur, etc. Such a pattern of employment and migration is not found among the Jains or among the intermediate and lower castes of Roopgarh.

A man from a family of the Darjee (tailor) caste settled in Guwahati about 80 years ago. He owned a *basaa* (an eating place) in Guwahati. The man was known for being a tough guy, and also for being helpful to his country cousins. A large number of people from the Shekhawati region of Rajasthan used to seek his help not only in getting jobs, but also in borrowing money and in making arrangements for boarding and lodging in the initial period of their stay. He was regarded as an inspiring soul. A Brahmin from Roopgarh also used to undertake *musafaris* (trips) to Guwahati, but he never inspired others to take up jobs there.

The traditional structures of the market, merchanthood and moneylending were characterised by these methods of operation: caste allegiance, feudal networks, and the obligations of merchants and moneylenders towards their debtors. For all their monetary needs and economic requirements, the *dhurias* were dependent upon their respective *seths* and *sahukars*. Compound interest, the mortgaging of land, crops and ornaments, and interest at an agreed rate in kind on fodder and foodgrains were commonly accepted features of the rural economic scene. The bonding of family members was also practised in order to clear debts. In such cases, an active family member would have to remain at the disposal of a moneylender, to work on his farm or in his shop for a fixed length of time.

Despite such exploitative practices and usury, the moneylender had certain obligations towards his *dhurias*. Normally, he would not withhold credit from his regular borrowers on occasions such as births, marriages, deaths and festivals. At the time of sowing too, he was obliged to facilitate the operation by lending money for the purchase of a pair of oxen, seeds and fertilisers. Of course he would expect his money to be paid back with interest at the time of the next harvest. If the money was not repaid then, he would expect compound interest. It was quite a common feature to pay compound interest, and many families remained attached to the same *vohras* (creditors) for generations. In normal circumstances the *seth* would not refuse credit to his *dhurias*, nor would the latter seek the assistance of another *seth* in his village. Such ties acquired a sort of mutual binding on both sides, but the system was slanted in favour of the merchant, since he was the dominant partner in this asymmetrical hierarchic relationship. If the *sahukar* denied timely help and credit to any of his *dhurias*, he was generally considered dishonest, deceitful.[34] The most renowned and trustworthy *mahajan* was one who, despite falling assets and income, came to the rescue of his clients in dire situations of drought, famine and illness, or for marriage or death feasts.

THE SITUATION TODAY

Today, the situation has changed drastically, due to the collapse of the traditional patterns of merchanthood, markets, moneylending and migration. There is no longer any dependence whatsoever on the village merchant, because the traditional merchant has disappeared. The *vohra-dhuria* (moneylender-borrower) relationship no longer exists. All the Jains have migrated to far-off places in other parts of India, with the exception of one family, and even this family is no longer engaged in traditional trade and commerce. Today the structure of trade and commerce has not only considerably changed, but its social base has also been transformed to a great extent.

There are none of the old type of merchants left in the village. The traditional village *sahukar* maintained a sort of general-store, catering to most of the needs of his clients, particularly the peasants, artisans and agricultural labourers. Today, there is nothing like a market or a market situation or the *vohra-dhuria* relationship. The traditional sort of general-store has altogether disappeared.

Why has the traditional merchant-role not persisted? One reason is that after Independence, land reforms led to major structural changes which particularly benefited local peasants, who had previously constituted a major segment of the *dhurias*. As the *dhurias* moved out of the clutches of their feudal lords, they started consolidating their own positions, first economically, and later, politically. A heightened level of socio-political consciousness was a natural consequence of the economic and political emancipation of the peasantry from the traditional authoritarian system.

A highly negative attitude towards the *sahukars* of Roopgarh finally crystallised in the early 1960s, when the very family which had previously enjoyed the goodwill of the people lost its benevolent reputation and ended up at the centre of a local dispute. The family had gotten involved in purchasing the substantial farm-land of a poor carpenter in lieu of adjustment of a loan advanced to him long before. Hundreds of villagers gathered to protest uproariously at the *seth's* activity. Senior police officers of the district had to intervene to suppress this short-lived uprising and rescue the merchant from the fury of the people. This was followed by a litigation process which has already lasted for more than 25 years so far.

After this incident, the family started winding up its mercantile enterprises within the village. Initially they moved to Sikar, and from there various members have migrated to places like Ranchi, Patna, Raipur and Calcutta. The family has disposed of all its agricultural and other assets in Roopgarh, except for the ancestral home.

Land reforms, the green revolution, better roads, and the availability of road transport are also among the key factors which have eroded the traditional institutions of merchanthood, markets, moneylending and migration. Roopgarh was one of the first few villages to receive the benefit of electricity for domestic as well as agricultural use. As a result of all these developments there is hardly any scope today for the role of intermediaries dealing in foodgrains. Most of the farmers take their produce directly to the markets at Sikar, the district headquarters, where they can dispose of it quickly. Similarly, most people buy major and expensive items from the bazaars of Sikar, and some even make purchases from Jaipur, the capital city of Rajasthan, which is about 100 km away from Roopgarh. This shows that the dependence of the peasants and other sections on moneylenders and intermediaries has almost disappeared.

Moneylending is not institutionalised today as it used to be about three decades ago. Interpersonal relations and connections, factional allegiances, caste-affinities, resourceful relatives and friends, credit cooperative societies, etc., are today being used to obtain monetary help and loans. Moneylending is no longer the monopoly of a single caste group. Well-off peasants, school teachers, government employees and some other categories of people have taken up moneylending as a subsidiary source of income. Most of them charge interest arbitrarily. The loans are given either after obtaining surety from some respectable person(s), or mortgaging ornaments and land. Such a pattern of moneylending is a new phenomenon. Previously, markets, merchants and moneylending had been more or less coextensive. The merchant was custodian of the market and protector of the norms of its functioning, and he was obliged to make loans available to his clients. A refusal was considered a violation of the age-old normative pattern of relationship between creditor and borrower Such a system and a sense of belonging have withered away.

Today, Roopgarh has no market, no merchants and no traditional moneylenders. It has petty shops dealing in cash transactions. No long-term borrowings or delayed payments are undertaken. There are no traditional *bahis* (account books) and *kalam dawat* (pen and inkpot) in the shops of Roopgarh. The shopkeepers deal in goods and articles of immediate day-to-day use. There is no cloth shop, which used to be an essential ingredient of the traditional market. No shopkeeper deals in the goods and articles required in agricultural operations People make these purchases from the markets of nearby towns. The fact is that there is no full-time shopkeeper today, whereas earlier the local market was full of economic activities. Gone are the days when people from nearby hamlets and smaller villages used to make purchases of goods and articles from the shops in Roopgarh.

One Jain, who has not been able to migrate from Roopgarh, is today sluggishly engaged in the foodgrains trade. His elder brother migrated long ago, and now has a well-established salt-business in the nearby salt town of Sambhar. An already-prosperous Brahmin school teacher has started shopkeeping as a subsidiary source of income. He is assisted in this by family members, including his octogenarian father. This family also owns and cultivates substantial land. Another Brahmin has taken up shopkeeping after remaining unemployed for a long time. A Khati (carpenter) school-teacher who owns and cultivates some land has also taken up shopkeeping as an additional means of income. Similarly, a Gujjar (shepherd) also owns a small grocery shop. Interestingly, a Raigar (shoe-maker) school teacher owns a grocery shop, and earns quite substantially from this secondary source of income; as with other shopkeepers, his wife and children help him in the business. Ignoring the traditional notion of untouchability, several upper caste families have become his clients. He also enjoys the patronage of the Jat Sarpanch and an influential Brahmin school-teacher.

Since Roopgarh is now linked by a pukka tarred road to Danta–Ramgarh (the *tehsil* headquarters), Sikar (the district headquarters), and the Jaipur–Bikaner National Highway, a lot of traffic consisting of buses, trucks, tractors, jeeps and two-wheelers take the route. Two tea stalls owned by Brahmins have come up close to the main road and bus stop. The Brahmin owners do not clean the *jutha* (defiled) tea tumblers themselves, nor do they keep servants for this job. In fact, they ask their clients to clean their own tea cups. However, normally they will not allow elderly and respected people of their own caste to clean their own cups. The owners will either wash these themselves or get some younger person to perform the task. They keep separate tea cups for 'untouchables' who visit their stalls to take tea. A Brahmin owning a tea stall and serving an untouchable is in itself something new to the village. This not only indicates an attitudinal change in the village, but also reflects the economic hardships and constraints which have led members of the upper castes to take up such a source of livelihood.

Change in the pattern of expenditure on marriages and other social occasions has prompted two Brahmin youths to start tent-houses in Roopgarh. One of them has taken this up as a subsidiary means of income. He is incharge of the local credit cooperative society. Agriculture is another source of income for him. The second Brahmin is a school drop-out who has taken up this new enterprise after remaining unemployed for a long time.

The questions that arise are: Can these shopkeepers be considered as merchants? How are they different from the Banias of yester-years? Is there a market today in Roopgarh? Who migrates? Why do they migrate? And what do they do in the towns they go to?

One of the important functions of the traditional Bania-trader was to assist other villagers to cover the expenses of such events as *japa* (birth of a child), *vivaha* (marriage), *mosar* (death feast) and *sukha* and *akal* (drought and famine). It used to be the responsibility of the *mahajan* or *seth* to arrange for all the expenses on these occasions and at the time of calamities. Today's shopkeepers in Roopgarh do not perform any of these functions, nor do most people expect them to. The bonds that existed in the past between the *vohra* and his *dhuria* are no longer applicable.

However, new alliances have been formed between local politicians and their respective followers. At times the former take care of the economic problems and hardships of the latter. Generally, politicians are well off and resourceful enough to come to the rescue of their followers. None of them would like to lose his following even if, in order to retain it, he has to take the pains to help people in solving their personal problems. Politicians also compete among themselves in extending patronage and help to their followers, with, of course, a view to gaining popularity. For example, a Jat Sarpanch and a school teacher, both active in village politics, have willingly undertaken the responsibility of arranging money in some cases to meet the expenses for marriage and death feasts. In several cases they have also helped the sick to get treatment at hospitals in Sikar. Obviously, they have done this to earn the political goodwill and confidence of the village people and to gain control over institutions of political power and authority in the village.

The concept of a market has practically disappeared from Roopgarh. The place which was once the shopping area has become nearly deserted. All the old shops remain locked. All the present-day shopkeepers have housed their businesses on the premises of their residences. Sometime ago an 'untouchable' opened a tailoring shop in the main old market, and nobody objected to this. Thus there is no market in Roopgarh today. The bus-stand on the main road attracts more people all the time, around the two tea-stalls.

Migration too has acquired a new character, as those who migrate today do not return to their village as people used to do in the old days. Once a person settles down with some sort of regular job, he takes his family away from the village. A large number of people have settled in towns like Sikar which is just 35 km away, or even in Jaipur, which is nearly at 100 km distance from Roopgarh. In Jaipur the people are employed as government servants, or in private firms and factories, and some have their own businesses and factories. Others are self-employed as tailors, shopkeepers, etc.

Migration has been stimulated by unemployment in the village, and also by a sort of revolution in the aspirations of the people.

These migrants to other towns in Rajasthan have not yet lost contact with their village, their relatives, kinsmen, and family members. Several of the villagers meet them in these towns; and on certain occasions the migrants too visit Roopgarh and other villages. But the Jain traders who migrated to far-off places like Kanpur, Patna, Calcutta, Ranchi, Raipur, Purulia, etc., have practically severed their ties with Roopgarh. Their relatives and kinsmen have also migrated to those areas in large numbers. Even for ceremonies such as *mundan* (the first time a child's head is tonsured) and *jat* (the first joint prayer by the newly married couple) the Marwaris have practically given up visiting their *kul devis* and *devatas* (family deities). Thus today migration has become multifaceted and is being determined by structural changes in the larger society as well as by parochial constraints and traditions.

CONCLUSION

Our observations about Roopgarh's merchants clearly show that in the past they were often associated with feudal and colonial interests. Nevertheless, when the princes and *jagirdars* began to levy heavy taxes on the merchants, they thought of migrating to other places. It is another matter that some of them were sent to Bengal, Bihar, Assam and other parts of India by *jagirdars* and princes in their own interest. A good number of these Bania-traders settled down in those far-off provinces and started their own trades and commerce. Their settlement established networks for subsequent migrants, and also provided a new twist to the existing nexus between the states of Rajputana and those eastern states of India.

At Roopgarh, none of the Jains were deliberately driven out of the village by the *jagirdar*, as sometimes happened in other parts of Rajasthan. Nor did they ever participate in India's freedom struggle, although the forefathers of Mahatma Gandhi's disciple Jamana Lal Bajaj hailed from Roopgarh. Part of Roopgarh's bazaar consists of shops owned by the Bajaj family. This family moved to a nearby village known as Kashika Bas. This village was renamed Bajaj Gram on the occasion of the late Lal Bahadur Shashtri's visit after the 1965 war with Pakistan. But Bajaj's patriotism did not have any noticeable impact on the merchants of Roopgarh.[35]

The merchants of Roopgarh migrated to remote places mainly because of the lack of a suitable entrepreneurial milieu in the village, with the motivation of becoming rich. Another factor was that the Jain traders of Roopgarh could hardly consider any other occupation than trade and commerce. After the initial migrations, it became easier for later migrants to follow, as earlier settlers provided a support-network for them.

As a result, the institution of the market has disintegrated in Roopgarh. It is replaced today by small-shopkeeping as a part-time activity. Moneylending too has changed to a great extent. Its former institutionalised character no longer exists. Today there is no merchant in the old sense, and also no traditional moneylender. Migration has become multifaceted, and migration to very distant places has diminished considerably.

NOTES

1. Walter Ruben, 'Outline of the Structure of Ancient Indian Society', in R.S. Sharma (ed.), *Indian Society: Historical Probings,* 3rd edn, People's Publishing House, New Delhi, 1984, p. 92.
2. Ibid., p. 92.
3. Romila Thapar, 'Social Mobility in Ancient India with Special Reference to Elite Groups', in R.S. Sharma (ed.), op. cit., 1984, p. 96.
4. Ibid., p. 97.
5. Ibid., p. 97.
6. Ibid., p. 98.
7. Ibid., p. 119.
8. Ibid., p. 119.
9. O.P. Verma, 'The Role of Traders and Guilds in Ancient India', in S.C. Malik (ed.), *Determinants of Social Status in India,* Motilal Banarsidas, Delhi, 1986, p. 113.
10. Richard Fick, *The Social Organisation in North-East India in Buddhist Times,* University of Calcutta, Calcutta, 1970, p. 253, quoted from O.P. Verma, op. cit., pp. 113-14.
11. O.P. Verma, 1986, op. cit., p. 114.
12. Ibid., p.114.
13. Ibid., p.114.
14. Uma Chakravarti, 'Towards a Historical Sociology of Stratification in Ancient India: evidence from Buddhist sources', *Economic and Political Weekly,* vol. XX, no. 9, 1985, pp. 356-60.
15. Helen Lamb, 'The Indian Merchant', in Milton Singer (ed.), *Traditional India: Structure and Change,* Rawat Publications, Jaipur, 1975, p. 25.
16. Helen, Lamb, op. cit., p. 60.
17. S. Nurul Hasan, 'The Historian and the Business Communities', 1984, in Dwijendra Tripathi (ed.), op. cit., pp. 5-6.
18. N.R. Sheth, 'Theoretical Framework For the Study of Indian Business Communities', in Dwijendra Tripathi (ed.), op. cit., 1984, p. 15.

192   Webs of Trade

19. See, for example Milton Singer, *When a Great Tradition Modernizes*, Praeger, New York, 1972; James J. Berna, *Industrial Entrepreneurship in Madras State*, Asia Publishing House, London, 1960; Milton Singer (ed.), *Entrepreneurship and Modernization of Occupational Cultures in South Asia*, Duke University Press, 1973; Satish Saberwal, *Mobile Men*, Vikas, New Delhi, 1976.
20. N.R. Sheth, 'Theoretical Framework For the Study of Indian Business Communities', in Dwijendra Tripathi (ed.), op. cit., 1984, p. 15.
21. G.D. Sharma, 'The Marwaris: Economic Foundations of an Indian Capitalist Class', in Dwijendra Tripathi (ed.), op. cit., 1984, p. 186.
22. Ibid.
23. James Tod, *Annals and Antiquities of Rajasthan*, 3 vols, Low Price Publications, Delhi, 1990. See vol. 1 for details regarding merchant castes.
24. R. K. Hazari, *The Structure of the Corporate Private Sector: a Study of Concentration, Ownership and Control*, Asia Publishing House, London, 1966, pp. 371-438. See also V.I. Pavlov, *The Indian Capitalist Class*, People's Publishing House, Bombay, 1964; Ghanshyam Shah (ed.), *Capitalist Development: Critical Essays*, Popular Prakashan, Bombay, 1990.
25. Thomas A. Timberg, op. cit., p. 11.
26. Ibid., p. 11. See also Girija Shankar, *Marwari Vyapari* (Hindi), Krishna Jansevi & Co., Bikaner.
27. Ashim Dasgupta, 'Indian Merchants in the Age of Partnership, 1500-1800', in Dwijendra Tripathi (ed.), op. cit., 1984, p. 33.
28. Thomas A. Timberg, op. cit., pp. 15-40.
29. See, for example, L.I. Rudolph and Susanne Hoeber Rudolph, *The Modernity of Tradition* (rpt), Orient Longman, New Delhi, 1987; and *In Pursuit of Lakshmi*, Orient Longman, New Delhi, 1987.
30. Thomas A. Timberg, op. cit., p. 37.
31. See Girija Shankar, op. cit., pp. 47-67.
32. David C. McLelland, *The Achieving Society*, Vakils and Ferrer and Simons, Bombay, 1961.
33. K.L. Sharma, *The Changing Rural Stratification System: a Comparative Study of Six Villages in Rajasthan*, Orient Longman, New Delhi, 1974.
34. David Hardiman, 'The Bhils and Shahukars of Eastern Gujarat', in Ranjit Guha (ed.), *Subaltern Studies V*, Oxford University Press, Delhi, 1987, pp. 1-54.
35. See for example Bipan Chandra, *The Rise and Growth of Economic Nationalism in India*, People's Publishing House, New Delhi, 1966; and *Nationalism and Colonialism in Modern India*, Orient Longman, New Delhi, 1979. In these and several other writings Bipan Chandra and some of his colleagues hold the view that the big capitalists and small traders and merchants actively supported the national movement and that they had an independent base and were not subservient to the colonial masters and the feudal lords. However, barring big personalities like Jamanalal Bajaj and G.D. Birla, most traders from Rajasthan were not concerned with the national movement and the anti-feudal uprisings. The small village traders and merchants remained, in fact, busy in trade and commerce, moneylending and usury.

REFERENCES

Berna, J., *Industrial Entrepreneurship in Madras State*, Asia Publishing House, London, 1960.
Chakravarti, Uma, 'Towards a Historical Sociology of Stratification in Ancient India: evidence from Buddhist sources', *Economic and Political Weekly*, vol. XX, no. 9, 1985.
Chandra, B., *The Rise and Growth of Economic Nationalism in India*, People's Publishing House, New Delhi, 1966.
———, *Nationalism and Colonialism in Modern India*, Orient Longman, New Delhi, 1979.
Dasgupta, Ashim, 'Indian Merchants in the Age of Partnership, 1500-1800', in Tripathi, D., *Business Communities of India*, Manohar, Delhi, 1984.
Hardiman, David, 'The Bhils and Shahukars of Eastern Gujarat', in Ranjit Guha (ed.), *Subaltern Studies V*, Oxford University Press, Delhi, 1987.
Hasan, S. Nurul, 'The Historian and the Business Communities', 1984, in Tripathi, Dwijendra, *Business Communities of India*, Manohar, Delhi, 1984.
Hazari, R.K., *The Structure of the Corporate Private Sector: a Study of Concentration, Ownership and Control*, Asia Publishing House, London, 1966.
Lamb, H., 'The Indian Merchant', in Milton Singer (ed.), *Traditional India: Structure and Change*, Rawat Publications, Jaipur, 1975.
McLelland, David C., *The Achieving Society*, Vakils and Ferrer and Simons, Bombay, 1961.
Pavlov, V.I., *The Indian Capitalist Class*, People's Publishing House, Bombay, 1964.
Ruben Walter, 'Outline of the Structure of Ancient Indian Society', in R.S. Sharma (ed.), *Indian Society: Historical Probings*, 3rd edn, People's Publishing House, New Delhi, 1984.
Rudolph, S.H. and Rudolph, L.I., *The Modernity of Tradition* (rpt), Orient Longman, New Delhi, 1987; and *In Pursuit of Lakshmi*, Orient Longman, New Delhi, 1987.
Shah, Chanshyam (ed.), *Capitalist Development: Critical Essays*, Popular Prakashan, Bombay, 1990.
Shankar, G., *Marwari Vyapari* (Hindi), Krishna Jansevi & Co., Bikaner, 1990.
Sharma G.D., 'The Marwaris: Economic Foundations of an Indian Capitalist Class', in Tripathi, D., *Business Communities of India*, Manohar, Delhi, 1984.
Sharma K.L., 'Country-Town Nexus in India: a macro view', in K.L. Sharma and D. Gupta (eds), *Country-Town Nexus*, Rawat Publications, Jaipur, 1991.
———, *The Changing Rural Stratification System: a Comparative Study of Six Villages in Rajasthan*, Orient Longman, New Delhi, 1974.
Sheth, N.R., 'Theoretical Framework For the Study of Indian Business Communities', in Tripathi, D., *Business Communities of India*, Manohar, Delhi, 1984.
Singer, M., *When a Great Tradition Modernizes*, Praeger Publishers, New York, 1972.
———, (ed.), *Entrepreneurship and Modernization of Occupational Cultures in South Asia*, Duke University Press, 1973; Satish Saberwal, *Mobile Men*, Vikas, New Delhi, 1976.

Thapar, Romila, 'Social Mobility in Ancient India with Special Reference to Elite Groups', in R.S. Sharma (ed.), *Indian Society: Historical Probings*, 3rd edn, People's Publishing House, New Delhi, 1984.

Tod, James, *Annals and Antiquities of Rajasthan*, 3 vols., Low Price Publications, Delhi, 1990.

Verma, O.P., 'The Role of Traders and Guilds in Ancient India', in S.C. Malik (ed.), *Determinants of Social Status in India*, Motilal Banarsidas, Delhi, 1986.

Contributors

FREDERIQUE BOURGEOIS is a geographer at Economie and Humanisme (Lyon). She has contributed various articles to learned journals about urban management and commercial activities in India.

PHILIPPE CADÈNE is a geographer who is currently teaching at the University of Montpelliers (France). He is the author of various contributions about Indian geography and sociology in collective books and he has co-edited *L'Inde dans les sciences sociales*, Paris, ORSTOM, 1987.

VÉRONIQUE DUPONT is a demographer at the French Institute of Scientific Research for Development through Cooperation (ORSTOM, Paris). She is currently a visiting fellow at the Institute of Economic Growth, Delhi and she is also associated with the Centre de Sciences Humaines (CSH, Delhi). She is the author of *Decentralized Industrialization and Urban Dynamics; The case of Jetpur in West India*, Delhi, Sage, 1995 and she has co-edited *Mobilités spatiales et urbanisation*, Paris, ORSTOM, 1993.

PIERRE LACHAIER is a social anthropologist at the Ecole Française d'Extrême-Orient (EFEO, Pondicherry). He is the author of *Réseaux marchands et industriels au Maharashtra; caste, sous-traitance et clientelisme*, Paris, EHESS, 1994.

K.L. SHARMA is a sociologist who is currently teaching at the Centre for Social Studies, Jawaharlal Nehru University, Delhi. He has edited *Social Inequality in India: profiles of caste, class, power and social mobility, Essays in honour of Prof. Yogendra Singh*, Rawat Publications, Jaipur,

1995, *Social Stratification in India*, Manohar, Delhi, 1992 and *Social Stratification and Mobility*, Rawat Publications, Jaipur, 1994.

EMMA TARLO is a social anthropologist at the School of Oriental and African Studies (SOAS, London). She is a Post-Doctoral Research Fellow of the British Academy and is currently a visiting scholar at the Centre for Social Studies, Jawaharlal Nehru University, Delhi. She is the author of *Clothing Matters, Dress and Identity in India*, Delhi, Penguin, 1996.

DENIS VIDAL is a social anthropologist at the French Institute of Scientific Research for Development through Cooperation (ORSTOM, Paris). He is currently a visiting fellow at the Centre for Study of Developing Societies (CSDS, Delhi) and is also associated with the Centre de Sciences Humaines (CSH, Delhi). He is the author of *Le culte des divinités locales en Himachal Pradesh*, Paris, ORSTOM, 1987 and *Violence et Verité, Un royaume du Rajasthan face au pouvoir colonial*, Paris, EHESS, 1995. He has co-edited *Violence et non violence en Inde*, Paris, EHESS, 1994. The English translations of the last two books will be published shortly in India.

Foundale / 951 / 16/8/05